Reaching Out to
Children and Families

Reaching Out to Children and Families

Students Model Effective Community Service

Michelle R. Dunlap

ROWMAN & LITTLEFIELD PUBLISHERS, INC.
Lanham • Boulder • New York • Oxford

ROWMAN & LITTLEFIELD PUBLISHERS, INC.

Published in the United States of America
by Rowman & Littlefield Publishers, Inc.
4720 Boston Way, Lanham, Maryland 20706
http://www.rowmanlittlefield.com

12 Hid's Copse Road
Cumnor Hill, Oxford OX2 9JJ, England

British Library Cataloguing in Publication Information Available

Library of Congress Cataloging-in-Publication Data
Dunlap, Michelle R.
    Reaching out to children and families: students model effective community
service / Michelle R. Dunlap
        p. cm.
    Includes bibliographical references and index.
    SIBN 0-8476-9115-2 (alk. paper)—ISBN 0-8476-9116-0 (pbk. : alk. paper)
    1. Student service—United States. 2. Social service—United States. I. Title.

LC220.5.D86   2000
370.19—dc21   00-031106

Printed in the United States of America

♾™ The paper used in this publication meets the minimum requirements of
American National Standard for Information Sciences—Permanence of Paper
for Printed Library Materials, ANSI/NISO Z39.48-1992.

Dedicated to my parents, with love and appreciation, always:

My father, Robert Edgar Dunlap

My mother, Wanda Marie Johnson Boyd

And in loving memory of my other mother,
Dollie Ola Mae Bell Dunlap

Who was called to heaven on
Palm Sunday morning, April 16, 2000

"It is not enough to prepare our children for the world; we also must prepare the world for our children."

—Luis J. Rodríguez,
America Is Her Name

Contents

Foreword

As we enter a new century, the character and the goals of American higher education are changing. Students may not notice this shift since their contact with higher education is either relatively brief or occurs in small units integrated into the rest of their busy lives. However, to faculty and administrators as well as others who have spent a good deal of time studying and working at colleges and universities, the change is quite apparent. Consider, for example, the changing make-up of the student body (Hansen 1998): between 1970 and 1995, the proportion of college students twenty-five and older grew from 28% to 44%; between 1976 and 1995 the number of minorities rose from 15.7% to 25.3%; between 1985 and 1995, while the number of men rose 9%, the number of women rose 23%. On many campuses nationwide, women are now in the majority; on some campuses in urban areas, minorities are now in the majority.

Changing also are students' cultural experiences, academic attitudes, and personal interests. Television has become such an accepted part of young people's lives that the average adolescent now views approximately thirty-five hours of television per week (Hansen 1998) while, perhaps not coincidentally, "just 34% of freshmen report having spent six or more hours per week studying during their senior year in high school, an all-time low." At the same time, "students' political interest is at an all-time low. In 1997, only 27% considered it very important to keep up with politics." Motivation for going to college, it would seem, is increasingly identified with "increasing one's earning power."

Whether or not any of these particulars apply to you, such statistics are leading more and more educators to question their assumptions about what today's students need to learn and how they can best learn it. If practical, career-oriented skills are more important than ever before, how do we develop those skills in a way that helps students become truly *reflective* practitioners (Schon 1995)? If students show less and less interest in the formal political process, how do we help guide them toward a "new citizenship" (Rimmerman 1997), one that taps their interest in making a difference in ways they can see and feel?

Surely the answers to questions like these must somehow include a reexamination of the teaching-learning process. Since most of today's professors were in college, we have learned so much about effective teaching and learning that many of the old educational assumptions simply will not stand up to rigorous examination. To take but one example, research has repeatedly shown that one of the most important aspects of the learning process involves an opportunity to apply, test, and modify abstract generalizations in new settings and real-life contexts (Ewell 1997; *Report* 1998). However, such a focus on experiential learning has traditionally not been part of the way most faculty either teach or learned themselves. As one researcher (Schroeder 1993) summarizes:

> As faculty, we have generally espoused the common belief that students learn and develop through exposure—that the *content* is all-important. . . . Many of us prospered under the traditional lecture system, where the focus was on coverage of material through teaching by telling. This approach may work for us but it may not work for the majority of today's students.

"Service-learning" is the name that has been given to one of the most popular—and promising—forms of experiential education recently to emerge. The basic principles behind this approach are deceptively simple: by combining (1) students' interest in helping others (so long as they can see that their involvement makes a difference), (2) our growing appreciation of the importance of building active, real-world learning into the curriculum, and (3) the willingness of many community-based organizations to partner with colleges and universities for their mutual benefit, we can develop a win-win-win educational strategy.

Reaching Out to Children and Families: Students Model Effective Community Service represents one especially important contribution to the service-learning phenomenon, because it is one of the first texts to address directly *student* needs, especially as they relate to service assignments with underserved children and families. Perhaps not surprisingly, these are precisely the kinds of service assignments the vast majority of students prefer. According to Campus Compact (Caron 1999), the country's leading service-learning organization, the populations most frequently served by campus service projects are children, grades K–12. As dozens of statements quoted in this book make clear, students find working with still younger students not only a very effective vehicle of social and academic learning but also a source of deep personal satisfaction.

But as other statements make equally clear, there is a lot more to effective work with children and families than may at first be apparent—especially when those children and families come from socioeconomic and/or racial/ethnic backgrounds different from those of the student workers. Taking seriously what it means to relate successfully to people outside one's own social group is one of the ways in which service-learning differs from much traditional student volunteerism. Since the "learning" in "service-learning" is as important as the "service" and, indeed, inseparable from it, instructors using this approach need to make sure students have been well prepared and are able to reflect upon their work in ways that will deepen their understanding not only of community members and course concepts, but also of their own values and assumptions. In this case "Just do it!" clearly does not apply.

That is why this volume is so valuable: it guides students through the entire service-learning process, and it does so largely through the voices of fellow students. Whether your task is arranging a community placement, dealing with statements and even behavior you find shocking, or finding a way to say goodbye to people of whom you've grown fond, Dr. Dunlap helps you accomplish that task by learning from the strategies her own students have used in similar situations.

As someone who has taught service-learning courses for over ten years, who has sponsored service projects in literature, writing, philosophy, and business classes, and who has run a campus-wide service-learning program, I am very grateful to her for creating such a guide. Service-learning instructors need resources like this as much as our students do, for to sponsor service projects is to take many risks: the risk that students will feel abandoned or even irrelevant in learning situations outside the classroom, the risk that service projects will wind up being educationally counterproductive—mis-educative—rather than powerfully liberating experiences, the risk that in our ignorance we may wind up doing harm to the very people we wish to help. With Dr. Dunlap's book as our guide, such situations are far less likely to arise.

I began by noting that American higher education is in the midst of a significant transformation. Will the changes taking place result in something better than we have had, something that more effectively meets students where they are, that builds on their interests and strengths? Will those changes result in more effective ways to link career preparation and active citizenship, intellectual stimulation and personal understanding, skillful analysis and broad sensitivities? Or will the entire enterprise go aground on our failure to adapt liberal learning to the needs of a student generation born into an ever more commercialized society? Over 150 years ago, the English poet Shelley lamented what he already saw as "a cultivation of the mechanical arts in a degree disproportionate to the presence of the creative faculty" (Shelley 1819). It is my hope that *our* use of this text—by students, college faculty and staff, and community partners—will help the next generation of student learners become the most perceptive, productive, and humane we have ever seen.

Edward Zlotkowski
Senior Faculty Fellow, Campus Compact
Senior Associate, American Association for Higher Education
Professor of English, Bentley College

Preface

When I was in college, I engaged in community service as a volunteer at a nursing home. In spite of my good intentions and love for elders, I was almost fired from my position. How do you almost get *fired* from a volunteer position, you ask? I was working at a nursing care facility that consisted primarily of senior citizens who were wheelchair bound or bedridden. I would go each Saturday for two or three hours with another volunteer. We would read to the residents, sing songs, or just sit at their bedside and talk with them. Many of the residents appeared to anticipate our visits, and therefore we were careful to be consistent in our attendance. I recall vividly Mr. "Leroy,"[1] one of the residents with whom I noticed myself developing a familial attachment.

A year into my work, I found myself facing a dilemma in regard to Mr. Leroy's safety. When I arrived one day, I found him improperly bound in a convalescing chair; the chair seemed to be in danger of tipping over and falling forward. I did not know how to properly secure him, and it would have been inappropriate for me to try, even if I had known how.

I alerted the nursing personnel several times about Mr. Leroy's condition and my concern that he might tumble over. Finally, a nursing assistant came to "fix" the chair by simply tightening the belt around Mr. Leroy's waist, which made the chair tip even more. I tried to diplomatically suggest that the tightened belt might not solve the problem, but the assistant ignored me. At that point, I went to the nursing supervisor's office and passionately complained about the treatment of Mr. Leroy, expressing my fear that he would fall over in his chair. In return, the nursing supervisor passionately instructed me to leave. She appeared offended by my noting the careless manner by which Mr. Leroy was bound in the chair. I left, but I felt confused and anxious that I had done something wrong, and I was still worried about Mr. Leroy's safety.

That Monday I called the volunteer coordinator of the nursing home, Ms. "Vicky," and explained what had happened. Ms. Vicky let me know that she had already heard more than enough about it; the staff were quite upset with me and were requesting that I not be allowed to return because they felt that I was "sticking my nose in matters that should not concern me." I tried to explain to Ms. Vicky the dilemma that I felt in that situation and the careful steps that I had taken to try to address my concern for Mr. Leroy. She told me that she understood and that she felt that this was a matter of miscommunication. She would try to work with the staff about my returning. Later that week, Ms. Vicky called me to let me know that I could return the following Saturday but needed to "keep a low profile" because the nursing staff did not appreciate my activist stance about Mr. Leroy and his chair.

For the sake of my relationship with Mr. Leroy and several of the other residents, I went back and kept a very low profile. I volunteered for another year, during which time I was careful to take any questions or concerns that I had to Ms. Vicky, who was able to see a broader range of the issues involved and advise me. Even though I did not completely understand what I had done wrong, I was extra congenial to the nursing staff to avoid suffering the possible consequences of offending them.

Since that experience at the nursing care facility, I have tried to practice examining the situation from the perspective of the nursing staff and the others involved. I have also tried to use my expertise in social psychology and human development to help me examine the situation from a variety of perspectives.

The nursing aides were mostly young African American women, and most of the nursing staff supervisors were European American women. Ms. Vicki was the only person of color among the administrative staff. I am an African American woman with multiracial roots that are evident in my physical appearance (Dunlap 1999a). I was the same age or younger than most of the aides, who, although young themselves, still had many more responsibilities than I. These women had families to feed and had to work long hours of hard labor in order to take care of themselves and their families. I had to work hard also, but not as hard as they did. In addition, I was in college and had the luxury of "volunteering" some of my time. There may have been an invisible partition of sorts between the aides and myself that I did not perceive.

I had not considered the differences between the aides and myself, only the similarities. As far as I was concerned, they were my sisters. They reminded me of myself, many of the women in my family, and the women with whom I grew up in the inner city of Detroit. I was no stranger to hotel housekeepers, nursing assistants, licensed practical nurses, security guards, automobile factory laborers, farmers, and the like, as I come from a diverse immediate and extended family of working-class folks. And I was no stranger to long hours of local five-and-dime retail cashiering myself, sometimes working three jobs at a time to support myself and my education. So when I saw the nursing assistants at the nursing care facility, they seemed familiar to me. They hustled to get their work done, like me and the folks in my family. They talked like me and the folks in my family. I took it for granted that I knew them and that they knew me. I had not considered their possible perceptions or misperceptions of me on any number of possible dimensions, for example, my college "educated" talk or my fair skin and what they might have assumed to be the unearned privileges that often come with light (and even more so, white,) skin in our society (McIntosh 1990; Russell 1993).

As for the nursing supervisors, it must have been difficult to hear a black woman speak with such assuredness, confidence, and directness (Goodwin 1996; West 1995), when they were used to giving young black women orders—young black women who had to take those orders so that they could feed their children.

Unknown to me at the time, the various experiences at the nursing home had already primed me for an in-depth interest in the experiences I would encounter years later. I was already primed for having an intense and methodical concern for the emotional processes, adjustments, and resources that would affect my students during their work in environments that might initially seem unfamiliar to them.

My interest in assisting people who work in unfamiliar communities also began several years after the nursing care facility experience. I worked for two years to support myself and my child while finishing graduate school. As a counselor in an early enrichment and family support program at a community mental health facility, I worked with children and families of various ethnic backgrounds, socioeconomic status, and family situations. That particular position had been set up to allow the counselor to provide support and services to families in their own familiar environment rather than have them drive or take the bus to an office. I had an office but only used it to do paperwork. The overwhelming majority of my time was spent in the clients' own environments.

The clients with whom I worked were from many different cultural backgrounds and situations. I saw black, white, Hispanic, Asian, biracial, single-parent, two-parent, adoptive, foster care, kinship care, straight, gay, lesbian, small, large, urban, rural, middle-class, working-poor, poverty-stricken, transient, and homeless families. The majority of my clients were from working-poor families. I saw them in their homes, on their jobs, in their children's classrooms, at the park, at fast-food restaurants, or wherever we could meet to work together. It was my task to provide support to children and families who had parenting and discipline issues, domestic violence issues, and family trauma and loss issues. Over the course of those two years I provided thousands of hours of counseling, education, support services, and referral services, and I drove over 10,000 miles to provide these services. Traveling to so many homes, work sites, and educational settings and adjusting to so many families and their various environments was a very interesting and sometimes challenging task. For me, as for many of my own students who work in community settings, appearing young and fair-skinned, as well as sounding "educated," meant climbing many walls to begin to win my clients' trust. Also like many students who work in the community, I found that each family left me with an indelible impression which helped me grow personally and professionally.

Today, having years of training as a social psychologist, years of experience as a human development college professor, and years of experience as a parent, I am in a different place than I was many years ago as a young college volunteer and as a new counselor in the family support program.

As a social psychologist, I have been able to put my own past experiences into a broader social-cognitive perspective that takes into account the wider intergroup relations involved in many cross-cultural community experiences. I can recall feelings of awkwardness and uncertainty as I became acclimated to new clients and new environments. I now observe my own students expressing similar feelings and emotions. In reading my students' journals, I am reminded of myself, the nursing care facility, and the family support program, now dramatized in hundreds of different variations.

As a human development professor, I have had the opportunity to work closely with students, mentor them, and support them as they adjust to working with children and families in new environments. I have been attuned particularly to the developmental processes that occur during their community service experiences. I have been able to see their adjustments in light of the human maturational processes that occur over time. I see well-intended idealism, heroic desires, frustration, and personal growth and maturity gained through work with others (Conrad and Hedin 1982; Dunlap 1997). A spirit of idealistic charity exists among many youth; such a spirit is crucial because it helps propel social change. Therefore, it should not be discouraged but rather dealt with realistically (Coles 1993).

As a parent, I am sensitive to the community side of the equation and think of how I would feel if the workers were engaging with me or my child. There have been instances where, figuratively, it was me or it was my child. For example, while my child was in elementary school, he participated in one of several community after-school programs in which college students and civic volunteers supported the staff in one capacity or another.

One reason for writing this book is my belief that those working in unfamiliar community settings would fare better if they understood better the emotional processes involved in adjusting to children and families, especially in circumstances where they view themselves as more privileged than those with whom they work (Ward 1997). It is my desire to introduce to readers the voices of individuals experiencing community services as a psychosocial process.

When I first incorporated community service into my courses in human development, writing a book was the furthest thing from my mind. I was engaging in a model for teaching that historically had been used in my department. Like my colleagues, I incorporated curriculum-based service, critical reflection, and journal writing into my courses. My colleagues explained that having students keep journals would assist them in making connections between their course curriculum and real-life observations and experiences, which I later learned is consistent with good service-learning[2] practice (Eyler, Giles, and Schmiede 1996).

The idea for this book came out of reading and responding to hundreds of student journals over the course of six years. After reading the first hundred or so of the more than eight hundred complete students' journals that I have read to date, I had a clear vision for a series of research resources (i.e., Dunlap 1997; Dunlap 1998a,b,c,d; Dunlap and Coughlin 1999) and later a practical book. I knew that the voices and concerns expressed by students working with children and families needed to be shared so that other students would feel less isolated and better prepared for engaging in their community work. For example, many students initially expressed feelings of apprehensiveness and awkwardness in spite of previous training or orientation and group discussions about their community work. If they knew that many of their other classmates felt that same way, I reasoned, then perhaps they wouldn't feel as anxious about their own emotions and could more easily get on with the process of adjusting and moving on to the business of their community placement.

In this effort, 215 student journals were collected and included in the work that culminated in this book. Other than responses to a brief set of ten "journal reflection questions" (appendix A), which I created to assist students in the techniques of observing and responding in their journals, each journal was guided by the individual student's own interests, concerns, and academic connections. Each journal is therefore unique. Nevertheless, common themes have emerged among them, such as initial awkwardness, difficulty finding and balancing roles, and ambivalent emotions at the end of the experience when they had established bonds of affection with clients[3] and staff.

After receiving written permission from the student participants, the journals were transcribed manually and by computer into a 1,148-page document of small-font, single-spaced anonymous data that was later coded with help from a team of student research assistants (appendix B). It was then my task to organize into a manuscript the major themes present in the data, articulate for readers the surrounding context for the data, and strategically place the data for use in this book.

Compiling and extrapolating the relevant journal data and writing this book were two of the most massive, tedious, and *enjoyable* projects I have ever undertaken. Many times it has felt like a professional and personal journey of psychological, human developmental, anthropological, sociological, educational, and historical proportions! I have experienced joy in bringing to others the voices and personal journeys of these students from the very beginnings of their community service and learning experiences with children and families to the endings, as they say good-bye and move on. Each component of their journey brings amazing adventures. I hope that community workers, as well as you who support and supervise community workers, will find the book a valuable resource for assisting you in your preparation for work among communities, sites, citizens, staffs, and/or students who may seem unfamiliar to you.

Let us now begin our own journey into the community service and learning process through the eyes of students.

Acknowledgments

First, I thank my Lord and Savior, Jesus Christ, who gave me the vision, voice, and venue for this book. I also thank my ancestors, elders, and mentors whose sacrifices have afforded me opportunities and whose spirits of determination have given me inspiration and strength throughout this work. I thank my family: all of my grandparents, parents, sister, brothers, aunts, uncles, cousins, nieces, and nephews on all three sides and beyond, who all loved me, encouraged me, and kept me laughing, no matter how focused I was on this project. And I thank my friends, colleagues, and community comrades for their loads of support during the writing of this book.

Interestingly, I find giving specific acknowledgments, in terms of naming people, to be one of the most challenging parts of completing this book. I feel grateful to so many people for their help as I wrote this book, and I worry that I will erroneously leave someone out. If I do that, I ask your forgiveness and hope that you will attribute any omissions to my mind and not to my heart.

I gratefully acknowledge Lisa Atkinson, William Bassett '00, Bishop & Mrs. James A. Bell and family, Sunil Bhatia, Dean Birkenkamp, Donald Blake, Rachel Blumberg '02, MaryAnne Borrelli, Wanda Johnson Boyd, Jamie Bridges '00, Robert Bringle, Mark Brooks, Rev. and Mrs. Frank Bunkley, Johnny Carter, Joan Chrisler, Pinkston Clarke, Orenise Coleman, Willie Coleman, The Connecticut College (Children's Program, Holleran Center for Community Action and Public Policy, Library, Office of Volunteers for Community Service [OVCS], and the hundreds of students who shared their personal journeys with me over the years), Rev. W. Vance Cotton, Edwin Cruz and family, Jennifer Dahlgren '01, Jessica Henderson Daniel, Ted Daniels,

Stephanie DiFrancesco, Cynthia R. Dunlap, Devonna R. Dunlap, Dollie O. Dunlap and the precious community of folks and family who were there for her (and me) these past two years, Regina and Phil Dunlap, Robert B. Dunlap, Robert E. Dunlap, Glenn A. Eason, Joe Feagin, Don Filer, Eugene Gallagher, Paulette Galathe, Christine Gatliffe, Claire Gaudiani, Camille Hanlon, Beth Hansen, Ruth Hapgood, Porter Hill, Barbara and Jimmy Hoggard, Jeffrey Hward, Sue and Chet Ives, Barbara Jacoby, Karen Johnson, Roseanna Johnson, Andrew Kerbs '99, Judy Kirmmse, Ann Kohlman '01, David Lewis, Lewis Lipsitt, Otelia Locke, Towana Mace, Patricia Major, Lisa Mkwalo '94, Jennifer Monroe '00, the citizens of New London and its surrounding communities, Kelly O'Neal '98, Cheryl Olinsky '98, Jeannette Oquendo '00, Peni E. Plucker, Jerry Poirier, Lauren Portway '00, Mary-Jeanette Quinones, Sara Radlinski, Brian Ragsdale, Helen Regan, Tracee Reiser, Jessica Ritzo '99, Bill Rivera, Rochelle Dunlap Robinson, Pastor Ella Roffi and each member of the M.S. Jones Church, Jill Rothenberg, Allison Rourke '97, Chrisona Schmidt, Margaret Sheridan, Shiloh Baptist Church and Single Parent Fellowship, Jefferson Singer, Nancy Spears, Shanice Spivey, Sherwin Spivey Jr., Sherwin Spivey Sr., Loretta Springer, Reginald Stanford, Art Stukas, Beverly Tatum, Winston Taylor, Terri Thomas, Ruth Timmer, Israel Tribble and the Florida Education Fund McKnight Program, Faye Dunlap Truss, James and Sandra Vest, Andrew M. Walker, Pastor and Mrs. Benjamin K. Watts, Lynn Weber, Carolyn West, Brenda Williams, the Calvin Williams family, Les Williams, Sheila Winkelspecht, Jerry Winter, Carlos Wise, and Ed Zlotkowski. To everyone involved, I offer my heartfelt thanks for assistance, prayers, moral support, and all other forms of contribution to this book.

Introduction

To be honest with you, I just don't know what to expect, and I am quite apprehensive and wary about [service at an inner-city middle school]. Thoughts of deprived, deranged youngsters throwing scissors at my head and the idea of not knowing any of the answers to basic algebra questions consume me. I also have thoughts of children looking up at me with admiration and longing. (Female, European American)

This book is about what college-age people think, feel, and experience when they engage in service and learning with children and families in communities that are unfamiliar to them. The terms "service" and "learning" are included in this book because these participants, on whom the book is based, were engaged in an experience that allowed them to both serve the community and learn from it as a reciprocal, mutually beneficial activity. Community members provided a service to the students by allowing students to spend time with them and learn from them. Students provided a service to the community by trying to support the citizenry and the staff of local nonprofit educational institutions and agencies.

Likewise, in terms of learning, all participants—whether students, community members, agency personnel, or college faculty and administrators—had an opportunity to learn from one another. My students also had an opportunity to connect their learning to their course curricula. This method is a curricular-based form of service and learning known as "service-learning."[1] In brief, service-learning provides service to the community, views service as mutually beneficial and reciprocal in nature, encourages time and space for critically examining experiences and learning in the community, and attempts to tie those learnings to academic education. For the purpose of this book, neither service-learning nor other programs are assumed to be superior to one another. To whatever degree a community involvement program shares mutual learning, critical reflection, and/or a connection to a course curriculum, it would be expected that they also have in common some of the processes discussed here with regard to my service-learning students. While presentation of the issues and voices here, collectively, may be the first of many possible models of the community learning adjustment process, it constitutes a beginning that I hope will be helpful to novice community workers and their support staff.

It should be noted that there are many ways to be involved with the community. Some ways are oriented more toward service as a sacrifice (e.g., volunteering). Some are oriented more toward practical life experience and curricular education (e.g., practicums or internships). Some are more curricular and service oriented (e.g., service-learning). Others are oriented more toward social activism. Often these are not mutually exclusive. Wherever a particular experience may fall on the service, learning, and practice continua, there is much to be learned from involvement in the community. For this reason, I will most often refer to such involvement in the community as "community learning." Sometimes I use the terms "community learning," "community service," and "community work" interchangeably because of the intertwined nature of learning, service, and practice in the curriculum-based community involvement process. Therefore, whether you are interning, service-learning, experiential-learning, engaging in social activism, and/or volunteering, if you consider yourself a "learner" with respect to the community where you are working, then this book was written with you in mind.

In your capacity as a community learner, you may experience a variety of emotions, and sometimes struggle, as you attempt to come to terms with the challenges, both positive and negative, that you will face during your work in new community settings (ACTION/NCSL 1989). It is my hope that the things that I have learned from my students will be helpful to you.

For me, it has been an adventurous six years as a professor of Human Development courses that contain a community learning component. I have suffered through and learned right alongside my students as they have shared with me their hopes, dreams, fears, anguish, frustration—and the resources that helped them. I will share five examples that ring vividly in my memory.

"JOURNEY"

Journey, whose words are quoted at the beginning of this chapter, came to my office and confided in me that she was feeling very apprehensive about beginning her community work at an inner-city middle school.[2] Journey was a nineteen-year-old sophomore woman of Jewish heritage who grew up in a suburban household that strongly valued diversity and encouraged multicultural experiences. Yet there were negative socially constructed images that Journey could not yet remove from her mind as she awaited her first day's work in an inner-city environment.

I encouraged Journey to think about where such images originate—within our culture—and to consider the truth and/or the falsity of such images. I asked her to jot me a note after her first visit so that I would know how her first day went. In Journey's note to me, she observed that, to her surprise, the children had very good manners, were very inquisitive about her, and had skillful and resilient natures. Recalling our first conversation, Journey critically reflected upon the origins of her negative expectations:

Why would I have a prominent picture of a child throwing scissors at my head? Where did this fear come from? Was I conditioned to believe that since these children whom I am working with are more deprived, economically speaking, than I am, that they would behave differently? I am ashamed at myself for believing that just because these children were from more disadvantaged circumstances that it meant that they lack the manners and proper etiquette possessed by more "advantaged" children.

"TRAVERSE"

Traverse was an eighteen-year-old freshman male of European American descent who grew up in a rural/suburban environment. Traverse looked and behaved very mature for his age, and his journal entries reflected a wisdom more common to a much older person. Traverse already had several years of experience working with children in high school. He had a way of working with children that I have yet to see surpassed by a college student. But not even his past experience and incredible people skills could prepare him for some of the experiences that occurred during his community work. Traverse elected to work in a college-sponsored after-school mentoring program for boys from challenged circumstances.

Two incidents in particular seemed to shatter Traverse's confidence. First, a nine-year-old fourth-grade boy announced during a game of Sound Ball, in which children imitate and guess sounds, that he would "make the sound a girl makes when she is raped." Second, a member of a group of preadolescent boys of color, with whom Traverse had been trying to bond, looked at him and said, "But that white guy doesn't want to have fun, he doesn't know how to have fun." Traverse, by the way, prides himself on his hard-earned open-mindedness and respect for diversity:

It truly broke my heart. I come from [the Midwest] and my family is definitely racist. I have tried so hard to get away from that mentality my entire life and it is difficult, and to have that thrown back into my face by one of these guys I truly care about, was devastating. I am worried that somehow I treated these guys like I thought that there was a difference because I was white and they were black. I hope that the guys can come to see me as a friend and as a person who will help them and care for them no matter what.

Both of the situations that arose for Traverse shook his confidence in himself and in his community work. Traverse and I spent a great deal of time in communication about these incidents and examined them from many different angles, which he found to be helpful. For example, one of the ways that we explored the Sound Ball situation was to consider the role or effects of media images and the values of machismo and sexual conquest upon the development of boys in our culture. We tried to consider how those socializing influences might have played a role the boy's comments (Jensen 1998). We also grappled with the question of whether one of the adults had a responsibility to explore the situation further with the boy, and whether that responsibility was Traverse's. Traverse and I decided that he should confer with the boy's teacher about the incident. When he did, the teacher took further steps to investigate the child's statement so that it could, at the minimum, be a learning process for the boy or an opportunity for support if the boy had witnessed a sexual assault.

In terms of the "racial" situation, we considered whether the child was making a negative, inaccurate, "racist" comment or whether he was making an acknowledgment of race. Therefore, we explored whether the child was insulting Traverse based on racial group membership or whether, as an alternative, he was acknowledging Traverse's racial or ethnic group membership (e.g., white, black, Puerto Rican) in the process of raising a pressing issue about the activities. We also considered the child's possible motives for suggesting that Traverse was no "fun." We considered that the child might have meant, for example, that Traverse was not meeting his expectations as a mentor, that Traverse's specific interests and activities were not matching those of the children, or that the boy did not want to observe Traverse's limits and wanted to do what *he* wanted to do. We also considered whether the boy may have been trying to "test" Traverse to see if he could trust his affection and the bonds of closeness that they were just beginning to form. Traverse spent more time gaining experience and testing out his evolving skills. His confidence eventually returned, and his relationship with the children steadily improved. Four years later, Traverse is still among the top students on my list of those whom I would trust to spend time with or work with my own child.

"PASSAGE"

Passage was an eighteen-year-old female of African American descent who grew up in a middle-class suburban environment. Passage and her family strongly valued making sacrifices for success, being kind to others, and "giving back" to the community. Passage elected to work in an inner-city public school fourth-grade classroom. Passage struggled with feelings of apprehension when she initially entered her community service environment, and later she struggled with feelings of guilt whenever she would end her visits with the children. She found saying good-bye to them extremely difficult each time because she felt that she was "letting them down" by leaving. She found anticipation of the final visit particularly challenging because it meant letting them go more permanently. She shares from her journal:

> *I want to be there for them forever, to watch them grow and mature. I want to see what their futures hold for them. I know that I shouldn't worry about them, but I can't help it.*

Passage, her classmates, and I brainstormed and role-played methods that Passage could use to better prepare herself and the children with whom she worked for the end of each of her visits, as well as for her final visit at the end of the school year. What Passage seemed to find helpful was the idea of making, with permission from her site supervisors, a small scrapbook of pictures and artwork that she and the children created during the semester.

"QUEST"

Quest was a nineteen-year-old male of African American descent who grew up in an inner-city family that valued hard work, discipline, and obedience to elders. Quest elected to work at a community after-school program sponsored by a soup kitchen. During one of our periodic in-class small-group discussion times, he confided that he felt that the parents of the children at the center tended to let children get away with things for which his mother and grandmother would have disciplined him. He believed in the traditional, firm style of discipline that his mother and grandmother applied to him, crediting it, in part, for his educational success. He found it very difficult to observe school-age children "talking back" to their parents and sometimes felt tempted to lecture the children about their behavior toward their parents.

Quest also confided to me in his journal that one of the preadolescent girls with whom he was working touched him in a manner that made him feel uncomfortable. He was not sure whether to interpret it as affection, flirtation, or what. He shared the incident with me as follows:

> *Today a little girl that I was introduced to two weeks ago came back with her two sisters. All three of them fought over who would sit next to me and who would assist me. In addition, one of them put their hands on me in an inappropriate fashion and I had to verbally reprimand her. I told her if I had*

touched her in that manner, I would have been arrested. I think that I need to be more assertive, but I can't seem to do that with children who aren't mine. I don't want anyone's parents coming in my face talking to me about why I said or did what I did to their child. I am still trying to find out what I can and can't do to be a good volunteer.

Quest asserted during the group discussion that if the incident were to happen again, he still would not be sure of the best way to respond. During group time, he and his group mates role-played possible responses for redirecting a child on such a matter without criminalizing her or him. We also explored Quest's general concern about the children's need for firmer discipline and how he could find a balance or a boundary that would allow him to relate to the children in a manner that would earn their respect without his having to shoulder the responsibility of rearing or disciplining them.

"DESTINY"

Destiny was a twenty-year-old female of Asian descent who grew up in a suburban household that paid extraordinary attention to her social development and fostered respect for all human life. Destiny elected to work at a women's prison. She took painstaking care in selecting her placement site and preparing for her first visit. Because she valued conscientiousness, she read all of the prison orientation literature, called to confirm her appointment, obsessed over the right outfit to wear to be sure that she was dressed appropriately for her first day, and arrived a half hour early after making the thirty-minute drive. When she arrived and parked her car, she waved her arms to try to get the attention of one of the guards. As she approached the guard to ask a question, he grabbed her, shoved her against her car, and interrogated her about who she was. Later she learned that he had mistaken her for a prisoner because she was wearing the same color combination worn by the prisoners.

To make matters worse, each time Destiny visited the prison, she had to deal with some new mishap, usually involving prison bureaucratic procedures. Once she was made to wait for an hour and a half before she was given clearance to enter the prison. Another time she was told that the inmate she was assigned to visit had rejected her visit; later she was told that a clerical error had occurred. Destiny began to realize that she could not always prepare for or control all events that occur in the community learning environment. With that realization, she began to direct her energies differently. For example, she began to critically evaluate what was occurring and attributed some of the logistical difficulties to what she perceived as a general stance taken by the guards against community workers. She shared her reasoning:

The guards do not like volunteers because the guards believe that people should not empathize with the inmates. The girls are prisoners, and a prisoner is not considered by them to be the same as a person. They are incarcerated and therefore should be forgotten.

Destiny spent a great deal of her journal and group time sharing her frustrations and connecting her experiences to the broader issues of sexism, classism, and racism. She also considered ideas for future women's rights activism within the criminal justice system. In spite of all of the challenges, Destiny managed to remain committed and made the most of her community work for the duration of the semester.

THE TAPESTRY OF VOICES AND THEIR PURPOSE

Journey, Traverse, Passage, Quest, and Destiny represent just five of the 215 students whose experiences contributed to this discussion of concerns, issues, and approaches that arise for college students engaging in community learning in environments that are often unfamiliar. Community learning has been a journey and an adventure for these 215 students, and for me. With each challenge that they have shared with me, I have been transported into unique situations—situations full of emotions, anxieties, worries, resources, resiliency, and connections to human development curricula.

The goal of this book is to offer you helpful suggestions and ideas as you begin organizing and preparing for your community work. The experiences of past community learners suggest that you might be dealing with a variety of events, from children wetting their pants while sitting in your lap to children, parents, and staff members making comments that you might not have expected to hear them say. There may be moments of laughter, and there may be occasional tears of frustration and disappointment. But in the end, you most likely will be wiser, stronger, and more knowledgeable about yourself, the world outside your own house or dorm room, and your course curricula.

SETTING THE CONTEXT FOR THE WORK PRESENTED HERE

Like many of my colleagues, I have required of my students curriculum-based community involvement. In my courses, students engage in two to four hours per week of service-learning for the sixteen-week course period. Such short-term experiences, if well planned, can provide illuminating, significant experiences for students (Delve, Mintz, and Stewart 1990; Eyler et al. 1996; McCarthy 1996). They can also form the foundation for future community-related endeavors. Students in my courses were instructed to choose one service-learning environment from either the Connecticut College Children's Program, a model child and family-focused early childhood program for infants and young children of diverse backgrounds and abilities, or from among more than fifty public schools, after-school tutoring programs, day care centers, and homeless and domestic violence shelters in primarily inner-city locations throughout southeastern Connecticut, Rhode Island, and New York, with the majority in New London, Conn., the community that surrounds the college.

The diversity of New London and its educational institutions make it an ideal place for college students to learn about the strengths, challenges, and resourcefulness of ethnically and socioeconomically diverse communities. New London is an urban area with a population of 28,540, with 28 percent being people of color (U.S. Dept. of Commerce, Bureau of the Census 1992). At least 12 percent of the population of New London was born outside of the continental United States. The distribution of females and males is pretty much even. At least a third of the families of New London are headed by a single parent, with at least 11 percent of such families with children under the age of eighteen being headed by men (U.S. Dept. of Commerce, Bureau of the Census 1992). The 1998 per capita income was $17,387 (New London School District 1999).

New London has eight public schools and nine nonpublic schools. Children of color make up 73 percent of the population in New London's public schools (New London School District 1999). Of the public school enrollees, 37 percent are black, 32 percent are Hispanic, 27 percent are white, and 4 percent are of other ethnic minority categories. Thirteen percent of these children do not speak English as a first language. Seventy percent of the children are eligible for free/reduced-priced meals at school.

The profile of New London's surrounding communities is strikingly different; people of color make up only 6 percent of the suburban population (U.S. Dept. of Commerce, Bureau of the Census 1992). The Hispanic population, which makes up 12 percent of the city of New London's population, makes up only 2 percent of the population in the other cities in New London County. Likewise, the city and public school populations are overwhelmingly European American, with students of color making up only 3–11 percent of school enrollments in two neighboring towns and averaging less than 10 percent for the entire surrounding region (*New London Day* 1999).

Although New London is a relatively small and diverse community, it, like many urban areas in Connecticut and in the United States, has its share of challenges. For example, within the state of Connecticut, the majority of K-12 schools provide very little diversity in their teaching staff. Although minorities make up nearly 28 percent of the student population in Connecticut, minority teachers make up only 6 percent of the faculty. In addition, 70 percent of the school districts have two or fewer minority teachers; 31 percent of all Connecticut schools have only one minority teacher; and another 34 percent of all Connecticut schools have no minority teachers. In many of these all-white or nearly all-white teacher districts, students of color make up more than 70 percent of the student population (Connecticut Advisory Council for Teacher Professional Standards 1995). While these kinds of imbalances are reflected somewhat in New London schools among the teaching staff, with only 14 percent being minority, signs of progress are also visible, with two elementary schools and the only high school being headed by ethnic minority principals and the recently appointed superintendent being an African American.

Even though New London shares the structural and institutional challenges facing other urban areas in the United States, it also possesses many strengths and resources. It is a close-knit community that, for the most part, contains constituents who are creative, resourceful, and proactive in terms of trying to solve community problems. For example, in recent years 19 percent of the adults lacking high school diplomas have enrolled in and completed adult education programs, and that number is steadily growing (New London School District 1999). New London has many active community agencies and programs aimed at education, the arts and sciences, recreation and youth development, youth employment, and individual and family health and social services (Office of Youth Affairs/Citizen's Forum for Achieving Results [C-far] 1999).

HOW THIS WORK EVOLVED

When I began reading student journals, I was reminded of many of the worries and adjustment issues that I had when I started community work. But I was also surprised by the anxiety that many of my students felt about being involved in an urban environment. As noted in the preface, I was born and raised in the city of Detroit in a family and community that are quite diverse culturally and socioeconomically. For that reason, my apprehensions about urban and inner-city environments were less pronounced than what I observed in my students, the majority of whom come from European American, middle-class, upper-class, and suburban backgrounds. I am older than my students, I have more academic expertise about a wide variety of communities, and I have had considerably more experience in many kinds of environments, all of which may further contribute to differences in how my students and I perceive and interact with respect to urban and inner-city communities. Even so, adjustment in any environment is a day-to-day process—a journey that continues to evolve and unfold with new insights, no matter how knowledgeable or experienced one may be.

Even though the majority of my students are European American and middle and upper class, I also have students who are from many other cultural and economic backgrounds. All of my students have an extremely diverse range of personal life experiences, yet many of them have had a variety of issues about work in urban and inner-city environments. I have had to put myself into the place of my students of all backgrounds in order to understand the source of their worries, concerns, resiliency, and coping strategies. I have had to *listen* to them, letting them tell me their stories and their experiences so that I could find ways to assist them in their work and, more importantly, so that I personally and professionally could *learn* from them and grow with them.

I did not ask my students to tell me most of what they shared with me. I just watched and listened, trying to hear whatever they chose to say to me. And they shared plenty, as you will see in the pages of this book. I have found the students to be incredible human beings, full of life, strength, determination, good intentions, occasional pain and frustration, and, always, hope. It did not take me long to notice these characteristics through my students' work. After the first year of reading my students' journals, I noticed clear thematic patterns in the journals regarding the kinds of concerns and incidents that students were experiencing in the course of their day-to-day community work, and their emotional responses to those incidents. During the third semester, as I read the journals, I tried to document the recurring themes. I had the very clear impression that even though students were sharing their community experiences both inside and outside class, many of them assumed that these were isolated, personal incidents. Their journals indicated that experiences they thought unique to themselves were indeed very common among many students. Clearly, their journals, when taken collectively, were indicating that many of them were having similar experiences and ranges of emotions and were devising similar coping strategies. Their journals, while remaining unique individually, collectively were weaving a tapestry of common themes and issues (see appendix B).

The 215 most recent student journals that are drawn upon in this book were collected from eight sections in the following courses: Introduction to Child Development (100 level), Introduction to Human Development (100 level), Children in a Multicultural Society (200 level), and Social and Personality Development (300 level). Some 84 percent of the students were women, and 16 percent were men. The students were of European descent (81 percent), African descent (9 percent), Hispanic and Latina/o descent (7 percent), and Asian descent (3 percent). The students for whom age data was available ranged from seventeen to thirty-seven years, with an average of nineteen, the overwhelming majority of them being eighteen or nineteen and in their freshman or sophomore year of college. These students, collectively, came into contact with literally thousands of child clients[3] and family members, as well as hundreds of staff members, during their community learning.

For many of the students, this was their first hands-on experience within communities other than their own. For a few students, these communities were familiar yet still, in one way or another, may have posed a challenge. In any case, the students were very creative and resourceful in how they approached their community work.

HOW TO USE THIS BOOK

This book is intended primarily for college students who are taking courses that have a service-learning, practicum, internship, experiential-learning, or fieldwork component. It will be especially helpful to those who have community work assignments that involve children and/or families. It may also be useful to non-curriculum-based and nonstudent volunteers working in community settings that initially seem unfamiliar.

Senior-level high school students engaged in community learning within unfamiliar environments may also find this book helpful, depending upon the nature of their assignment. Also, international students who have come from overseas to attend college and engage in community learning may find this book helpful. They may find themselves relating to the experience of trying to (1) find their place in their new surroundings; (2) build rapport with individuals; (3) find and set appropriate limits with those with whom they work; (4) respond to things that they find shocking; and (5) say good-bye when it is time to leave at the end of the program. I hope that because of this book you will be better prepared to act in partnership with the community members and agency staff with whom you engage during your community work.

Although this book was written with the novice community worker in mind, it will also be helpful to those who help facilitate the community learning process. Faculty members, college and community administrators, high school teachers, principals, hospital personnel, community agency supervisors, child care workers, and other agency staff will find issues discussed in this book helpful in understanding and preparing for their own community work and for guiding students in their community involvement. In this regard, additional resources are provided at the end of each chapter with facilitators of the community learning process in mind. Novice community learners will find these additional resources helpful as well.

The material in this book will be of particular interest to those involved in courses whose curricula focus on children, on families, or on issues that affect them in our society. Thus anyone taking courses in human development, child development, business, education, government, health, sociology, psychology, anthropology, economics, and other social science courses will find this book helpful. Rothman, Anderson, and Schaffer (1998, 49) report that "a majority of campuses of virtually all types and in all locations" including urban, suburban, and rural, as well as the majority of nonprofit, community agencies, report trying to address issues and support programs that affect children and families. These issues include health, women's issues, child care, elementary and high school tutoring, multicultural issues, housing issues, poverty issues and economic development, arts and media, work with the elderly, services to the disabled, and environmental issues (Rothman et al. 1998). Although this book has a child and family community learning focus, such a perspective is a strength and an advantage because many communities and campuses are working hard to better support and work in partnership with child and family constituencies for a healthier society.

Thus, a central focus of the book is on improving community work with children and families. It should be noted, however, that the manner in which students make specific connections between basic child, adolescent, and adult concepts in their human development course curricula and their community learning experiences is not a central focus of this book.[4] Rather, it focuses on the workers' *emotional adjustment* and the *resources* that they draw upon for psychosocial assistance. Nonetheless, curricular connections to human development theories and concepts will be evident as I share students' emotions, experiences, and resources with respect to their community work. For example, in chapter 6 a worker shares a dilemma about not knowing how to redirect a preschooler who was scratching other children while pretending to be a cat. She notes on reflection that the child appeared to be in Piaget's "preoperational stage" of development (Berger and Thompson 1998) because of his need to literally scratch during the pretend play and because of his lack of awareness of how his scratching would feel from the other children's perspective. These are the kinds of connections that motivate me to include service-learning as part of my course curricula. However, while these kinds of academic connections are extremely important and visible in the book, the emotional development of the community worker takes precedence over them in this context. This allows me to stay within the primary mission of the book, which centers on the *adjustment* and *successful functioning* of the *community workers and their partners*.

The quotes selected for the book are representative of many similar comments that could not be included. Any experience that tends to be more singular is noted as such. I also try to acknowledge the influence of gender, socioeconomic status, "race," ethnic culture, and personality differences on interactions. The representative quotes are intended to familiarize you, the reader, with the overall process that occurred for many within the collective of 215 students.[5] While I hope that the book will familiarize you with the overall experience of community learning and help you at every step of the process, it is not meant to encourage a self-fulfilling prophecy. A self-fulfilling prophecy occurs when your knowledge or expectations about a person or situation lead you to prematurely behave in ways that confirm those expectations (Brehm and Kassin 1996). The concept of the self-fulfilling prophecy is mentioned here to caution you against expecting your own community learning to take place in exactly the same way that occurs for the service-learners here. Rather, you need to become familiar with the variety of approaches and resources that you will find helpful in the event that you need them. My intention in writing this book is to help you gain a familiarity with, and an understanding of, the issues experienced by these students and to use that information to your benefit *if* the challenge or opportunity presents itself. Each community experience is as distinctive as the combination of the circumstances, characters, personalities, resources, and maturity of those present in the situation. Therefore, it is important that you keep an open mind and flexible expectations as you learn about the experiences provided here because other community learning situations may unfold differently.

As you read the book, you may find it helpful to consider or imagine how you might have responded in the various situations that arise, that is, how you might have responded as a community worker, as a client, as a staff member, or as a member of the client's family or community. Again, remember that there is no one way to respond and that helpful approaches and general guidelines will be provided in the latter half of each chapter. One worker speaks to her recognition of the uniqueness of each situation during her own service learning:

> *There is no set protocol for every new situation. It is up to the teacher, parents, and school to help the child as best they can. Although I knew this to be true before this semester, it became real to me as I saw this problem solving put into action. Working with [children at a public elementary school] has opened my eyes to a whole new side of education and school of which I have never been aware. It showed me how problems can arise with individual students; and everyone has a responsibility to figure out what to do about it. (Female, European American)*

It is also important to remember that the community learning process can be examined from many different perspectives: the child's, the family's, the teacher's or agency personnel's, the administrator's, the faculty's, and the student's. This book focuses on students' perspectives on the community learning process. As you hear the students' voices and issues, please also be aware that there are other important voices and perspectives on the very same issues.[6] I will try to offer, as much as possible, expertise from the literature and from my own years of living and working in a diversity of community settings in order to provide insight into other possible perspectives.

Thus this book may be used as a text, a reference, or a general guide for assisting students in their community work. However, please note that the suggestions offered in this book are not immutable. They are intended only as provisional guideposts. Similarly, this book is not intended to serve as a substitute for individual orientations and counseling. It is a basic guide and introduction to the experiences and emotions of other workers engaged in the community learning process, not a solution for every problem or challenge that may be encountered by community workers. Therefore, while this work will not present a definitive answer to every challenge and situation that can arise in your community work, it does provide a variety of experiences, perspectives, and general guidelines that you may reflect on and find helpful.

HOW THIS BOOK IS ORGANIZED

Each chapter but one presents an introduction to the chapter topic, defines emergent themes related to the topic, identifies challenges related to the topic, describes competencies and resources, and offers practical tips—in that order. Thus each chapter begins by providing a basic introduction to the topics in it. Second, information is provided to delineate the various ways that the major theme of the chapter manifests itself as part of a community learning process. Third, a discussion of the challenges to that particular part of the community learning process is developed. Fourth, specific competencies and resources that seem helpful to workers are presented. Finally, each chapter ends with a list of practical tips to assist you in your community learning. Chapter 2 is organized somewhat differently because of its theoretical nature—providing the philosophy and theoretical underpinnings of curriculum-based community learning.

Beginning with this introduction, you may have noticed that student journal comments are accompanied by the student's gender and ethnic/racial membership. The gender and ethnic/racial data are provided to help you consider the students' comments within a richer context. Gender and ethnic/racial socialization are two of several powerful determinants of the manner in which information and circumstances are perceived and interpreted by people when they are interacting with others (Gilligan 1982; Kanter and Stein 1980; McIntosh 1990; Tatum 1992, 1997; Williams, McCandies, and Dunlap, in press). For this reason gender and ethnic/racial data are included when student comments are presented. This information is most relevant in chapters 4, 7, 8, and 10. Age, years in college, socioeconomic status, and college major are several of many other very important developmental characteristics. These characteristics are not listed because this information was not available consistently across participants.[7] When specific situations are discussed in the book, I try to provide as much contextual information as possible about the community workers, the client(s), and the specific community site, without violating worker, client, staff, or site anonymity. However, the presence of client information, such as age, grade level, race/ethnicity, and socioeconomic status, varies depending upon the degree of detail students provided in their journal accounts.

Each chapter includes selected resources if you, your course professors, or other facilitators of the community learning process would like to read more on the chapter topics. Each chapter ends with a blank reader's notes page for you to jot your ideas, thoughts, comments, questions, personal reactions, connections to course curricula or other issues you might like to address in your own journal or other reflection methods. In general, the chapters in part 1 and part 3, as a group, are presented in an order that follows the community learning process from the very beginning, when you are just getting organized for the start of your community work, to the very end, when you are preparing to say good-bye to the clients and staff with whom you have worked. The chapters in part 2 relate to issues that could occur at any time.

In conclusion, the community learning process has been as much a journey for me as it has for my students because of the many trials and triumphs that they have shared with me. In the pages that follow, I will present to you the major issues that my students articulated as they engaged in their community work with children and families.

I

BEGINNINGS

1

How Do I Get Started?

Getting Organized for Community Service and Learning

> *When I was at the community service fair, I was basically looking for a placement where I could observe children while having fun at the same time. Also, I have a pretty full schedule and don't really have the time for a big commitment, but the director who was at the fair was very flexible about finding a time for me to serve that would fit into my schedule. (Female, Hispanic)*

This chapter identifies the logistical issues and challenges involved in getting placed into a community learning environment. It also presents suggestions and ideas to assist you as you begin organizing and preparing for your actual community work.

The procedures for arranging a placement often vary from college to college and even from course to course. In some courses, the community learning location is preselected by the course professor. In other courses, the students select their own location. My students arrange their service-learning placements in one of several ways. They may begin by visiting a counselor at the campus Office of Volunteers for Community Service (OVCS), which is the central community learning support office for Connecticut College. Its staff provides information, orientation programs, support services, and location monitoring to assist students, faculty, agency personnel, and community partners in the community service process. As much as possible, OVCS tries to match the interests of the students, the requirements of the course, and the attributes of the community site.

Rather than visit the OVCS office right away, some students opt to visit the OVCS-sponsored Community Service Fair, which occurs at the beginning of each semester. During this one-day event, students visit and collect information distributed by representatives from a wide variety of nonprofit community agencies.

As I have traveled throughout the country to different service-learning conferences, I have become increasingly aware of the fact that not all colleges have these kinds of support systems in place for their students. I have also discovered that there are as many possible ways to implement a program as there are programs, so there is no one exemplary model to follow. However, research in the service-learning field has revealed that there are "best practices" for supporting and sustaining curriculum-based community learning programs (Robinson and Barnett 1998; see also Bringle and Duffy 1998; Erickson and Anderson 1997; Hatcher 1998; Howard 1993; Kendall and Associates 1990; Nyden, Figert, Shibley, and Burrows 1997; Zlotkowski 1998). For example, programs that hold student orientations, involve students in the college's community involvement process, use the team approach, hold group reflection sessions, track outcomes, and recognize and celebrate community involvement efforts tend to be more successful than those that don't include these components in the community learning process (Robinson and Barnett 1998).

You are advised to begin early on the procedures that have been put in place for setting up your community work. For liability reasons, try to avoid going outside the placement boundaries set by your professors and administrators unless you can negotiate special arrangements with them.

Once a placement site is selected, you must work out (within the guidelines set by your professor, the campus community service office, and/or the agency) starting and ending dates and a weekly schedule. In my courses, students arrange two to four hours of service-learning in one or two visits per week for the span of the semester. They can also arrange, through the OVCS office, regular transportation to and from their placement location.

When you go through the process of arranging your community placement, you should concern yourself with determining *where* to work, the *appropriateness* of the site for the course, your *transportation* options, your specific duties or *tasks,* and the *time* commitment that you will be expected to make. Ideally, the placement should be one that your professor has approved and one that you genuinely find interesting. It should be one that will provide adequate connections to your course curriculum while also allowing you to work with clientele and staff.

HOW TO GET STARTED

My previous experiences suggest that many students have a relatively clear sense of the kind of placement they desire and the kinds of placements that

are expected for their course(s). Thus many, though not all, will feel motivated and ambitious about setting up their placements (Serow 1991; Stukas,
Snyder, and Clary 1999b) and may visit potential sites and make follow-up
telephone calls. Many will find that available placements match their interests. In addition, support from placement staff and college administration
can assist in making the community service adjustment process run
smoothly. One student describes a preliminary visit that she arranged in
order to put the various details of her placement into order:

> *[The supervisor at a children's dance program] and I finally got in touch with
> each other and arranged to meet today. The meeting was very productive. First
> of all, it served as an introduction to each other for both of us. Second, we de-
> cided on the days that I will go into the program to help out. After much dis-
> cussion, we came to the conclusion that it would be better for me to be involved
> with smaller children rather than work as an accompanist for the older, more
> advanced students. She purposely placed me in a class with two young boys.
> She feels, and I agree, that my influence as a male role model will be very help-
> ful to them. (Male, European American)*

For others, however, setting up the placements may not run so smoothly.
Despite your intentions and high levels of motivation, logistical challenges
outside of your control may exist and may delay your making a placement
decision or beginning your placement work with ease. Two students provide
examples:

> *[On Monday] I have been very frustrated in the last couple of weeks. I would
> like to volunteer at [a women's shelter], and the woman that I have at-
> tempted to contact about it has been playing phone tag with me! I call and
> leave a message for her and then she calls me back and I'm not in, so she
> leaves a message for me, and we keep missing each other. It is getting very
> upsetting to me!! [On the following Wednesday] I finally got everything
> worked out!! I'm going to volunteer on Tuesdays and Wednesdays from 3 to
> 4:15. (Female, European American)*

> *When I got no response [from the agency volunteer supervisor after three weeks
> of phone calls], I was perturbed and frustrated, and thus called her again, stat-
> ing on her voice mail, "Hi, this is _____ calling. I left you a note last week
> about a placement. I am still very interested in working with you. However, this
> placement is part of a class requirement and I really need to get going on it as
> soon as possible. So, could you please return my call and let me know if you're
> still interested in my help, or if I should move on and look for a different place-
> ment? Thank you!" Finally, I received a call from her on my voice mail, saying
> that she was indeed interested in my working with the children and she apol-
> ogized profusely. She has promised to have me placed in the program and
> working by the end of the week, and I'm excited to begin. (Male, European
> American)*

Ultimately, things worked out well for these students in their service-learning programs. It just took a little longer than usual to catch up with their agency contact persons so that they could get their schedules arranged.

There are also cases where you initially may not feel certain about your placement choice. If you prioritize your interests, you can work through this challenge with ease. As one student articulates:

> *I knew I wanted to participate in a community service position this term prior to learning of the course requirement, but there were so many options. I narrowed my options to tutoring and coaching sports, and the class's requirements led me more toward tutoring. I believed it would be easier to observe children's behaviors as a tutor rather than a coach. I also wanted to serve in a position that would honor my mother, as she was a teacher. Thus tutoring seemed appropriate. (Female, European American)*

Indeed, some of you will have community interests that are apt to be either diffused or, in some cases, absent. Some of you may feel ambivalent about engaging in community learning at all. You may feel a lack of motivation and ambition about setting up your placement, and may, consequently, be vulnerable to procrastination. If you procrastinate, however, you may find that there are no placements available that match your interests, especially if you do not have other alternative interests delineated. You must allow for processing time at the placement site and therefore should move swiftly. For example, some placements require letters of recommendation, interviews, background checks, and/or immunizations, so you do not want to delay. If you are reluctant to compromise on your site choices because of time restrictions and location limits, you may find the suggestions at the end of this chapter helpful.

Challenges such as difficulty in contacting the site personnel, arranging transportation, scheduling, and communicating can occur when you are arranging your placement. It is important that you do not become overly discouraged and that you persevere until all of your community work arrangements have been made. For example, you could make telephone calls and visits, and you should consult with community service support staff as soon as it seems that things are not progressing as well as expected.

For freshmen and transfer students, the frustrations of organizing for community learning can be exacerbated by the complex set of other adjustments that come with entering a new educational setting (Chickering and Schlossberg 1995). On the other hand, having community experiences in the "real world" can help to keep you grounded as you realize that life on campus, though far from trivial, may be relatively simple in comparison to the complexities that may exist elsewhere. Students describe this:

> *It is so nice when you are having a stressful day or things in life just seem so confusing that you can have a conversation with a [preschool] child and they will put everything into perspective. A child never thinks about getting an A on*

that math test or getting into that one college that you really want to go to or even how much it costs to go to a movie. (Female, European American)

These [elementary school] children have taught me more than I could ever have taught them. Whenever I felt things were out of place or not going right, these children have reminded me to take each day for what it is worth. They reminded me of innocence, of pure hearts, and of eager minds. I have seen them endure the economic stigmas, the language barrier, and their cultural differences, and I have seen them embrace their situations. So, although I didn't help anyone with their math today or correct any English as a second language papers or hang up any of their artwork on the wall, I felt as if today was the day I learned the most and did the most. I was able to see the impact I had on them. I saw the impact they had on me. (Female, Asian American)

Likewise, there may be occasions when transportation systems may not run as smoothly in everyday life as they appear to on paper or on schedule cards. This too may be very frustrating when it happens. For example:

Today is November 16 and again the school van is late. I am sick and tired of standing out in the cold for twenty minutes to half an hour. I love seeing my [elementary school] kids and being with them. It is just the ending when I have to say good-bye five minutes early in case the van is there so they won't leave me, but then they are not there. (Female, African American)

When these kinds of circumstances occur, you must exercise as much patience as possible. To coordinate transportation services, a college may set up hundreds of vehicle runs per day to get students to and from their community work locations. Even with the best planning and scheduling, there are bound to be glitches in the implementation of the transportation schedule from time to time. And even when logistical glitches occur, opportunities for learning and connecting with others may still abound, as illustrated in the following example:

I went today [to a soup kitchen community after-school program] prepared to do volunteer work. I entered the building only to find out I was not yet needed. The secretary was about to leave and offered to give me a ride back because [our campus] was on her way home. She was extremely friendly and informative about working at the [site]. I now have a pretty good picture about what to expect and I am superexcited. I got a lot out of simply visiting the site even though I was not yet needed. (Female, European American)

There may also be difficulties in terms of coordinating your time and schedule with the schedules and activities that are available for community work at particular agencies. For example:

One thing that bothered me about my service-learning project was that the only time I could fit into my schedule to volunteer was the period that included the children's rest hour. I felt that this was kind of a lost hour in my time with them and that if I had a chance to be with them in the morning, perhaps I would have learned just a little more. (Female, European American)

Although from time to time confusion or disappointment may be present in the initial phase of the community learning process, it is important that you remain as consistent and dependable as possible, even if you do not see others behaving that way. When discouragement and other difficulties occur, you are advised to report such challenges to the appropriate parties (e.g., the community learning coordinator at the college). In addition, you should be prepared to exercise patience and consistency when things do not run as smoothly as planned. Patience and consistency are appreciated by the staff with whom you will work and by the clients who come to rely on your presence. The following incident illustrates this point:

The first thing my little buddy said to me when I saw him was "bend down." I bent at the knees and placed my head on his level. He preceded to grab my nose with a moderate grip and said, "You owe me an apology. You said you were going to come in last week and you didn't." What happened was that the last time I saw him I told him I would see him next week. What I failed to remember was that I had my spring vacation. I smiled and was about to explain the mixup when I decided that it would be better if I just apologized, and I reassured him that it would not happen again. (Male, European American)

ARRANGING COMMUNITY LEARNING: HELPFUL APPROACHES

As you arrange community learning, it is helpful, first, to be organized, second, to think critically about your work on a regular basis and, third, to keep a journal.

My previous experiences with community learning students suggests that you are more likely to begin your community assignment with ease if you approach it in an organized and flexible fashion. This requires you to be clear and realistic about your schedule, to know exactly when the available times are in your schedule, to persevere in trying to find placements that will match your schedule, and to be willing to compromise, when necessary, in order to meet your other obligations. For example, some students have selected their second- or third-choice placements because they provided evening or weekend hours rather than their first-choice placement, which would have put them into an uncomfortable time crunch during the weekdays. The following student shares an example of forfeiting a first-choice site because of a time crunch; a recommendation from a friend prompted her toward another option:

I came across my site on a suggestion from a classmate. After many weeks of repeatedly searching, I was becoming really frustrated and welcomed my classmate's suggestion. It proved successful in accommodating my schedule. Personally, [my service-learning site] wasn't my first choice. I wanted to get more involved with the social services, i.e., [an HIV/AIDs support center], a women's center or a child abuse center, but at that moment there wasn't any-thing available for Saturdays or Sundays. (Female, European American)

Taking an appropriate degree of responsibility for your own community service experiences will help you to treat your work as a personal benefit rather than as just a course requirement (Stukas et al. 1999b). By valuing your community service as personally beneficial, you will be more likely to readily set up and organize the placement, especially when you are provided support from the facilitators within the community service environment. You will also recognize the mutual and reciprocal nature of your service and learning in the community and will behave responsibly not only for your own sake but also out of consideration for those with whom you work.

REFLECTING CRITICALLY

You can engage in critical reflection by talking, writing, or communicating in some other manner about your experiences on a regular basis. If you talk or write critically about your community experiences with your peers, and your professors, and administrators who can help facilitate the community in-volvement process, you tend to feel better supported in the community learning process. It is important that you reflect critically, without violating the privacy and confidentiality of those with whom you are working (see appendix C). Thus it is helpful to refer to clients or staff, for example, by initials instead of using names. Group discussions and journal keeping are two commonly used methods of facilitating critical reflection.

Group Discussions

Some find it easy to participate in group discussions about community service experiences. Others, especially those who are very shy, may find these discussions awkward at times because of their personal nature. Whether it initially comes naturally to you or not, processing your experiences with others in similar circumstances will prevent you from feeling isolated in terms of the challenges and rewards that you experience during the community learning process. A student shares:

Our reflection time during class gave me the chance to share the stress of the situation with my classmates. I now have a place to put my frustrations. Many of my classmates offered wonderful feedback that allowed me to process the situation. (Female, African American)

Keeping a Journal

Your course journal keeping is very important. Making time for written and oral reflection is a key component of community service and learning (Cooper 1998; Eyler et al. 1996; Goldsmith 1993; Kahne and Westheimer 1996; Norrell et al. 1997; Robinson and Barnett 1998; Sigmon 1994; Wade 1997).

Although some may find journal keeping to be sheer drudgery of only tangential value, most consider this way of reflecting on their community service as vitally significant. Journaling provides an opportunity to clarify thoughts and ideas, and it also provides emotional relief. Reflecting on your experiences and writing about them in a journal, while not always easy to do, is cathartic.

The particular method of keeping a journal can vary depending on the community learning project and the course professor (Eyler et al. 1996). I instruct my students on the technique of journal writing (appendix A) and expect them to discuss in their journals any course concepts that become apparent to them during their community service. I also ask them to describe the manner in which a concept becomes apparent to them. The following student, for example, notes the concept of sex stereotyping and shares how it became revealed to her in her community learning environment:

> *The children in [a particular preschool] classroom love to engage in sociodramatic play. I observed that the children were making "food" for their babies. One boy brought over a baby to the table. The two other boys began to laugh at him because he had the baby in his lap. The boy retaliated, "Now my baby is crying because you guys laughed at her." He picked up the baby and looked at it. The boys continued to laugh, and the boy told them to cut it out, and he continued to play with the doll. The children were working through their ideas about sex stereotyping. Even though the boys teased him, they eventually stopped and continued to play with him. (Female, European American)*

Thus this student was illuminated on the concepts of sex stereotyping and sociodramatic play (Berger and Thompson 1998). Although she does not use the term "gender socialization," it is implied in her discussion of sex stereotyping.

Students are encouraged to be sensitive to the psychosocial climate and their own emotions and reactions as they engage in the community (appendix A). In the following quote, a worker notes that a client appears apathetic, she also provides clear evidence for *why* she perceives him that way. She also describes her own thoughts in response to his demeanor:

> *When I first met [a particular elementary school boy], I thought that his body language was apathetic: he was usually frowning or hunched over a table, or*

he was fidgeting with something while staring off somewhere. I felt that I needed to touch him or direct his eyes to mine to even make eye contact with him. (Female, European American)

The following student comments suggest that they find journal keeping extremely valuable, and they offer a diversity of insights into the value of their journals:

Processing these experiences and ideas in the journal allowed me to explore some of my own feelings. Had I not processed these observations [at a preschool] in the journal, perhaps they would have just faded away. (Male, Hispanic)

The journal really helped me to recognize that human development concepts occur in real life. Although sometimes it was a real pain to write in the journal about my experiences at [a child care center], I think that without it, I would not have realized many of the things that I know now. (Female, European American)

I often can't relate [my child care center] activities to the text or to the class right away. I just often see them as kids and having fun. I am more likely to make accurate comparisons of the textual information with my visits when I reflect versus when I interact with the children. (Female, European American)

Thus it is healthy for you to talk about and to reflect on your community learning experiences with others in order to make appropriate connections to course curricula, to help you critically analyze your perceptions regarding your community environment, and to help you realize that your feelings and concerns are quite often a common and normal part of the community service process. Whatever your inclination toward writing, you are strongly encouraged to take journal keeping seriously (using the method provided by your instructors). You are also encouraged to be diligent and consistent about journal reflection, and to make connections as much as possible to your course curriculum and personal knowledge base. It is during the articulation of your experiences, reactions, issues, and curricular connections that you reveal to yourself and your course instructor what your curricular and personal revelations actually are. Without such articulations, much of the richness of the community learning experience and connections to the course curriculum may be lost.

In closing, with some planning, organization, and flexibility, you should be on your way to beginning your community work assignment. The following practical tips recap the approaches that are helpful at this stage of the community learning process.

PRACTICAL TIPS

- Start getting organized for your community learning as early as possible. You can minimize feelings of being overwhelmed by not waiting until the last minute to arrange a community learning location. Start early by making calls and visits of inquiry.

- Research available placements. Use the resources accessible for exploring placement options, beginning with your central office for community service. If your college does not have a central office, your course instructor will most likely provide instructions for arranging your community site. In some circumstances, you may research community agencies yourselves before selecting a location. In this case, recommendations from previous students, faculty, and administrators will be essential.

- Attend community service showcases and orientations. If there is a community service fair or some other orientation for acquainting yourself with community learning options and processes, make every effort to attend it. If this resource is not available, then you might consider tapping into whatever resources are provided by the college or by your professor for identifying potential placements. At a minimum, the college or your professor should have a working list of sites where students have worked in the past. Investigate your placement options within the limits of what is feasible, given the resources that are available to you.

- Determine your interests. One of the first things you will need to do is envision the kinds of community work that most interest you. Ask yourself what your community interests are. Create a list of the kinds of places you might find rewarding. Rewrite the list in the order of the jobs most desirable to you. Include alternate interests and placements in case your first choices are not available. See which placements provide experiences that match your interests. After you have created your initial list, remind yourself of the purpose of the course and your instructor's expectations regarding the community learning assignment. Put an asterisk next to those placements that match the objectives of the course.

- Consult available resources. Begin early by taking advantage of any support services that are available to acquaint you with programs and the community learning process. If there seems to be no overlap between your own interests and the placements that are available, you may want to consult with the professor. Central community service office staff can also be helpful in this regard. You may find it useful to refer back to your course syllabus to refresh your memory about the professor's guidelines on community learning placements. In some cases, the community learning location has been predetermined. If you missed the first class meeting, refer to the course syllabus and consult with your course professor to be sure that you are clear about placement criteria and expectations. In general, when it comes to your community learning experience, do not hesitate to seek support from the appropriate faculty and administrators.

- Network and explore within appropriate limits. So that you do not put yourself or your college at risk for liability, avoid striking out on your own when selecting a placement. You should first establish that the agency you are considering is reputable and that it or its constituents have some past or current history with your college. You are strongly advised to select your placement in consultation or negotiation with your professor and/or other college staff.

- Be practical. When deciding on your placement and designing or negotiating your placement schedule, be sure to consider your daily course schedule and other day-to-day obligations. Be both practical and efficient in the use of your time. Similarly, be realistic and practical about your transportation needs concerning all potential community service positions. Remember that buses, vans, and taxis do not always run on time. You need to build a little cushion of time into your schedule to account for tardiness in transportation so that you are not late for your assignment, your courses, and your other obligations.

- Be reliable. Once you have negotiated and agreed upon a schedule, commit to being on time for each visit. Commit to being consistent, reliable, and conscientious in your work at your community service site, not only for the sake of your own reputation but also for the sake of your college's reputation and that of your placement. In addition, do not treat the clientele or community members with whom you will work in a manner that you would not want to be treated yourself, for example, by showing up late or inconsistently for your work and your learning with them.

- Take journal keeping seriously. Whether journal keeping comes naturally to you or not, keep a journal and write in it regularly. Much of the learning and connections to course curricula will be revealed as you try to articulate your observations and experiences.

- Take verbal reflection seriously. It is during your struggle and others' struggle to articulate community work experiences, reactions, issues, concerns, and connections to your curriculum that you have an opportunity to discover the similarities and uniqueness in your experiences. Such discussions provide an opportunity for people to share ideas and offer support to one another.

- Exercise discretion. It is good to share your experiences with your classmates, faculty, and administrators who are involved in the community learning process. However, it is equally important to share discreetly, honoring the privacy of the personnel and clientele with whom you are working. I advise my students not to use client names and agency personnel names when communicating with one another about their experiences. In their written communication, such as journals, I ask students to use first initials rather than names. For additional guidelines governing privacy and confidentiality, see appendix C.

FURTHER READING

Chickering, A., and N. Schlossberg. 1995. Time management, learning, and test taking. In *Getting the Most Out of College*. Boston: Allyn & Bacon.

Dunlap, M. 1998d. Methods of supporting students' critical reflection in courses incorporating service learning. *Teaching of Psychology* 25, no. 3: 208–210.

Eyler, J., D. Giles, and A. Schmiede. 1996. *A practitioner's guide to reflection in service-learning: Student voices and reflections*. Nashville, Tenn.: Vanderbilt University Press.

Goldsmith, S. 1993. *Journal reflection: A resource guide for community service leaders and educators engaged in service-learning*. Washington, D.C:. American Alliance for Rights and Responsibilities.

Hatcher, J., ed. 1998. *Service-learning tip sheets: A faculty resource guide*. Indianapolis: Indiana Campus Compact. 850 W. Michigan, Suite 200, Indianapolis, IN 46202.

Robinson, G., and L. Barnett. 1998. Best practices in service learning. *Project brief 98/3*. Washington, D.C.: American Association of Community Colleges. one Dupont Circle, NW, Suite 410, Washington, D.C. 20036-1176.

Rothman, M., E. Anderson, and J. Schaffer. 1998. *Service matters: Engaging higher education in the renewal of America's communities and American democracy. Campus Compact lessons from the field*. Providence, R.I.: Campus Compact Brown University.

University of Colorado–Boulder 1995. *Service-learning handbook*. Boulder: University of Colorado–Boulder, Student Employment and Service Learning Center. http://csf.colorado.edu/sl/cu/handbk95.html.

Wade, R. 1997. "Preparation" and "Reflection." In *Community service-learning: A guide to including service in the public school curriculum*. Albany: State University of New York Press.

Reader Notes

2

While You Are Getting Ready

Community Service and Learning in Context

> *Service-learning [at a middle school] gives me a visual application for the course material. In addition, it allows me to create relationships with the students. It is my hope that through these relationships I can gain a genuine understanding of the students. The things that I learn during this experience will be extremely valuable to my future in working as a legal advocate for children. (Female, African American)*

The above comment shows that curriculum-based community work has a way of helping you bring a course more fully to life, providing you with many opportunities to connect course content to the real world. The comments also suggest that often your hopes and dreams are tied in to the work that you do, even though it is part of a course assignment. For others, the personal relevance of your community work may not be apparent until much later, and for still others, perhaps never. In any case, the next few chapters will explore the emotional processes in depth. But for now, while you are finalizing your community placement and schedule arrangements, I would like to present information on the philosophies and underpinnings of community learning, so that you will have a greater understanding of the definitions, history, and evolution of such programs.

CURRICULUM-BASED COMMUNITY WORK

When professors and teachers include service-learning[1] and other curriculum-based programs in their courses, they provide students with real-life opportunities to cognitively grapple with the "theories acquired in the classroom and

17

to concretize abstract thought . . . leading to a deeper grasp of course material" (Campus Compact 1993, 7). Thus, for the purpose of this book, "service-learning" and other curriculum-based forms of community service, though similar to volunteerism in many ways,[2] are differentiated from volunteerism in that they assume *mutual* learning between workers and community members, require workers to regularly devote time and attention to reflect on and communicate about their experiences in the community where they are placed, and encourage workers' exploration of the relationships among observations, experiences, and course curriculum materials through a critical reflection process. To whatever degree a volunteer or other community learning experience includes these components, the workers' adjustment process is expected to parallel that of service-learners in some respects.

The process that you will encounter as you engage in curriculum-based community service has been identified as one of the top ten most important community learning research issues to be addressed in the coming years (Giles, Honnet, and Migliore 1991; Giles and Eyler 1998). Studies indicate that in addition to assisting in the learning of course concepts, community involvement can also increase your sense of social responsibility and connectedness to communities, your sense of community efficacy, your valuation of systemic approaches to social problems, and your racial tolerance (Berson 1997; Boss 1994; Eyler and Giles 1999; Eyler, Giles, and Braxton 1997; Giles and Eyler 1998; Primavera 1999). However, because there are many issues and processes to be addressed and assessed, researchers have only scratched the surface in terms of understanding the psychological effects, personality adjustment, and emotional outcomes involved in community learning (Driscoll et al. 1997). Thus community learning and its different forms is an area of inquiry that is continuously evolving and is growing at a rapid pace (Rothman et al. 1998; Stukas, Clary, and Snyder 1999a).

THE HISTORY OF CURRICULUM-BASED COMMUNITY WORK

Community work in the United States dates back to the Native peoples who helped each other plant and harvest crops (Wade 1997). Although community work has always been a part of our American culture, more recent pioneering efforts on a college-wide level became overwhelmingly popular in the 1960s and 1970s (Coles 1993; Delve et al. 1990; Stanton, Giles, and Cruz 1999; Weigert 1998). Students then were guided by a determination, an idealism, and a concern for society that motivated them to take to the streets in a spirit of community activism for social change. During the 1980s, student community activism significantly waned as the political climate and the economy changed. Students became more conservative in the use of their "free" time. Currently, there seems to be a resurgence of community service and learning as a vital part of high school and undergraduate education because of the work of college community service organizations such as COOL (Campus Outreach Opportunity League), VISTA (Volunteers in Service to America), Campus Compact (Rothman et al. 1998), and public calls such as President Clinton's and General Colin Powell's "call to service" to the youth of our nation (Wade 1997). The resurgence in volunteer and curriculum-based community learning has been apparent in the growth of women's centers on and off campus, antiviolence campaigns, building programs such as Habitat for Humanity, and after-school programs for children and families. The popularity of movements such as the service-learning movement has grown with each passing year since the 1980s (Delve et al. 1990; Orr 1999; Ryan 1999; Stanton et al. 1999; Wade 1997).

THE BENEFITS OF COMMUNITY LEARNING

Those of you who are new to the curriculum-based community learning experience might take some comfort in thinking about the many benefits that you will potentially gain as a result of your engagement in such a process. The benefits include bringing theories into active learning and practice, visualizing concepts through real-life experiences, assisting participants in perceiving the strengths and weaknesses of specific environments, improving self-knowledge, making connections to communities that otherwise might remain unfamiliar, and providing multicultural experiences and improving competency skills (Berson 1997; Dunlap 1998b; Eyler and Giles 1999; Eyler et al. 1997; Harkavy and Benson 1998; Hatcher 1998; Hatcher and Bringle 1997; Primavera 1999). Students share examples of these kinds of benefits:

In observing what I was learning about in my child development class, I found that the subject came alive for me. Not only did I learn about child development and the children I was working with, but I know that I learned a lot about myself. (Female, European American)

I arrived that first day to see that not only was I the only white teacher assistant but I was also the only white person in the whole center. I was overwhelmed with questions. How would they treat me? Would I have nothing in common with these people? Would the students like me? I learned quickly that love was all these kids cared about. They didn't care what color my skin was or where I lived. I had never been the person who was in the minority. I met children age 3-5 that were so happy and loving that it shocked me that they came from challenging situations. (Female, European American)

Community learning experiences are also useful to students for clarification of their career path and for motivating them toward future work in the community. Workers often speak of the benefit of their being provided experience for future employment and social activism. For example:

Coming into this, I knew that I wanted to be a teacher; I just didn't know what age group I wanted to teach. Every week I became more and more sure, and now I know that I want to work at an elementary level. I can only hope that I can spend the rest of my life helping children learn, hopefully making a difference in their lives, and, in return, gaining such a rewarding feeling for myself. (Female, European American)

This has been an incredible way to do some serious self-discovery. I think the most important thing I got from this [elementary school] experience would be that I realized I want to work with kids. Right now I am aiming to become an art teacher for a middle school. I wonder if I would have discovered this aspect of myself if it weren't for this experience. (Female, European American)

After each visit I am more and more convinced that I want to practice dentistry with children like the ones that I am working with in the inner city. (Male, European American)

Service-learning and other forms of curriculum-based community learning are not without their difficulties. There are many challenges in comparison to traditional teaching paradigms. Such programs may, in part, translate into increased work for faculty and students; increased reliance on college resources in order to facilitate the logistics of providing community service experiences; concern over transportation and other logistical needs and issues; and greater difficulty in defining, articulating, and assessing learning objectives (Berson 1997; Hatcher 1998). These challenges, as revealed through the eyes of the student participants, will be explored in detail throughout the book. It should also be noted that not every student is sold on the idea of community learning as a component of their course (Stukas et al. 1999b). For example, the first student below did not care for service-learning at all yet found that it informed her desires about career choices. The second disagreed with curriculum-based service as a matter of principle.

The service component was so annoying. If this service-learning experience has taught me anything, it is that I definitely don't want to work with kids at any point in my life because I can't deal with them. I was just glad to be done because I didn't feel like this was a beneficial experience at all. (Female, European-American)

I never felt comfortable about the fact that I was doing this "for a requirement." This should be work that is done without any repercussions of a grade. This is not saying anything about the class. This is saying that I would like to continue this out of my own free will, and I feel that others should as well, and they should not only be doing it for a requirement or for a good grade. One should not have to be asked to serve the community, it should be implied. I am learning something new about children every time I visit, helping them, myself, and this nation's future. (Male, European American)

Making greater strides in providing resources and models for coping more effectively with the various difficulties, and increasing the benefits, have been recommended as part of the future research agenda in service-learning (Giles and Eyler 1998). As mentioned earlier, curriculum-based and other forms of community learning, like any other area of inquiry, are "in progress" and are constantly evolving. The following student articulates the reality of the challenge of engaging in community work with children and families. In doing so, she helps to articulate the purpose of the work presented in this book:

Community work is difficult. Anyone who is going to romanticize this experience into an easy and fun time cannot possibly understand the complex dynamics that occur. For example, in three hours at [an elementary school] I felt a huge wave of feelings ranging from intimidation and frustration to great motivation and satisfaction. Sensitivity to individual differences—while keeping the necessary tools of cultural, social, and psychological knowledge in one's pocket—remains a continuous challenge for me. With each encounter I have with these children, I am constantly thinking about meeting their individual needs in the context of a cultural whole. (Female, European American)

In summary, the community service and learning process is a complex one with no set or fixed formulas but rather dynamic, ever changing and evolving processes and approaches. As you continue along your path and begin your community work, you should keep in mind that there may be times when complex issues will reveal themselves. Quick-fix, straightforward solutions to every challenge often will not be available. Hopefully, however, the material and resources provided throughout the book will shed some light along your unique path of experiences as you serve and learn.

PRACTICAL TIPS

- Think on some of the issues discussed in this chapter. Consider the definition(s) and meaning(s) of the kind of community work that you are doing. Whom should your work benefit? Is your work with the clients potentially mutually beneficial? How can you benefit from your work? How can the clients benefit? What are the possible costs for you? What are the possible costs for the clients? Do the potential costs outweigh the benefits? Why or why not?

- While you are waiting, review the practical tips listed in chapter 1 and be sure that everything is in order concerning your community work. Be sure that you have covered all of your bases, confirming the start date, the schedule of your visits, the duration of each visit, and your ending date. Try to find out to whom you should report upon your arrival. Be sure that your transportation and other supports are in place.

FURTHER READING

Bringle, R., and D. Duffy, eds. 1998. *With service in mind: Concepts and models for service-learning in psychology.* Washington, D.C.: American Association for Higher Education.

Chickering, A., and N. Schlossberg. 1995. Maximizing learning beyond courses and classes. In *Getting the most out of college.* Boston: Allyn & Bacon.

Coles, R. 1993. *The call of service: A witness to idealism.* Boston: Houghton Mifflin.

Delve, C., S. Mintz, and G. Stewart, eds. 1990. *Community service as values education.* San Francisco: Jossey-Bass.

Driscoll, A., et al. 1997. *Assessing the impact of service-learning: A workbook of strategies and methods.* Portland, Ore.: Portland State University Press.

Eyler, J., and D. Giles. 1999. *Where's the learning in service-learning?* San Francisco: Jossey-Bass.

Rhoads, R., and J. Howard, eds. 1998. *Academic service learning: A pedagogy of action and reflection.* San Francisco: Jossey-Bass.

Wade, R. 1997. *Community service-learning: A guide to including service in the public school curriculum.* Albany: State University of New York Press.

Weisbard, P. 1999. *Feminist collections: A quarterly of Women's Studies resources special issue on academy/community connections* 20, no. 3. Madison: University of Wisconsin System.

Reader Notes

3

What in the World Am I Doing Here?

The First Visits

*The longer I wait to do this, the more anxious I get with nervous antici-
pation. I just want to get started. I am still nervous about beginning my
work with these sixth graders. . . . [Several days later] Finally, I got to go
today, and I was a little nervous at first, but that wore off as soon as I was
actually in the classroom. (Female, European American)*

This chapter will acquaint you with some of the emotions and experiences
of community learners as they actually began their work. By now you should
have selected your placement site and arranged your schedule. Perhaps it is
now almost time for that first or second visit. Your first couple of visits can
set the tone for later visits and in some cases for the entire placement.

When I first started reading student service-learning journals, the emotions that students expressed about their initial visits caught my attention.
The feelings and experiences seemed so diverse and yet recurred throughout the journals. Most interesting were the different approaches that students take. Some students approach their service-learning requirement as
if they just want to complete it as quickly and painlessly as possible, and
move on. A few try to avoid the task altogether. A few indicate that they
expected service-learning with children and families to be akin to baby-
sitting. They learn quickly that such learning with children is different from
baby-sitting. Sitting tends to take place with a smaller number of children,
in a more personal setting, and with less moment-to-moment supervision
than does community work. Overall, student journals reflect that first visits
can be one of the most challenging yet wonderfully exciting parts of the
community learning process.

THE FIRST VISIT

You can expect to grapple with several issues during your first visits—(1) your initial impressions of your site, (2) your initial emotions, (3) the welcome you receive at your site, and (4) the balancing of your roles and expectations.

First Impressions

The journals of my students suggest that if you are not accustomed to environments that are socioeconomically, historically, and commercially challenged, you may be surprised by the physical appearance of some of the facilities within which children and families reside, earn their education and livelihood, and receive social services. Students comment:

The [child care center] was not what I expected, to say the least. It was located in a low-income neighborhood. The inside of the day care center was typical for a day care center. It was fairly clean, but the furniture and supplies were all old and run-down. (Female, European American)

Any feelings of doubt and fear I had were greatly magnified when I finally arrived at [a child care] center. The outside is a little run-down, almost warehouse looking. A strange looking center in a strange place. Embarrassing as it may be, I was ready to turn on my heels and run after the van. As I turned the corner, I saw a happy playground full of screaming children. This wasn't going to be so bad after all. The kids came pouring over to the fence and started riddling me with questions: "Who are you? Are you going to play with us? Is she a stranger? I don't know, she doesn't look like a stranger." I just smiled. I found my way inside and was introduced to the director of the center. She is a wonderful and friendly woman who truly seems to enjoy her work. The center on the inside is an amazing place. (Female, European American)

Regardless of appearance, eventually you will be able to distinguish between the physical appearance of some of the buildings and the quality of the services that are provided within. In spite of first impressions about the buildings and facilities, you will most likely feel more comfortable with each additional visit. For many, the community learning experience starts off well and remains positive. For example:

This service experience is extremely challenging and beneficial for me because I am working with students of color who are from the inner city. A lot of the children are very socially mature and they talk back frequently. Nevertheless, I must relate to them in a very caring manner regardless of their attitudes. Most of the kids warmed up to me very fast and started to ask me questions: Where I was from? Am I their new counselor? And did I see that new movie with Jamie Foxx and Vivica Fox? I enjoyed answering these questions because they made me feel that the students were feeling comfortable with me and accepting me. (Female, African American)

Initial Emotions

Many of you will feel some initial discomfort as you begin your community learning experience (Dunlap 1998a). To one degree or another, you may feel overwhelmed, awkward, anxious, confused, inadequate, isolated, in the way, and/or unwelcome. Such emotions are a normal part of most adjustment processes and are usually transitory (Dunlap 1998a). Try to remain optimistic about your work in spite of your normal apprehension. Several students describe their feelings and outlook:

> *Personally I feel frightened. I have never worked with children with special needs. In spite of this, I see this service-learning as an important opportunity and challenge. I am excited and happy about my placement. I will try my best to help these children. (Male, European American)*

> *As of now I still feel like an outsider [at a crime remediation after-school program]. At this point I think they are still checking me out, trying to find out what's my angle. I don't think it will be difficult; they think I'm kind of cool. I have not reached a connection with anyone yet, but I have tried to talk one-on-one with most of them. (Male, Caribbean/Hispanic/African American)*

> *Personally I feel really stupid doing a lot of the things that we do in this [preschool arts] class, and the kids have fun with it. I'm trying, but I just can't get out of my mind how stupid I must look at times. Honestly how I feel in this service-learning project at the moment is fairly awkward. I've only had one day so this may change in the future. (Female, European American)*

Warm and Cold Welcomes

Many of you will feel warmly welcomed when you first arrive at your site, which can aid in the adjustment process. You may be hugged by children and greeted kindly by staff. For example:

> *[The teacher with whom I will work at the child care center] came into the room and greeted me. I was really impressed by the teachers. I think that they provide a nurturing and loving environment for the children and service-learners. (Female, European American)*

There may be some instances, however, when you feel rejected by the agency staff or clientele during the very first visits. The people there initially may not make you feel welcome or they may "keep you out." For example:

> *The fact is, this teacher [at a child care center] was so unfriendly to not only me but to all the children. It seemed to me as if someone had once said to her, "so, where is the last place you would ever want to work, because that is where you are going." She acted like it was a toss up between working with children at the*

[child care center] and shoveling coal in the pits of hell. By her attitude, if that person asked her again, she would say the pits of hell. The whole time I was there, she never once spoke to a child except to reprimand. And I think she hates me. (Female, European American)

Today was my first morning with the young children at the [child care center]. When my friend and I first walked in, I felt somewhat out of place because none of the four teachers there bothered to introduce herself, with the exception of one. I felt as though they thought of us as rich snobs from [the college] and that was making me feel really uneasy. After a few minutes, though, we began to mingle with the toddlers and play with them as though we were best buddies. I chatted with a few of the teachers for a moment, and in fact, they were very pleasant to me, despite the fact that I still do not know their names. In all, I had fun! (Female, European American)

I have this feeling of dread when I think about the next few months [at a re-medial after-school program]. I really hope it gets better. Maybe when [the preadolescent children] get used to me, they will feel more comfortable asking me for help, and maybe when I get used to them, I will feel more comfortable also. They seem to have a lot of inside jokes. They all know each other and the directors, but they don't know me, and I don't know them. I hope that I can get to know them all before I am done. (Female, European American)

What students eventually learn is that in most circumstances, rapport and trust among clients, community workers, and agency personnel take a period to develop but do tend to improve with time and experience (see chapter 5).

You may also struggle with the myths, expectations, and other preconceived notions that you might carry with you as you encounter your work environment. In the first example, a student shares her and her partner's reaction to a young male adult client with muscular dystrophy with whom they worked in the role of community peer companions. In the second and third examples, students share their initial expectations in regard to working with clients of diverse backgrounds. Notice how each one struggles with myths or inaccurate stereotypes of sorts:

I think we were both a bit nervous because we didn't know what to expect. I no-ticed that the house [of a twenty-two-year-old with muscular dystrophy] was well equipped for a wheelchair. It had ramps going up the front and back doors. He was very different looking than I expected mostly because he looked normal. I guess I was expecting him to look a bit retarded and to talk with a slur, but this was not the case. (Female, European American)

My previous tutoring experience was with children from my hometown, a pre-dominantly white, upper-class suburb. So obviously, my expectation of [an inner-city middle school] was that the kids would be unruly, like the typical stereotype of underprivileged children. Although I have to admit that I was feeling a little nervous as my alarm went off this morning, I was also looking forward to the first tutoring session. I was actually very pleasantly surprised with my first day. The teacher gave me a warm welcome and several students smiled in my direction. So far I am proud of my job! (Female, European American)

I hate to think about the things children [of an inner-city preschool] go home to. Maybe it's not that bad—they all seem to be happy kids with none of the stereotypes or symptoms you usually hear about. I am planning on discussing it more with their teachers and learning more about their histories. I think they deserve that much. (Female, European American)

Methods for coming to terms with initial inaccurate stereotypes are explored in chapters 4 and 8.

Balancing Roles and Expectations

Many challenges or problems can occur early on. One common difficulty concerns balancing your roles as a community learner with other roles that may be expected at your site. For example, frequently students report that they are trying to find their appropriate "place" or are trying to balance roles such as observer, learner, student, adult, mentor, role model, and disciplinarian. Thus you may feel confusion regarding your role(s) and may feel uncertain about what is and is not appropriate. Confusion may result from such seemingly simple matters as your being called "Miss" or "Mister," especially if you are also just beginning to adjust to a new status as an adult living away from home. Examples of how workers reflect on this issue include the following:

I was asked today if I was a "grown-up," and I said I don't know. Instead of a puzzling look, the [elementary school] girl just smiled and said "good." (Female, European American)

Today a few things struck me as kind of funny. One is the way the children [at a child care center] react to me. They see me as an "adult." They will listen if I tell them not to do something or to do something. They respect what I say and do. I really started to notice this after their math teacher referred to me as one of the adults in the room. I thought about that for a moment. Oh no, I'm an adult now! That is what I was thinking. Actually it is nice to know that the students do respect me. (Male, Hispanic)

I heard one [sixth-grade] girl whisper to a friend: "She even looks like a college kid." It was very cute, and it was then that I remembered how much kids at this age look up to anyone older, and that it was my responsibility to use this honor wisely. (Female, European American)

Methods of negotiating a balance in your roles, particularly with respect to your relationships with clients, are explored further in chapter 6. For now, you might observe the environmental norms and try to speak with your supervisor about your appropriate role at the site.

In addition to trying to find your proper place or role within the community learning environment, you may discover other challenges. For one, you may feel discomfort in, or be put off by, community environments in which the clientele present may not be the same from visit to visit. Many students feel that this impedes their ability to form bonds of trust between themselves and the clients. The following extracts are from students who faced this issue:

> *Although most of the children at [an after-school tutorial program] are what one might call "regulars," there is no guarantee who will show up from day to day. The center discriminates against no one. (Female, European American)*

> *It is good to be back, but it was kind of a sad day. I have no idea what happened to [one of the preschool children]. She never came back after the last day I talked in my journal about seeing her. Now for sure, she is not even in the school anymore. (Male, African American)*

Navigating through these kinds of situations is discussed in chapters 5 and 11. For now, realize that not all clientele will be present for every visit and try not to be overly discouraged by it.

You may also feel ill at ease when school or agency staff appear unduly firm or permissive with clients or staff. In this regard, you may feel ambivalence, discouragement, and disappointment concerning the agency, its staff, or its clientele when they do not measure up to the ideal images you may hold concerning them. The following student shares her disappointments with a site bus driver's approach to discipline:

> *The bus driver scared the [first-grade] children and even me with her extreme yelling and angered voice. I felt horrible. I understand the importance of safety, especially on a bus, but I do not understand her ways of obtaining this safety. I felt very uncomfortable. Once we finally reached the gym, the children got off the bus and ran inside. She is such an isolated, horrible woman. The school needs to hire a new bus driver because it is not good for the children to be around such a pessimistic woman. (Female, European American)*

I am quick to remind students that they can learn as much from observing environments and staff whom they consider to be inappropriate as they can from situations and staff whom they admire. I tell them to let the former instruct them on how they do not want to behave in their future careers, whatever those careers may be, and to let the latter instruct them on how they do indeed want to behave in their careers.

An overwhelming majority of students who report initial discomfort with their job site, site director, teacher, and so on, also report within two to four visits that their situation has begun to improve because they feel more familiar with the site and their role within it (Dunlap 1998a). In the meantime, however, it is fairly common for students to report feeling uncertainty and nervousness, as well as anxiety, sadness, anger, disappointment, mild disillusionment, and sometimes guilt. You may also experience mildly debilitating yet transitory feelings of being overwhelmed by the community work experience when you encounter clients who are suffering within various situations, and you find that you have little power, by yourself, to alleviate their stresses. Many examples of this are presented in chapters 4 and 10, as well as the variety of methods and resources that students draw upon in response to such emotions if they appear.

Thus you may feel that, in spite of a great deal of orientation and training, you do not know what to expect and may feel an initial queasiness at some point during the first visits. During these initial periods, it is not uncommon for students to consider quitting or changing their placement. Generally, notions of quitting usually fade with each subsequent visit, even with the toughest of situations. Within several visits, you will most likely feel more comfortable with your community environment and begin to find balance in your roles (Dunlap 1998a). Two workers articulate their struggle and the tendency for things to improve:

In the beginning the children regarded me with curiosity and a bit of disdain, but as soon as I began to interact with them and help them with their work, they were extremely welcoming. They listened to me when I told them to sit forward and do their work quietly, while also knowing that I was also their "friend." I think that this equilibrium will be very important in the weeks that we have ahead together. I do not want to be a commanding authority figure, but I also do not want to be taken advantage of. (Female, European American)

I remember going to [an after-school tutorial program] my first day. It felt like the first day of kindergarten. I was overwhelmed by the noise, the activity, and the number of children in what is a relatively small area. Feeling small and uncomfortable but trying hard not to show it, I introduced myself to the teachers. Although busy, they were extremely welcoming. Still, it was hard. The kids knew each other and all of the teachers. Plus, in a room consisting of mainly Spanish and African Americans, I felt out of place because of my light, freckled skin and red hair. Moreover, I could not understand the kids when they spoke back and forth in Spanish, so that also made me feel isolated. I was really fighting a feeling of helplessness, but now, a couple of months later, I love going. (Female, European American)

CHALLENGES DURING FIRST VISITS

Several of the challenges to the initial adjustment process include: the new-
ness of the situation; undeveloped perspective regarding the site; undeveloped trust among the community worker, clients and staff; and multiple
adjustment processes.

The Novelty of the Situation

One of the reasons that some students report feeling emotional discomfort
during the first few visits is simply that a sense of awkwardness or insecurity
is normal for a wide variety of new or unfamiliar situations (Weinman 1990;
Wong and Wong 1998). In addition, people tend to be less flexible, less intu-
itive, less creative, and less efficient in processing information and perform-
ing tasks in novel situations than in more familiar situations (Charness 1989).
With increased experience, we tend to handle situations more easily. Further,
it takes time for us to get to know one another and to feel comfortable communicating and interacting. In cross-cultural therapeutic situations, for example, a minimum of eight visits may be required before a rapport or trust is established between client and therapist that helps to assure the client's return
(Collins et al. 1990; Greene 1986; Jones 1974; Meier and Davis 1993). Community learning situations do not necessarily equate with therapist and client
relationships, but such results suggest that you should not be surprised if you
require several visits before feeling comfortable in your community setting.

Undeveloped Perspective

Another factor that may contribute to difficulties with initial adjustment is
that sometimes students do not realize that staff and clients in the agency environment may be busy, tired, or even overwhelmed themselves. It is not unusual for people working hands-on with clientele in agencies to be paid
salaries that are surprisingly low and for the agencies themselves to be oper-
ating on slim budgets and less than adequate staffing. In addition, some agencies are run on "soft" or temporary money. In some instances personnel may
not know from month to month if they still have a job. Furthermore, agency
personnel may have family responsibilities that they are trying to juggle while
also depending on that job for their and their family's basic economic survival
(Belle 1982; Bullock 1995; Scott 1991). All of these factors can put pressures
on the staff that the workers may not initially understand. Some students are
perceptive in regard to these kinds of situations, for example:

> *It is obvious on my first visit that [an inner-city child care center] is under-
> staffed and overworked. There are eighteen children ranging in age from three*

to six years. There are two teachers, three teacher aides, a cook, a secretary, and several volunteers making alternating visits. (Female, Hispanic)

Today was a pretty depressing day at [an inner-city child care center]. When I got there, the director told me right away that they are going to be shut down by the end of June. They had no warning that this was going to happen at all. No one even hinted that this was coming. The staff is extremely upset for several reasons. They are worried about their jobs. Now they all have to go find new work. They talk about how it will be hard to find work, and once they find it, how hard it will be to adjust to a new environment and new kids. They are also worried about the kids. It will be hard for them to adjust to a new place with new surroundings, new teachers, new children, and new routines. Many of these kids have been there a long time. (Female, European American)

Clients at the site may also have pressing concerns. As articulated by one worker:

I noticed that many of the parents are the guardians of several children as well as the parents of several of their own. Also, all of the parent/guardians work. Obviously these families are working hard to support their children and make "ends meet," and I am sure that they love their children. But stress can cause them to be less patient at times. These are not two-parent, white-picket-fence, two-children families that I was taught to be normal in school. It is very hard to unlearn something like that. Yet none of these children seem maladjusted. (Female, European American)

The Issue of Trust

In addition to the fact that client families have their own burdens, a client's (or a client's family's) trust is not something you should assume will be present. Therefore, you should not take for granted that clients and families will feel comfortable communicating beyond a superficial level with you (Ward 1997). Trust among all members in the community service situation takes time to develop, and it cannot be rushed or even guaranteed. In the meantime, however, while you are trying to build trust, you may occasionally feel that you are being overlooked, ignored, or rejected by agency personnel and clients. Fortunately, these feelings are often short-lived, as you become better acquainted with your site and the personnel.

It should also be mentioned that agency supervisors often suggest that one way for improving worker performance is for students to ask more questions and to be less hesitant about participating in site activities with clients.[1] On the workers' part, such a course may feel risky. You have to trust your intuition, while not allowing fear to overwhelm you to the point that you do not try anything. Suggestions for working on this are provided in chapter 5.

Concurrent Adjustments

Finally, as mentioned in chapter 1, freshmen and transfer students, in particular, are apt to feel initial discomfort in the community learning process. While you are engaging in community work, you are also adjusting to college, perhaps to living away from home for the first time, having new roommates, and a myriad of other issues. However, having a focus that occasionally takes you away from your college issues could assist in your adjustment to college.

HELPFUL APPROACHES DURING FIRST VISITS

The approaches that may be most helpful to you during the first visits consist of properly introducing yourself at your site and finding ways to familiarize yourself with the site in order to ease feelings of apprehension.

Proper Introductions

When you meet clients during your first visits, clients may want to know why you are there. Your answer to this question may set the tone for communication for the rest of the semester. You do not want to be patronizing in the answer or evasive. A genuine, age-appropriate response is best. One student tells how she dealt with the question of why she was there:

> *There was one [sixth-grade] girl, who as soon as I walked in the room, said: "Hi, I'm _____. What's your name?" So, I amiably replied that I was _____ and that it was nice to meet her. And then another girl asked me why I was there and what I was going to be doing. So, I explained that I was there to help the teacher out with anything she might need and to work with them. There were other kids who acted as if I wasn't even there and just continued with their work, while there were some who kind of checked me out, when they thought I wasn't looking. (Female, European American)*

This worker's answer to the client's question is a good one in that it was honest and age appropriate. However, I would have included in my comment the fact that I am there to learn about the school and the community as well.

Coping with Initial Emotions

Comments in student journals suggest that you can be assisted in three ways when dealing with any initial discouragement or feelings of being overwhelmed. First, you can try to gather as much information as you can about your community learning site that may help you to feel better equipped. For example:

I found posted on the Parent News bulletin board policies and beliefs that the museum supports, i.e., it's holiday policy, mission statement, and vision plan summary. I found these very informative. I now have a lot more respect for the museum. (Female, European American)

When I first started volunteering, I was not sure exactly what I was supposed to be doing. In order to make myself feel more comfortable, I quickly studied the daily schedule so that my actions would not seem out of place. This really helped me out a lot. (Female, European American)

Second, as suggested in chapter 2, when you and your fellow classmates share your common experiences with one another, you will tend to feel better. Robinson and Barnett's (1998) "best practices" for service-learning indicate that community service programs are better sustained when they contain group reflection periods for students, and when students feel that they are a part of a team.

Third, when you can share your experiences and emotions with the appropriate college faculty and staff, you will most likely feel supported and consequently will perform better. The provision of opportunities for mutual sharing of concerns with your colleagues, professors, and other facilitators of the community service process helps them to support, sustain, modify, and ultimately improve the community service process.

Fourth, some workers spend the first few visits, if there are no objections to their doing so, just "being there" and observing at their placement location. Others not only observe those in the placement location but also model their own behavior after the staff in their site. Students provide examples of different helpful approaches to handling the first visits:

Today [my first day] I just casually sat in [the preschool] class and observed. I did not force any interactions because I think it's important for the kids to feel comfortable around me and not feel as though I expect something from them. (Female, European American)

When I arrived at [a child care center], I wasn't sure what exactly I was supposed to do, and I was slightly nervous. I wasn't actually instructed on what to do with the children, so I just followed the lead of the woman in charge. One of the children asked if I would rub her back during nap time. I felt a little uncomfortable with that idea because I wasn't sure if that was appropriate, but when I saw the other teachers rubbing the children's backs, I assumed it was acceptable. (Female, European American)

I am nervous about it being the first day, but in my experience, if you act like you know what you're doing and you seem to be having a good time, kids will usually follow the lead. (Female, European American)

Thus the more time you spend at your site and the more familiar you become with the site norms, rules, philosophies, and expectations, the more comfortable you will begin to feel about your work there.

PRACTICAL TIPS

- Try not to panic over normal first-visit jitters. Previsit and first-visit jitters and anxiety, if you should experience them, are usually normal. Many workers report such emotions. Realize that with most new experiences there is a period of adjustment. Allow for that. Be kind yet firm with yourself. Try to remember that no matter how cool and calm your colleagues may appear on the outside, you are most likely not alone in your concerns and emotions. At the same time, do not throw caution to the wind. If something happens that seems beyond what is discussed in this chapter, be sure to immediately consult with the appropriate persons in your support system. Also, exercise caution and safety as much as possible in all circumstances, as discussed in the previous chapter.
- Have a good attitude. Try to keep an open mind and a positive demeanor. Remember that you can learn as much from difficult experiences and challenges as you can from easier or more favorable experiences. Also remember that surrounding yourself with appropriate support when needed will assist in the adjustment process.
- Draw upon available resources. If documentation is available that explains the purpose and philosophy of the program where you are placed, you are advised to read it. Without buying into inaccurate negative stereotypes, gain as much public-access information as you can about the school or agency and community before and during your tenure there.
- Properly introduce yourself. If available, take a copy of an introductory letter from your professor or administrative staff with you to the community learning site so that agency personnel do not over- or underestimate your professor's or college's objectives. A sample of such a letter is provided in appendix D, and professors can use it as a model. If you are not properly introduced by others, try to cordially introduce yourself using your own discretion. For example, you might try approaching whoever seems to be in charge and, putting your hand out to shake saying, "Hello, I am Robin, one of the stu-

dents from _____ College or University, who has been assigned to work in your program to assist with tutoring. I am very happy to be here and was wondering if you could point me in the direction of the community service coordinator or the person I should see to check in."

- Dress and carry yourself appropriately. Wear clean, comfortable attire that is appropriate for the environment in which you are working. For example, if you will be working with children, you may want to wear comfortable shoes and washable clothes that you can easily move around in. If you are not certain about what to wear, consult your supervising staff, administrator, or professor.

- Avoid taking notes during your community service periods so that you can be completely present and experience what is going on without the distraction of taking notes. You also do not want to become a distraction to the people there who may become self-conscious about your presence if you are taking notes. It is better to take notes and critically reflect right after the session, being sure to make as many connections to your course curriculum as possible if that is one of the objectives of your community learning. Also, remember the rules for discretion and privacy as mentioned in chapter 1 and appendix C.

- Try not to take things personally if clients or agency staff seem distant or distracted. With time, you may get to know them better and learn much from your work with them. On the other hand, do be open to constructive criticism from supervisors and others who have been charged with assisting you through the community learning process.

- Reach out for support. Don't hesitate to seek support from the appropriate professor(s), college administrative staff, or agency staff. If you feel the need for support beyond what they provide, do not hesitate to seek the support of the college counseling services. As already mentioned, community service does not occur in isolation from the rest of one's life experiences. If by chance you begin to feel overwhelmed beyond what seems typical, seek support for yourself quickly.

FURTHER READING

Anderson, C., and J. Witmer. 1997. Administrator voices from the field. In R. Wade, ed., *Community service-learning: A guide to including service in the public school curriculum,* pp. 238-249. Albany: State University of New York Press.

Boynton, D. 1997. Classroom teacher voices from the field. In R. Wade, ed., *Community service-learning: A guide to including service in the public school curriculum,* pp. 217–224. Albany: State University of New York Press.

Dunlap, M. 1998. Adjustment and developmental outcomes of students engaged in service learning. *Journal of Experiential education* 21, no. 3: 147–153.

Keith, N. Z. 1997. Doing service projects in urban settings. In A. Waterman, ed., *Service-learning: Applications from the research,* pp. 127-149. Mahwah, N.J.: Lawrence Erlbaum.

Thomas, T. 1997. Student voices from the field. In R. Wade, ed., *Community service-learning: A guide to including service in the public school curriculum,* pp. 225–237. Albany: State University of New York Press.

Reader Notes

II

INTERMEDIATE ISSUES

4

Looking in the Mirror

Images of the Self, the Hero, and the
Mutual Learner

> *The hardest thing today, I think, was realizing just how lucky I am.*
> *That sounds so cliché—everyone always says that, but there is definitely*
> *truth in it. One of the children at [a community family support pro-*
> *gram] came in with her mom, and she had holes in her shoes because*
> *they were so old. Never in my life have I had shoes with holes in them*
> *because my mom wouldn't ever let that happen. But for this mom, she*
> *must not be able to afford to get her new shoes. That is so hard for me*
> *to deal with because I have always had what I wanted. I don't mean to*
> *sound snotty about it, but I know that I am lucky. I know that I am for-*
> *tunate to have received a private school education and new clothes*
> *when I needed them. It's not fair that everyone can't have that. I feel*
> *guilty in a sense because I have so much and so many people don't. It's*
> *a weird feeling. But I am looking forward to helping these children,*
> *and understanding them and where they come from and how their*
> *lives are different from mine. (Female, European American)*

This chapter will familiarize you with some of the initial motivations, emotions, and experiences that influence the way community learners position
themselves with respect to the clients and environments they encounter.
The "self" or self-concept is defined here as the collective set of "beliefs that
people hold about themselves that guide the processing of self-relevant information" (Brehm and Kassin 1996, 53). The beliefs that we develop about
ourselves over time have been shaped in part by our familial upbringing
and our cultural socialization (Fiedler, Mitchell, and Triandis 1971; Markus
and Kitayama 1991). Thus our self-concept is fostered in part by the mes-
sages about who we are from our family and significant others, as well as

by the larger surrounding culture. Our self-concept assists us in positioning ourselves with respect to others (Rhoads 1997; Schlenker 1985). It also acts as a filter that influences our perception of incoming information concerning others and our relation to them (Lamb, Suomi, and Stephenson 1979; Schlenker 1985). Our cultural socialization and subsequent beliefs about ourselves also help shape the actions that we take with respect to others in our community service environment. Thus how you, as a community learner, view yourself in relation to the community has a tremendous impact on how you approach your work. It also influences your expectations regarding the experience (Rhoads 1997; Ward 1997). The greater awareness you have regarding your own worldviews and your own sense of self, the better prepared you will be for understanding others who may live in circumstances that differ from your own.

You may be engaging in community work as part of your course curricula in part because you are required to do so. However, you may also be motivated for other reasons (Clary, Snyder, and Stukas 1996, 1998; Serow 1991; Stewart and Weinstein 1997; Stukas et al. 1999b). First, such work enhances and helps develop your image of yourself as a helpful and responsible citizen. Second, you may be motivated to engage in such work because of idealistic desires that are normal at the adolescent and college age. These desires are crucial to social activism and have propelled a great deal of favorable change in our society (Foos 1998). Finally, you may be motivated to engage in community service in order to learn from the community as well as to teach, in other words, in order to have a mutual learning experience. Whatever your motivations, the image or concept of your self can have an impact on your community work.

HOW THE "SELF" IS MANIFEST IN COMMUNITY LEARNING

When we enter any situation, familiar or not, we bring our sense of self to it. When we enter new or unfamiliar situations, the self functions in several ways. First, it has presentational value in that we elect to show different aspects of our self depending on the situation and what we feel is appropriate. Often we try to present ourselves as favorably as we can (Schlenker 1985). This is the self that is known by others through their observations of us and their interactions with us.

Second, as already noted, our sense of self tends to act as a perceptual filter for all incoming information. The filter consists of past experiences, beliefs, stereotypes, and styles of assimilating new information. This aspect of the self acts as a lens through which we view the world. It is the self that acts as a seeker and interpreter of information, particularly social information (Schlenker 1985). It is because of this aspect of the self that two people can witness the same events yet interpret them differently (Dunlap 1999b). Our sense of self can influence how we see or interpret any given situation, particularly our community service, both initially and in later stages (Rhoads 1997). Our sense of self can influence how we interpret relationships and communicate with people. It can also influence how we view power in relationships and where we see ourselves fitting along continua of power and relationships relative to others.

Reciprocally, the community learning experience can also influence how we see ourselves in relationship to the world (Dunlap 1997; Markus and Kitayama 1991). Thus community learning and our sense of self can influence each other. They do so because we enter the community learning experience with a certain sense of who we are, what our values are, what we think is normal, and what we think is not. As we enter new environments, we are exposed to other peoples' lives, their challenges, and their ways of coping and existing. At the same time, we often initially enter the community learning environment with particular expectations or preconceived notions about the clientele, staff, and the purpose and function of the organization. Some of our expectations may be correct and on target, and others may not. If we have tried to start with some open-mindedness, then more room may be immediately available for not only our own ideas and preconceived notions but also for other realities. If, on the other hand, we do not have an appropriate degree of open-mindedness, then we may tend to evaluate all that we see there from an ethnocentric perspective, viewing ours as the standard or norm by which everything is to be evaluated. The latter can easily lead to a sense of disappointment and disillusionment about the community service environment or experience (Dunlap 1997).

Our sense of personal power (Miller 1997), our maturity (Dunlap 1997), our academic work, our mastery of course concepts (Berson 1997), and our acceptance of diversity can also be influenced by the community service experience (Giles and Eyler 1998). Studies have shown that such experiences are associated with a greater sense of humility with respect to other communities (Dunlap 1997; Miller 1997; Stewart and Weinstein 1997). Thus our sense of self affects our community learning experiences as much as our community learning experiences affect our sense of self. The two processes work interdependently.

You may enter the flow of community work in a manner that does not seem to cause too much emotional and introspective upheaval. Or you may face a major challenge, involving coming to terms with who you are in relationship to the world, its inequalities, and its surprises. Student journals suggest that when students, from privileged economic backgrounds in particular, engage in community learning, initially their sense of self is enhanced. As they become more aware, firsthand, of the inequities that exist in our society, their sense of self becomes temporarily threatened.

Finally, as they begin to come to terms with these inequities, their sense of self is revised to consider the larger world in a more mature, realistic way (Dunlap 1997). Thus as you engage in your community learning, if you find yourself questioning the operation of social structures and institutions, the justice and injustice of the world, and your place in all of it, do not be fearful of that. Such questioning is healthy, and it suggests that cognitive and maturational growth are in progress.

There are several ways in which the self may be reflected as you begin to encounter the complexities of life in communities that may differ from yours. You may recall your own past and present as you are reminded of them by your community work, you may be reminded of your own privilege or poverty, and you may be challenged by multicultural issues.

ISSUES OF THE PAST AND PRESENT

Your past and current personal issues may affect your community work. For example, your current personal circumstances can weigh on how you respond to situations in the community learning environment. Those who have experienced particular illnesses or other serious issues may tend to show a little more sensitivity or may more readily write in journals regarding such issues when they emerge. Here workers share heart-wrenching examples:

[A particular preadolescent, middle school child] lacks the day-to-day relationship with a mother because her mother is in jail. She is having to face issues that are easier to deal with when a mother figure is present. My own mother died recently, and to some degree [this child] and I are both learning how to live our lives without that relationship. Although we have lived through different traumas with our mothers, both have affected our lives. (Female, European American)

A child at [a child care center] has a rare kidney disease and is a candidate for a kidney transplant. The teacher said that if I ever notice any sign that she might be ill, I should let them know immediately. When the teacher told me this, I had a very hard time not crying. I thought of my father, who is at least forty years older than she, and he needs a heart transplant. I thought back to all the times where I was so angry at the unjustness of it all. Then I thought about this little girl, who has so much to live for and how she's so very young, and I thought that nothing could be worse than this. Nothing could be more unfair than a child whose life is at risk, and nothing could compare to the pain that her family must feel. Just as I wish I could give my dad my heart, I wished I could give this little girl one of my kidneys. (Female, European American)

Second, you who engage in community work with children may tend to reflect back to your own childhood experiences, for better or worse. For example:

I watched the children [at an elementary school] play and I flashed back to my childhood times on the monkey bars and the slide, almost wishing that I could be that young again. (Female, European American)

I'm still slightly uncertain of myself. I'm not used to being in such a large school, and I remember seventh grade as a very painful and mildly traumatic time in my growing up. (Female, European American)

I forgot what it was like to feel chained up in high school—like I was in prison and could not get out. Sitting there, in that classroom, in those desks, brought it all back: the annoyance, the boredom, the temptation to daydream all came back. I found myself empathizing with these students and their plight. I just hope that we college students can somehow help alleviate this feeling. (Female, European American)

Even those of you who are placed with older clients may be reminded of yourselves from time to time. For example:

At [a nursing care facility for the elderly] one woman in particular stands out because she shared many of my qualities, likes, and behaviors. She was very cheerful and seemed to want to please me. She enjoyed recounting stories of her experiences yet listened attentively. She loved reading and had the habit of unintentionally interrupting people. I share in all these characteristics. (Female, Hispanic)

Some of you may be not only reminded of your past but also motivated by it. In the following examples, students share how family and personal issues motivated their placement selections:

I know I could make a difference with these girls [at a middle school]. I feel so drawn to it. I think it may have to do with my sister. She was a difficult child. She had everything—she was pretty, smart, and popular. But in high school she started cutting her classes and acting out in very dramatic ways. She would scream, curse, and yell at the family, would not attend family functions, and would never obey house rules. Then she ran away. She has had a very troubled life. She has so much potential, but she still has not gotten even close to realizing it fully. Maybe my attraction to this placement is that I rationalize that some of the girls I will see might be like my sister. If I could intervene with just one girl to keep her from doing what my sister did, is doing, and unfortunately will do, I would feel so good. I just really want to do this one. (Female, European American)

I honestly see no excuse for parents who don't spend enough time with their kids, stressed or not. My father used to try to tell me that love meant putting a roof over my head, clothes on my back, and food on my plate. But I have suffered the consequences of a home life without love, care, or consideration to a child's emotional needs. So, if I can give to children who may not be given enough care at home, it makes me feel like I can possibly make a difference in their development, which is why I chose this placement to begin with, rather than with privileged children who have a lesser chance of facing these problems. (Female, European American)

Today was a bad day for [a second grader with attention deficit hyperactivity disorder, or ADHD]. He was off the wall and was upsetting his classmates. As I watched him interact with the other students, I remember myself behaving the same way. No one likes to be told to shut up, but that is what the ADD/ADHD child hears several times a day, from many different people. The biggest thing to keep in mind is that their actions are not meant to irritate you. My biggest hope is that I can somehow help him get through this time in his life with as little unhappiness as possible, while at the same time getting others to understand the uniqueness and talents associated with ADD/ADHD. (Male, European American)

The point is that we all bring our own personalities, experiences, communication styles, memories, personal issues, and motivations with us when we engage in interaction with others. We bring our self-concept with us when we engage in community work. Part of the struggle is to acknowledge these issues within ourselves when they arise without letting them interfere with the work at hand, as the students above have attempted to do. Methods for navigating this process are presented later in this chapter.

ISSUES OF SOCIAL STRUCTURE AND PRIVILEGE

Previous studies have shown that community learners, particularly those who are at the adolescent and postadolescent stages of development, tend to grapple with their own values and sense of self as they engage in their work in communities that differ from their own (Dunlap 1997). Some of you will have an eagerness to make a significant difference in communities that you perceive as needy and will experience a sense of frustration when you find that making that difference is far more difficult and complex than you once anticipated. You may begin to come face-to-face with your own sense of earned and/or unearned privilege relative to the difficult situations experienced by many of the clients with whom you may work. You also may become increasingly aware of the social structures and institutional impediments that tend to hinder people who are poor and people of color. You may begin to realize that the world is not the meritocracy (or just world that has fair and equal access to privileges and success for everyone) that you may have once thought it was (Belle 1982; Fine et al. 1997; McIntosh 1990; Tatum 1992). The following students articulate the complexities involved in their trying to deal with their emerging awareness of privilege and related issues:

Having experienced service-learning in such a different environment was very good for my own realization of what else goes on in the world. When I thought of elementary schools before this, I thought of them as these massive, beautiful schools with everything they needed, including huge fields as playgrounds, etc. But now I also see them as small, tight classrooms with just enough for learning; a gym that is also the auditorium, library, and lunch room; and concrete as the playground. It has definitely changed my idea of the average elementary school. It has been a great experience for me. (Male, European American)

I wish [these middle school children with special needs] had greater access to specialists on mental, physical, and emotional disorders. I wish they had teachers who looked like them, shared the same cultural backgrounds, and lived in their neighborhoods. In my town, we know all of the police officers. There is a mutual respect. Therefore, when people break the law, they are not only thinking about if they are going to get caught. They are also thinking about the community's response, the police officer's, their parents', and the school's. In [my town] there is a community that is rooting for them to do well. I just find myself feeling so overwhelmed. These children are told that they are lazy, but they are not. I feel like there are links missing in the children's life. I wish I could fill them. I hope that my service part will help. (Female, European American)

I grew up in a small town with all the privileges in the world that I know many of these children will never get. I can relate to some of the problems the children may face in school because I know at one point I was lost in the system. I was behind in my reading and math skills, and frustrated with school. I know that it can be very difficult when you feel you are inferior to others. I also know that I was very lucky to have a mother who could find the resources to recognize and deal with learning disabilities. I have trouble believing that most of these [child care center's] children's hard-working, but young and minimally educated, parents have those same resources. (Female, European American)

The journals of students from traditionally disenfranchised backgrounds tend not to mention issues of heroism and guilt with respect to privilege, although they do tend to express desires to be role models for urban and inner-city youth. Interestingly, however, I did come across a journal in which a student from a challenged environment resisted being placed in a similar community environment. I found his comments particularly insightful as I attempted to understand his resistance to the placement that he reluctantly selected. He quickly transferred out of the placement after his first visit. In his journal he explained:

> *When I walked into [an inner-city after-school tutorial program] I had this "vibe" that I was not going to enjoy this. The walls were deteriorating and cracked with chipped paint. To be sincere, this is not what I want to do, but let me explain. I am from [a larger urban city]—the bad parts, not the ones that you might imagine as elegant in a movie. The first impression I got brought back some memories of home. I applied to colleges in hope of getting away from the noisy and often poor city life. The first step into the [after-school tutorial program] reminded me of the "ghetto." The truth is the children there are too similar to the kids in my neighborhood back home. And bluntly put, I may have gotten sick and tired of seeing the same faces. (Male, Asian American)*

Later, when this student and I met to discuss his experience and reactions, he repeated that the earlier placement had elicited overwhelmingly painful memories of inner-city life at a time that he was trying to escape that life and find better opportunities for himself. He described his daily struggles with the negative stereotypes that people have of youth from the inner city (e.g., an assumption that inner-city youth are drug dealers). He also eloquently explained that his initial placement struggles "touch upon deeper and larger social issues that cannot be explained in the context of one journal entry or a whole journal or five hundred pages." "Nor," he said, "can they be easily resolved."

Whatever your initial reaction with regard to privilege or lack thereof, if a mutual and balanced connection with the client(s) does not appear early on, you may feel insecure, frustrated, or even overwhelmed in reaction to it. You may need to remind yourself and be reassured and encouraged to give it more time. If all other efforts have been exhausted, you may need to be supported in your consideration of a placement change . As discussed in chapters 3 and 5, comfort, connections, and relationships can take some time to develop.

CHALLENGES RELATED TO THE HERO SELF

Many college students are in the later stages of adolescence, a period frequently marked by a certain degree of idealism concerning the ability to change the world (Berger and Thompson 1998; Dunlap 1997; Elkind 1967, 1984; Gilligan, Murphy, and Tappan 1990; Muuss 1988). Adolescent idealism, to whatever degree that it may affect a person, is extremely important and useful for propelling or motivating social movements and change in society. You may genuinely want to help. At the same time, however, age-appropriate idealism can also present a challenge to you, especially in the earlier parts of the community learning process (Coles 1993; Dunlap 1997). For example:

> *Admittedly, I am an idealist, but I thank God every day that I am. Without idealists you never reach ideals. I see myself as helping to stop the cycle. For those who don't make it, there is so little to fall back on, and the vicious cycle continues. If I can get [high school] students to understand that true respect can only be attained through education, and if I give them the self-confidence and means to succeed, then I will be making a difference. There will be many important factors I will have no control over. But I think I can do this, I think I can make a difference. (Female, European American)*

Previous students' comments suggest that you may begin with a great deal of enthusiasm, motivation, and desire to make a difference. As you work, you are naturally provided with more information about the realities and complexities of life in challenged environments. You may experience feelings of guilt and frustration as you reach an emerging awareness of your own privilege relative to others. While you go through a period of struggle adjusting to the differences and similarities between your lives and the lives of the community members with whom you are placed, you may begin to shift your personal expectations and goals. Most likely you will maintain your desire to assist. If you are properly supported through your community learning process, by the time that experience ends, you will have begun to gain a better understanding of the realities and complexities of the world, and a greater realism about your ability as an individual to effect the kind of changes that you may originally have had in mind (Dunlap 1997; Miller 1997). You can begin to move toward a social action that is more practical and beneficial.

Students also sometimes assume that their clients are maladjusted because the challenges of their communities are more visible than the challenges in middle- and upper-class communities. Therefore workers frequently express a desire to "help" or even "save" the "needy" with whom they work. The following excerpts illustrate these desires. Notice that the first worker has an extremely high goal for one semester of work. The second also has high goals but is more realistic about what can be accomplished in a relatively limited period of time. He realizes that he needs time and experience in order to accomplish all that he would like, so in the meantime, he adjusts his goals in order to maximize his chances of success.

> *Hopefully with the time I am volunteering with these kids [at an inner-city child care center] I can help them grow to be happy and well-adjusted adults. (Female, European American)*

There is so much I want to be able to do to help children. I just wish I had the experience to give all of the help that is needed. I don't want to save the world, but I do want to touch a few of the ones that I meet. I want to make a difference in some of these kids' lives. (Male, European American)

When students have the desire to heroically help less privileged community members in a very short period of time, it may grow out of the process of examining similarities and differences between themselves and the clients with whom they work (see question 6 in appendix A). As students ponder their similarities and differences with others and gain an awareness of the inequities that exist in society, they may be naturally struck by an emerging awareness of the privilege that they may experience in their own lives relative to those with whom they work. As mentioned earlier, this awareness may cause them to experience guilt (Dunlap 1997, 1998b). The initial guilt is transitory, especially when students can focus on goals that are more realistic. For example, the following student decides to continue to serve without any course requirement, so that he will have time to more realistically attempt to reach his goal, which will move him farther in the direction of quality social activism.

There is almost never a day that I don't leave feeling that I didn't do enough. My goal for the next semester is to try to find a way to really help [a particular elementary school child] enjoy school. I will discover ways to teach him. (Male, European American)

As you begin to accept your humanness, your own frailty, and your own limitations, as well as your strengths and competencies, you should gain a greater sense of satisfaction. You should also improve in your ability to assess the strengths and weaknesses of the clients with whom you are working. In this regard, a student shares how she uses her own strengths and the strengths of the clients to bring about change:

The more and more I go to [an elementary school] the more I become dedicated to these kids. Every time I go, I look at them and say, "You are part of the future." They have so much energy and potential. They really want to learn. In the bilingual class, the children bring books to me to help them read. We take turns reading, so they won't become bored. Recently, they found out that I speak and understand some Spanish. They kind of test me sometimes to see how much Spanish I know. Boy, they were shocked when they discovered that I knew what they were saying. (Female, African American)

MULTICULTURAL ISSUES

The comments quoted from many of the workers suggest that the community service environment may be one that is new or unfamiliar to you. Often this means that you must come face-to-face with issues that are either unfamiliar or uncomfortable. These issues may include race and ethnicity, socioeconomic status, educational level, employment status, family configuration, community support systems, historical issues, gender, sexual orientation, and diverse physical, cognitive, and social needs and abilities (Belle 1982; Bullock 1995; Lynch and Hanson 1998; Okun 1996; Scott 1991; Tatum 1997). Many of these issues are mentioned in more detail in chapters 7–9. But for now, it should encourage those of you who are struggling with multicultural and related issues to know that this is the time and place to make a start and to move forward. Before and during college is the time to think about, learn about, grapple with, and grow with respect to multicultural and diversity issues. You do not want your first encounter with these issues to occur during a job interview or during the first day on your new job after college. One student shares his realization about this:

> *Since I was raised in narrow diversity, racially and socioeconomically, I need to get experience in diverse environments because I could quite easily find myself teaching in such environments two or three years from now. (Male, European American)*

I have had the privilege of sitting on job interview committees for educational institutions and various community agencies. I often pose to candidates the questions of what they can offer the community and what the community can offer them. I have been told by some candidates who are from outside of the community, but who feel confident that they know the community, that they can help save a community that is dysfunctional, selfish, uncaring, irresponsible, and lazy. Such statements are made with a tone of well-intentioned sincerity. I recall once being told that inner-city parents tend to miss agency events because they do not care about their children and would rather sit at home and watch soap operas. These kinds of responses demonstrate an ignorance about inner-city families, the love that they have for their children, the hard work that it takes for them to survive, and the sacrifices they make for their families. There is also little recognition of the structural hindrances that face many communities, and the strengths and survival skills that are exhibited by families.

Research has shown that cultural awareness and understanding of diversity is one of the major benefits of community learning experiences (Berson 1997; Dunlap 1998b, 1998c; Eyler et al. 1997; Ward 1997). Because learning about and growing with these issues is a lifelong process, brief stints of community work are not a panacea. Nonetheless, short-term community learning can constitute a beginning or a segment of the road in your journey to knowledge and understanding of these issues (Mabry 1998). In today's diverse and ever changing world, you must have a solid understanding of the strengths, vulnerabilities, histories, and resiliency of members of challenged communities. You must also have some notion of

how to deal sensitively and effectively with others who do not look exactly like you, talk exactly like you, or live exactly like you. One important step for gaining an understanding of the diverse and ever changing world is to spend time in communities that are unfamiliar to you. You are encouraged to gain a perspective of your self-concept by considering your own views with respect to others (Shujaa 1994; Tatum 1992, 1997). Again, you must do so realizing that this is a process—a lifelong one at that (Dunlap 1999a,b). You must allow yourself to be challenged toward greater growth, no matter how far you feel you have already come. The following student shares her realization of the need to gain experience in multicultural environments:

> *With the growth of America's minority population, I cannot help but feel excited to continue my multicultural knowledge by putting all that I have learned "into my pocket" and extending it to learning about myself, my family, my friends, my future students, and extended environments. I grew up in a very homogeneous suburb of Boston, and the variations of culture were slight and often times not capitalized upon. I feel from this course and from my experience in the diverse elementary schools where I engaged in service-learning, I have found a deeper sense of desire to understand and learn more about the many cultures that surround me and our world. (Female, European American)*

THE "MUTUAL LEARNER" IN ACTION

In terms of the community learning process, it is important that you realize that you are as much a learner within the new community environment as you are a community servant or teacher. In other words, you should expect that the community learning process will be one of learning and growth on both sides. Moments of cognitive discomfort are frequently a signal that you are in the process of revising the information that you had stored about a particular group or community. Although it may be uncomfortable to feel that tension, resistance, and/or upset within yourself, often it is a necessary part of shedding simplistic, inaccurate stereotypes and finding new ways to conceptualize the world around you (Williams, Dunlap, and McCandies 1999). During these difficult times, you might remind yourself that (1) you come to the situation with your own cognitive filters or ideas, and even "baggage," concerning those who are different from you; (2) those whom you encounter will also come to the situation with their own filters and "baggage"; and (3) some of what is experienced may have little to do with you personally but may reflect social and structural tensions that have existed historically, long before the moment you are experiencing.

Excerpts from student journals reveal that you can resolve challenges and confrontations between your sense of self and the realities of other environments in a variety of ways. First, it is important to know that, given time, you can adjust your expectations and make them more realistic or appropriate for the situation. The following students illustrate how they and their peers came to realize that their expectations may have needed adjusting. They also try to recognize that the communities with which they are working already have strengths:

> *If I can help turn around the life of even just one child in my entire career, then it will be worth it. I want to be there for all the children who don't make it and do all I can to make sure they do have something to fall back on, even if it's only my love. (Female, European American)*

> *At this point I feel I know little more about the children with whom I will work than the stereotype that intrigued me to volunteer. Thus I feel ill-equipped to draw many conclusions. However, if this stereotype can be considered valid, it could be said that these children come to [an after-school homework program] bearing certain developmental deficits. However, they also bring with them resilience, eagerness, and untraditional intelligence and modes of learning. I wish to know where they are coming from and why they may be uncooperative at times. In this way, I feel I could be more patient, compassionate, and understanding. The more I know, the better chance I have of improving myself as a tutor and peer model. (Female, European American)*

> *Going into this, I just wanted to accomplish something, anything, before I left. Leaving, I feel like I have accomplished more than I could have ever imagined. To think that [an elementary school child] could hardly multiply two times two when I first came, and now he knows all his multiplication tables, partially due to my help, is the greatest feeling. I have tried very hard to make him understand that there is nothing wrong with him just because math is hard for him. I actually think I may have succeeded. Again, the way that makes me feel is indescribable. I can only hope that I can spend the rest of my life making children learn, hopefully making a difference in their lives, and, in return, gaining such a rewarding feeling for myself. But even if I got nothing out of it, I still think I would want to teach. (Female, European American)*

A second way of resolving challenges and confrontations between your sense of self and the realities of other environments is to keep a determined spirit when going through difficult times of frustration and discouragement. Try to not give up and try to continue to learn. A third way is to try to shift your focus from your immediate feelings and experiences to the bigger picture, or the higher good in your experience, and its significance for you and your intellectual or personal growth.

Fourth, you can try to exercise critical thinking as you encounter and adjust to the emotional challenges that can accompany your work. Such critical thinking can include reflecting on your own behavior. Attempt to objectively examine yourself, your motivations, and your feelings and emotions with respect to your community learning environment. Try to recognize your own biases and analyze the impact they may have on your adjustment. You can make a concerted effort not to judge the clients or environment prematurely. The following students provide examples. The first tries to avoid having preconceived expectations, and the second revises her expectations as she encounters new experiences during her work:

> *I really have no expectations of what I will learn during my time at [a children's dance center]. This way, I will not be disappointed and will be pleasantly surprised by what I do gain from the experience, I hope. (Female, European American)*

> *I am most impressed with the art teacher at [an after-school tutorial program]. For Thanksgiving we all made Pilgrims and needed to write on their clothes what we were most thankful for. What struck me was my own mind-set. I had thought how unfair it is to ask these kids to write down, for all to see, what it was they were thankful for, when it was so obvious they had nothing. Well, as usual, my stereotypical thoughts slapped me in the face. These children do have things to be thankful for. I forget sometimes that many (not all) of these children still believe and hope for their futures. Also, they are getting reinforcement in their community that they do matter. (Female, European American)*

Fifth, you can attempt to approach your community learning assignment as a mutual learning task in which you expect to learn or to receive as much or more than you yourself teach, share, or give. Your learning experiences then become conceptualized as multidirectional between you and the client rather than unidirectional, extending only from you to the client (Gelmon et al. 1998). For example:

> *I am starting to feel that it is me who is going to get the most out of this deal. This project is taking me back to where I was in high school and bringing [high school students] forward toward college, all at the same time. I think we are meeting somewhere in the middle, in a place where both can share and learn from each other. I am really excited to see where this experience takes each of us. (Female, European American)*

> *Working with children is a continual learning process and I have only just begun. The children [at a family/community support center] were brilliant and have been a pleasure to teach all along. I feel that I have also grown and learned a lot as a person as well. They have taught me about what it means to be a child nowadays. I see the innocence of my little brother in all these children, but unfortunately, many of these children have lost this innocence and have become little adults. Many of them go home to find their caretaker is not there, only to have to stay with a neighbor until their caretaker arrives. Some take care of younger brothers and sisters as if they were their own children. This*

is a heavy responsibility to place on the shoulders of a ten-year-old. When these children look back and evaluate themselves, they will be stronger for the battles they have fought. They were a breath of fresh air in a choking society, I am forever grateful. (Male, African)

To summarize, your past history and experiences will likely play a role in how you view the community in which you are placed, and how you view yourself and your role within that community. You may experience a variety of emotions as you grapple with your own history and experiences relative to what you witness in your community service environments. It is important to realize that this is a normal part of the process of experiencing new environments. You will find your "place" and comfort level with time. It may be helpful to take a mutual learning approach and to seek support if needed.

PRACTICAL TIPS

- Remember that you do not have to be an "authority" or an "expert." Rather, you can consider yourself a partner in a mutual learning process that, at best, is beneficial to both you and those with whom you come in contact.
- Balance desires and realistic expectations. Keep alive your desire to be helpful and to make a difference in the world. However, remember that the issues which people face are complex and multifaceted, and whole solutions may require a larger system of support. Also keep in mind that change is a process that takes time, and each step in that process is worthwhile.
- Avoid creating a negative self-fulfilling prophecy. Realize that sometimes community learning experiences are accompanied by an initial questioning of your own values, privileges, and life experiences. If you experience self-questions, try to take it in stride. If you do not experience them, that is all right too. You may want to keep focused on other aspects of the community learning process that can provide enough challenges of their own.
- Allow time for adjusting. Without shirking your responsibilities, give yourself time, space, and support for your personal, emotional, and intellectual growth and adjustment during the community service process.
- Use recommended resources available to you. The better use you make of resources, the better prepared you will feel. Helpful resources are provided at the end of this chapter. Your professors, other staff, and experienced student colleagues may recommend additional resources.
- Try not to take things personally. You do not want to overinternalize events for which you are not responsible. At the same time, you do not want to fail to accept responsibility for learning to behave appropriately

and competently in your community work situations at all times. The balance between accepting responsibility and not overinternalizing events is a delicate and serious one that you should continue to work on. It is a balance that comes more naturally with time and experience, so challenge yourself to grow in this way while also giving yourself room to do so.

- When in doubt, get advice. When you are feeling personally responsible for an uncomfortable situation, or when you are feeling particularly bothered by something and are not sure whether to take it personally, or are not sure what to do about it, consult as soon as possible with one of your community learning advisers, administrators, professors, or counselors.
- Seek additional support when you need it. Reach out to those who are in place to assist you in the community service process. When you feel that you need to, seek the administrators, staff members, professors, and student colleagues who have made themselves available to listen and provide support.

FURTHER READING

Coles, R. 1993. *The call of service: A witness to idealism.* Boston: Houghton Mifflin.

Dunlap, M. 1997. The role of the personal fable in adolescent service learning and critical reflection. *Michigan journal of community service learning* 4: 56–63.

Fine, M., L. Weis, L. Powell, and L. M. Wong. 1997. *Off white: Readings on race, power, and society.* New York: Routledge.

McIntosh, P. 1990. White privilege: Unpacking the invisible knapsack. *Independent school* 492: 31–39.

Rhoads, R. 1997. *Community service and higher learning: Explorations of the caring self.* Albany: State University of New York Press.

Tatum, B. 1992. Talking about race: The application of racial identity development theory in the classroom. *Harvard Educational Review* 62, no. 1: 1–24.

VIDEO RESOURCES

Kanter, R., and B. Stein. 1993. *A tale of O: On being different.* Cambridge, Mass.: Goodmeasure.

Mennonite Central Committee 1995. *Free indeed: A videodrama about racism.* Akron, Penn.: Mennonite Central Committee and MCC U.S.

Reader Notes

5

Is It Getting Better Yet?

Building Trust and Nurturing Relationships

One little girl started talking about me and the other volunteer, and how all kids at our college were weird. She said we all dressed funny. Then she walked around in a funny way saying, "We're hippies, man!" The other volunteer and I laughed for a while because it was so funny. Then the kids started begging me to come back again, so I told them I would see if I could make arrangements. They jumped around, especially [one in particular], and said thank-you about a hundred times. It was a good feeling, like they really wanted me to come back. (Female, European American)

Community learning environments almost always require significant interaction with other people. Those of you who have placements in soup kitchens, child care centers, nursing care centers, elementary schools, after-school tutorial programs, rehabilitation centers, and other similar facilities will have opportunities to interact with children and adults on a regular basis. Thus for you and those with whom you will work, communication and trust, and the building of bonds, will be essential.

By now, your assignments have become well established, and you are engaging in a regular pattern of interaction at your site. Moreover, you may have noticed some of your initial feelings of awkwardness, if you had any, beginning to subside. Some attention may now be turned to communicating with and building relationships with those with whom you work. Most of you will notice rapport beginning to gradually develop. Rapport is the communication and bond of trust that begins to form between you and the clients, staff, and/or others in the work environment. Some of you may experience frustration because there seems to be little progress toward rapport. Typically, rapport becomes more natural, comfortable, and/or fulfilling with time.

If all goes well, a sense of belonging will begin to develop. If not, then you will have to accept that a sense of belonging is not always easily achieved within the community learning process. Sometimes it requires more time, trust, or depth of relationship than you and the client have available.

BUILDING RAPPORT

Developing a rapport, or bond of trust, with those at the community learning placement site is a process that usually occurs gradually. For some, however, the process may seem to occur more quickly, depending on the temperament and styles of those involved in the situation. For example:

> *So far, I have only visited twice, and I feel a very close connection with most of the children in the [child care center] class. They are a very welcoming group, and right from the very start I felt like an important asset to the classroom. Also, the teachers in the classroom have made me feel important. I hope that over the course of the semester I can become even closer to the children and can build a special bond with each and every one. (Female, Hispanic)*

While a community service environment may have an overall tone of welcome, individuals within a particular site may differ with respect to rapport and temperament styles. Students articulate this diversity in the following examples:

> *I have everything, from a girl who constantly clings onto me and says I am her mommy to children who don't even acknowledge my existence. (Female, European American)*

> *[One elementary school child] is probably the smartest in the class, but her moods are almost like that of a teenager. Some days she is in a great mood while other days watch out, bad mood, don't mess with her! This all proves to me that kids grow and change at different rates, and they are all at different levels socially, cognitively, and psychosocially, and eventually the majority of them will all catch up. (Female, European American)*

> *A funny thing happened when [a child at the child care center, boy A] woke up. I picked him up, and he screamed. I put him down, and he screamed. One of the workers came and got him, and for the rest of the time he wouldn't let go of her. He looked at me and cried some more. He has severe stranger anxiety, it seems, and it happens every time a stranger comes into the room. But [boy B] was my star of the day. He was easy to adore, he held his arms up, and he loved to be held. (Female, European American)*

You and other workers may also vary in your styles of connecting with others. For example, some of you may feel that it is not appropriate to form bonds with a client when you are not going to be involved in the client's life for an extended period of time:

I don't want to get too attached to any individuals, nor they to me, since I'll only be there for a short time. (Male, European American)

Others may yearn to form bonds immediately. For example:

[Prior to the first visit] I want to establish some sort of a link with these [middle school sixth-grade] students. It seems like such a crucial yet vulnerable age. I also hope that my experience will help me better understand my sister who is this age. (Female, European American)

Whether workers desire them or not, attachments frequently do form. One student explains how, after just four visits, one child has become very attached to her, and how this presents a struggle for her:

I kind of feel guilty whenever I leave the fourth-grade bilingual class. There is one boy who always sulks when I leave. I feel so guilty. I always ask why he is sulking, and he says, "don't go." I try to explain to him why I have to go, but I'm not sure if he understands. Hopefully, he will get used to it over time. (Female, African American)

Situations like this tend to work themselves out within a few visits as students learn to set appropriate limits (discussed in chapter 6).

You may experience rapport ups and downs with respect to your community work as your comfort levels and satisfaction wax and wane throughout the process. Given this, it is important that you allow time for building rapport with clients, staff, and others with whom you may come in contact during your visits. In the end, when you reflect on the overall experience, you will most likely remember it as more favorable than unfavorable:

I remember walking in the first day in September thinking that this was going to be such a big time commitment. . . . I left with countless memories, and even a new sense of self, a more enlightened, patient, happier self. The impact of a few children on my life will be forever. (Female, European American)

As noted in chapter 3, it typically will take two to four visits before you will begin to feel that you are adjusting and making significant progress in your community learning environment. The length of time required to make a full adjustment can depend on a number of factors, for example, the social atmosphere that exists at the placement site. Within any placement location there can be a range of personality types that vary in friendliness and temperament. As illustrated earlier, you may perceive some clients and staff to be extremely friendly early on, whereas others tend to warm up as time passes. My students have reported encountering a range of temperaments and have suggested that those temperaments affect their comfort levels.

Regardless of the social climate of the community environment and the temperaments of those within it, it is usually better to build bonds and rapport slowly rather than push ahead too quickly. At the same time, however, you must not be so withdrawn and cautious that communication breaks down between yourself and those with whom you are working. One student illustrates how, even during his eighth visit, he tried to carefully balance not pushing too quickly while also keeping the lines of communication open:

> *Every time I see [a particular adolescent at a crime remediation after-school program] he asks me about school. Today he asked me what my major was. I told him I am interested in filmmaking. He got really excited and told me that he had done a film storyboard in art class. I always carry my art supplies in my book bag, so I gave him some drawing pencils and a drawing eraser. I have never seen him so excited. We talked about art for a while, and then we began to play basketball. At this point, I felt comfortable enough to ask him what he had done to get arrested. He sharply told me he didn't want to talk about it and that he was trying to put it behind him. I told him that I really respected that. After he beat me badly in basketball, I asked him if he wanted to go next time to the college to see the art exhibit. He said yes without hesitation. (Male, Caribbean/Hispanic/African American)*

Notice that with this client, the worker finds a point of mutual interest (art and basketball) for engaging the client and for building rapport with him after they have already had some contact with each other over a period of eight visits. Admittedly however, this service-learner has an advantage in this kind of situation relative to many workers in that he has had eight weeks to become mutually familiar with the clients. In addition, he comes from a background similar to that of the clients, and he is very familiar with their struggles and resiliency. Therefore establishing rapport may be just a bit easier for him because he entered the situation already feeling a connection to the clients. He explains:

> *I could write a thesis on the similarities between some of these children and myself. In general, we are from the same socioeconomic background. I was raised in [an urban] single-parent family household, and my grandmother was also a major part of my life. In many Hispanic families, older generations are very much a part of the family. When I was growing up, I turned to my peers and the streets for guidance and lessons I felt I needed to learn. [A particular inner-city area] was the world to me. I think many of the children in the [crime remediation] program could relate to a lot of the issues I have dealt with growing up. (Male, Caribbean/Hispanic/African American)*

Even if you do not feel that same sense of familiarity, with time, patience, sensitivity, and resources such as those provided in this chapter, you are likely to build bonds of trust.

You may be tempted to prematurely jump to conclusions about a client and his or her family, which can also affect the rapport-building process. For example, you may prematurely assume that an affectionate child client, with whom it is easy to build rapport, is deprived of affection at home. If the affectionate child is from an impoverished background, you may be more likely to think that you have uniquely bonded with the child and that the child is insufficiently bonded with his or her own caregivers. Moreover, you may be tempted to believe that not only does the child have an abnormal attachment at home but the assumed abnormal attachment causes the child to seek a compensatory attachment with you. In addition, the normal youthful heroic desires discussed in chapter 4 may compound misunderstandings about the life conditions and attachment needs of the clients. In fact, however, the children may be exhibiting temperamental differences and not necessarily deficiencies in their familial attachments. As an alternative explanation, the client may come from cultural or familial backgrounds that are more tactile and expressive of affection (Hale-Benson 1986; Shade 1989), or they simply may be excited over the additional attention that they receive from you as a community worker. The following student reveals some of her assumptions about a client's need for affection while attempting to remain unbiased in her assessment:

> *It seems evident to me that [a particular four-year-old boy] is experiencing some type of neglect at home. If what I am told is correct, he is out of the house from early in the morning until late in the evening, placed in the care of other adults while presumably his parents work. Looking at his somewhat rebellious behavior and constant craving for attention, lack of proper attention, jealousy of his brother, and exhaustion, his neglect is obvious. However, I must keep in mind that I am making judgments about his family situation based on what I have been told by the teachers. I have not seen what happens at home, nor have I met his parents or observed how the family acts privately. Therefore these generalizations are not carved in stone, nor are they necessarily true. (Female, European American)*

On the other hand, as noted in chapter 3, when a client or staff member does not talk to you or respond warmly toward you, you may inappropriately blame yourself. A transitory sense of failure and frustration may result. Even if this happens, you are very likely to find that things get better with time and that the client and staff also need time to adjust to you. As each week passes, you are more likely to find yourself building an increasingly stronger rapport with some of the clients and staff. In the following examples, workers describe how rapport improves:

> *I am starting to feel more attached to [these elementary school children] because they know me and they talk to me more like an older sibling than a teacher. I am starting to be able to relate to them much more than I did the last two times.*

Now they ask to sit in my lap or hug me, or sometimes grab my hand on the way out to recess. I hope that they will want to talk to me as they would to one of their friends or siblings. (Female, European American)

It took the kids a while to get used to me and to realize why I was there, and that it could be fun. I feel that the fact that it was such a struggle that I have gone through some sort of rite of passage. It gives me a sense of what I would be able to accomplish if I continue to go next semester also. (Female, European American)

Journals also suggest that there may be a relatively small number who never feel any progress toward building rapport or forming a bond of trust within the community service environment. If you see things moving in this direction, I recommend that you communicate with professors, community service administrators, and other community workers about such experiences so that you can be supported through them. It is also vital that professors or administrators monitor your progress sufficiently through course journals, group discussions, site visits, and/or individual consultations so that they can be alerted to such circumstances and provide appropriate support. However, do not leave the responsibility of discussing such challenges on the shoulders of your professors and administrators, who probably have their hands full with many other responsibilities. Be proactive and take the lead in approaching them if they have not yet checked in with you.

As you become more comfortable in your placements, you will become increasingly able to add new, successful approaches to your repertoire of community service behavior. With increased levels of comfort and adjustment, you can turn your attention to not only fulfilling whatever duties you have been assigned but improving your ability to observe and communicate with others. You can focus more on making connections to course curricula, can reflect on your own behavior, and can integrate more information between your own previous experiences and your current experiences. For example, you may find yourself better able to notice and appreciate the strengths demonstrated by others who are resolving conflicts in the community learning environment. As discussed in chapter 4, you may also feel a greater readiness for mutual learning with the community members, who often have a wealth of strengths, skills, and resources to share with you.

CHALLENGES TO BUILDING RAPPORT

Some barriers to building trust in relationships during community service include expectations of quickly forming relationships with the people at the site, uncertainty about your specific role with respect to clients, inconsistency in clientele attendance across visits, and higher expectations about how staff and family should treat clients than what you witness during your work.

Expecting to Form Bonds Quickly

Service-learning journals suggest that some of you may have very high expectations for yourself and may put a lot of pressure on yourself to build relationships quickly. But just as you begin to feel you are making progress toward bonding, your assignment comes to an end for the semester or permanently (Dunlap 1998a). In other words, just as you are becoming comfortable and are feeling that you belong in the community setting, you must begin to deal with ending the experience. Therefore it is important for you to understand that from time to time you may feel conflicting emotions and ambivalence with regard to building relationships within your community service assignment. In fact, as mentioned earlier, some of you may prefer not to make significant or enduring attachments with clients, since you know your time with them is temporary. You may resist getting too close to the children or adults with whom you are working. But if you do desire to bond, try not to assume that others are eager to bond with you (Ward 1997). One student explains that after her third visit she assumed, with some idealism, that because she was from a similar ethnic cultural background and saw herself as a role model to adolescent clients, they would automatically be eager to embrace her and her message to them. She was taken aback when the clients tested her by giving the impression that they were not eager to hear what she had to say to them about the importance of setting goals:

> *Today we were supposed to talk about the process of setting goals. Dream on! We got no farther than the first couple of sentences in our curriculum guide when [the small group of adolescents] started interrupting the class with their rendition of [a popular rap song that had curse words in it]! They all had the audacity to agree [with the lewd words and said that the message of the song] was their goal, and they assured me that they would work hard toward reaching it! I guess I was more hurt than angry. I thought that my presence and my tall physical stature demanded an amount of respect without my having to ask for it. Well I was obviously wrong. After this incident we accomplished hardly anything in accordance with our curriculum guide. I spent most of the class time explaining, without expressing my own feelings of hurt, why that wasn't a "good" goal and why one shouldn't strive toward it. (Female, African American)*

This worker, as well-intentioned as she was, might have benefited from trying to engage the clients more informally and personally when she saw that they were not responding immediately to the structured curriculum. As

I explain in the next chapter, she could then redirect the clients toward her curriculum in the process.

Uncertainty about Your Role

You may also experience ambivalence and confusion in regard to your specific role within the community learning context. Although you may understand very well that you are serving and learning as a community worker, you may not always be clear about what your duties are and what your relationship should be to the clients. In addition, supervisors may not be sure about their expectations regarding your role. Even when professors and community service administrators have clarified expectations and roles, there may still be initial awkwardness as you and the other parties involved adjust to one another and establish a flow of responsiveness. Typically, you may feel hesitant initially, and you may struggle to find a balance between being a student, an observer, and a worker. The following student provides an example of this struggle:

> *If there is something that I have found particularly challenging, it would be the difficulty in finding a balance in being a volunteer and being an observer. I have to get into the class and be comfortable with the environment so that I can interact better with the kids. But at the same time, I have to keep an objective perspective on everything I see and hear in the classroom involving me. Finding a balance in this is not easy. (Male, European American)*

Agency supervisors of my service-learning students, while delighted to have them to call on and also very pleased with their performance, indicate that they would like them to be more active, more hands-on, and not as hesitant to get involved.[1] However, as mentioned earlier, to the degree that there is flexibility in the environment, it may be better for you to move cautiously at first and then, as you become better acquainted and comfortable, increase your involvement and interaction.

Inconsistency in Clientele from Visit to Visit

As mentioned in chapter 3, you may find yourself surprised that clients, and sometimes staff, vary from week to week. You may, at times, find such variation frustrating because it can make connecting psychologically with the clients and staff more difficult. Related to this issue is the fact that you may see the client for only a few hours each week. Students articulate the challenge of building rapport and trust when they work with clients on a limited basis:

> *My only regret is that the group of children changes from week to week, so the children I interact with are sometimes unfamiliar with me, and I feel al-*

most as if I have to "start over" with a new child each week. (Female, European American)

I cannot try to really help him because I am only there for two hours, once a week. I feel as though my time spent with him is a waste. I am unable to accomplish what I wish I could. He could benefit from some very personal and concentrated attention. (Female, European American)

Even under these challenging circumstances however, the tendency is for bonds of affection, rapport, and trust to eventually be established to some degree, as exemplified by journal comments throughout this chapter.

Expectations about How Clients Are Treated

Finally, one of the greatest challenges to building rapport is coping with frustration when you think that staff, or in some cases parents and other family members, do not care as much about the clients as you feel that they should. The staff or parents, on occasion, may appear to be nonchalant, overtaxed, or overly harsh. You may feel the most satisfaction in settings where teachers, staff members, or parents exhibit a healthy balance of both setting limits and expressing compassion toward clients. You may feel shocked if you observe teachers, parents, and staff members engaging in apparently "stressed" approaches with clients. For example, you may witness teacher "burnout," which is a form of stress and fatigue that is often accompanied by severe frustration and significant decreases in effectiveness. If you are not aware that teacher and staff "burnout" exists and have no understanding of it, you may experience disillusionment or irreconcilable resentment toward the teacher. Several students share their experiences and insights as they identify staff members who are overly stressed in their approaches with clients:

There was one staff woman [at a battered women's center] who wasn't nice and was actually quite rude. She kept making comments about not wanting to be there, and I wondered whether she was "burned out." I wondered if the emotional stress of the job, seeing abused women and disadvantaged children every day, had gotten to her. (Female, European American)

If you can imagine a room full of children with Attention Deficit Disorder, you can understand the difficulty faced by the teachers of this sixth grade special education class. A class of twenty sixth graders is a big job by itself, but add to it that each and every one has their own different special needs, it is close to impossible. Anyway, one of the teachers snapped at me with a long, drawn-out answer about how they couldn't teach these kids anything because they have so many problems and they are so bad, etc. Keep in mind, this is all said right in front of the kids. It was demeaning and intentionally hurtful. Children's spirits are so fragile, and a comment like that can crush them. In her class, I see the self-fulfilling prophecy come into effect frequently. (Female, European American)

I don't believe that there are many teachers who really don't care about their students, but I think there are many who are frustrated and don't think that they can make a difference. It is hard to put yourself out on a limb, to care deeply, when there is always the possibility that the student will not make it, and you will be hurt after investing so much. I believe that we have to take this risk but that we should also be prepared for it. You have to be ready to let go when it's time, to not get so involved that one loss seems to outweigh all the wins. There is also a certain amount of ego that you must let go. You must always try, even though you will not always win. You cannot let your own self-esteem be completely dependent on your students or the losses will render you ineffective. (Female, European American)

Given the fact that people do get overburdened sometimes, keep in mind that the community learning environment is no place for you to make flip or unprofessional remarks. Try to exhibit dignity, sensitivity, integrity, respect, and professionalism in all of your communications with clients and staff in spite of how anyone else behaves. Insensitive remarks are a hindrance to building rapport and trust among the various constituents of the community service process. There should be, for example, no negative talk about clients and their families, and no cursing.

Please also keep in mind that such unseemly behavior among staff and clients does not appear to be the norm. If you witness such behavior and feel discouraged by it, you may want to report it to your professors or community learning administrators at your college as soon as possible. They may be able to assist you in processing the experience and in formulating appropriate responses. While you are not in a position to govern the behavior of school and agency staff, you are in a position to govern your own behavior and are strongly urged to do so. You are also advised to keep in mind that your own professional behavior is a representation of not only your personal values but also those of your college. Behavior that tries to illustrate sensitivity to the clients, staff, and others in the community learning environment helps strengthen rapport and trust among everyone involved. One worker shares his thoughts regarding careful communication in community work settings, especially where children or other vulnerable populations are involved:

I admit that children intimidate me more than people my age or older. I feel that when you tell children something, they hold on to your words and are less likely to dismiss you than people in my age group and older. You must always watch what you say around children. (Male, African American)

The challenges that you may experience regarding building rapport are as diverse and individualized as you and the community environments are. In the next section I discuss the techniques, skills, and resources that you can use to build healthy, trusting relationships in that environment.

HELPFUL APPROACHES TO BUILDING RAPPORT

The first step in appropriately building rapport and trust with clients is to recognize how different each client can be in terms of personality, temperament, communication style, age, maturity, and past experiences with others. Approaches that work with one client may not work with another. Students have commented that adolescents and adults must be engaged differently than children, which is consistent with child development theories (Berger and Thompson 1998). Workers comment on older children and adult clients:

> I learned a lot about interacting with adolescents and trying to be a role model for this age-group. I think it is hard to form close relationships with that particular age, especially coming in as an outsider, which I think they viewed me as. I am not sure if they were ever able to fully trust me. Had I been there longer and more often, I think this would have been different. In working with children of this age, I have realized it takes much longer to form trusting relationships than it does with, say, a three-year-old. (Female, European American)

> I did notice something out of the ordinary at [a children's recreational education center] concerning the adult staff members and their behavior. All of a sudden I noticed a distinct warmth and recognition. Today, I finally reached a point where the people seem to be used to me hanging around, and familiar with my ways (as I'm more familiar with theirs). I feel almost like I fit in now, whereas before I kind of felt awkward and in the way. My sensibility points out that adults take a while to warm up to somebody new, unlike a child, who makes a new friend on contact. Adults have a lot to do. An adult feels his or her life is very full already, with busy schedules, established relationships, families, jobs, and other responsibilities. (Female, European American)

As I have suggested throughout this chapter, regardless of the age, maturity, or personality of the client, when in doubt, the best approach is to proceed carefully while building bonds gradually.

Besides recognizing the differing paces, styles, and temperaments of clients, my students have identified several other techniques, skills, and resources as helpful for building trust. One involves focusing on the client in addition to the task. A second involves using sincere encouragement to build bonds with clients. A third uses the appropriate sharing of information about yourself with the client (i.e., self-disclosure). And a fourth consists of exercising your own patience and encouraging clients to be patient.

Personal and Task Orientations

One of the most important techniques for building rapport is using a "personal orientation" as well as a "task orientation" (Hale-Benson 1986; Ladson-Billings 1994; Shade 1989). The latter is, of course, the more common orientation in our culture. That is, when we are assigned a duty, we tend to focus on the end product more than the person to be helped. For example, if you were asked to assist elementary school–age children with their homework, your tendency might be to focus immediately on completion of the homework, possibly at the expense of emotional morale and bonding. Connecting socially, however, might be required in order to engage the client in partnership toward the task.

There is one technique in particular that students frequently mention in their journals that can help you consider the process as well as the task. Students try first to engage the client on an appropriate personal level before jumping right into the task. When they do this, clients seem much more receptive to the worker's communication with them and their assistance. You may notice that it helps your working relationships with clients to make age- and culture-appropriate light conversation about, for example, the client's interests (favorite games, sports, teams, educational subjects, television programs) and personal gear (backpacks, favorite colors, textbooks, sportswear). Such conversation is helpful sometimes because clients enter the community work situation tuning into the psychosocial atmosphere or "vibe" of it, feeling uncertain about whether new individuals can be trusted. This tendency to be cautious may be even more prevalent for clients from traditionally marginalized cultures (Collins et al. 1990; Hale-Benson 1986; Shade 1989). It is important that you exercise sensitivity and care when attempting to "break the ice" with clients. You should not treat clients as if they are subjects being analyzed under a microscope. You must not exploit clients in any way, for example, by probing into their extremely personal or private matters. Such treatment is not conducive to building rapport and is apt to elicit an opposite or undesired response.

The following journal excerpt illustrates how one worker tries to observe clients' interests and considers topics she may be able to use to engage them in the future:

> *I work with fourteen first grade–level students [at an inner-city elementary school]. They are from different ethnic backgrounds and social classes. There is a wide spread of diversity and, from what I notice, each student seems to come from a nurturing family. I have tried repeatedly to discover aspects of their lives beyond school, but they are more interested in discussing siblings, random facts, or me. (Female, European American)*

The next journal entry illustrates how that same worker used her knowledge to engage a client in a discussion during a bus ride. Without exploiting the client, she learned more about the way this client thinks:

While sitting on the bus, I sat with [a particular first grader]. I asked him about his brothers and sisters. He said he had five brothers and one sister. He said that he fought constantly with his younger brothers (while smiling) but loved his baby sister. (Female, European American)

Another worker illustrates how she and a service-learning partner began their visit with a young adult male client with muscular dystrophy:

[The social worker] was helpful in starting conversations. Sometimes there would be long pauses, and [my service-learning partner] and I wouldn't know what to talk about. At first we talked about ourselves—our interests, our family, college life, etc. Afterward [the young man] opened up and told us his many interests. (Female, European American)

The Power of Encouragement

Providing genuine encouragement is one of the most important techniques that you can use for improving relationships with clients in community learning environments (e.g., "you can do it" and "see, you were able to do it") (Pasztor and Leighton 1993). Workers share examples and insights on the importance of encouragement:

Most of the [first-grade] children I have worked with, when I ask them to read, consistently say "I can't read" with a small smile. I always respond with, "of course you can, let's do it together." And then I proceed to help them picture-read and, smiling, I tell them they are doing a great job, "and you said you can't read!" (Female, European American)

I tried to help [a preschool child], but he wanted me to do the work for him, so I said I would come back in a little while to see his progress. I made him look me in the eyes, and I said "you can build really well with the blocks, I know you can." When I came back later, he was working well, so I encouraged him and left. A while later, he called me over all excited. He had built the exact same copy of the blocks that his friend did! It was pretty cool that I convinced him to do it. (Female, European American)

I opened the box [with a little mirror in it and the young child] looked in and said, "It's me!" with such disbelief and wonder. It was so amazing to see. I told her that she was the most special person and that she could do anything. She seemed so happy. (Female, European American)

Related to this issue, another student comments on the reinforcing nature of physically putting oneself on the level of child clients when trying to communicate or work with them:

> *I sit down in the same small chairs that the children [at a child care center] use, and I talk with them at their level. I think that this helps them understand what I want to say a little better than if I was standing up looking down at them. (Female, European American)*

Another worker cautions that when it comes to building trust and rapport, that you should not attend to and reinforce the "cutest" children at the expense of those who are not as "attractive":

> *Unfortunately, I found myself following the children I found to be the "cutest," and I realized that I was doing it unconsciously. So, throughout the remainder of my volunteering, I tried to make a point to pay attention to all of the children equally. Some of the children were not as eager to play with me, but at least I tried to make the effort with every child. (Female, European American)*

Journals suggest that tuning in to or accentuating the positive is a similar technique helpful in building rapport and trust between workers and clients. That is, you should seek out, acknowledge, and focus more on the strengths than the weaknesses that you see. Focusing on strengths can include, for example, detecting and reflecting on instances of client resiliency, independence, and interdependence; clients' modeling appropriate behavior for one another; and clients' observing and learning from staff members and one another. You might also focus on instances of staff members learning from clients. The journal assignment in my course includes reflection questions (appendix A) designed to help students identify strengths and weaknesses among clients and staff. Regularly focusing on such strengths may allow you to seek new insights about clients and staff, remain hopeful regarding the present and the future, and anticipate that things will improve.

Self-Disclosure

You can use the technique of "self-disclosure" to enhance rapport with a client. Self-disclosure involves your sharing something personal, yet appropriate, with a client. For example, if you are trying to connect psychologically with a client, you might ask the client not only about his or her interests but you might also share information about yourself that clients might find interesting (e.g., your interests, hobbies, number of siblings). Thus, for example, if you are assisting a child who resists doing homework out of a dislike for it, you might share that you too disliked homework when you were younger while continuing to encourage the client to do the homework.

When conducted strategically, disclosure might help clients appreciate your humanness, which may help them feel more comfortable about communicating and identifying with you. It is important that your self-disclosure not be insensitive, overly personal, or too intense. It must also be age appropriate and genuine. The following examples illustrate appropriate, discrete instances of self-disclosure:

> *One of the little [child care center] girls was standing by herself during playtime outside. When I went over to her, I realized that she was crying. She kept saying over and over again that she wanted her mother. I knew that her mother would be coming soon, so I tried to keep her occupied for the time being. I told her that I missed my mother too. That seemed to give her great comfort, and before long, she was laughing and playing. (Female, European American)*

> *[A middle school boy] came in with something obviously on his mind. He seemed to be very preoccupied with the fact that he was one of about twenty Jewish students in his entire school. He was telling me that not many people knew what Passover was. When I told him that I too was Jewish, his eyes lit up. I explained to him the term "minority" and told him that he was part of a religious minority at his school. All of a sudden he thought it was "cool" to not be like "everyone else." He began to look at the fact that he was Jewish as a positive thing. After our discussion, I felt that he and I had bonded. I was very happy and proud of the progress we had made in one short hour. (Female, European American)*

> *Initially, none of the children were interested in my assistance, but I soon won them over with my own drawings. I told a couple of them about my homeland, Africa, and I was greeted with faces of disbelief. Questions arose about all sorts of impressions of Africa. I was happy to share my experience of my homeland with the students. I felt that this was important so that they at least know that people from Africa are just as capable as they are. (Male, African)*

You may also find it helpful to consider any site guidelines, ethical and legal, when sharing your religious faith and other personal information about yourself with clients. In addition, past workers caution in their journals that you observe the body language of the client, which may signal her or his comfort level with you and your disclosures. The following worker notes, for example, the importance of her being sensitive to the facial expressions of a physically disabled young adult who apparently was becoming depressed with another worker's disclosures:

> *Today was another visit to the house of [a gentleman with muscular dystrophy]. His life is really sheltered, and I imagine that he sits on the couch and watches TV for most of the day. My partner always makes references to the many places she wants go like Italy, France, Rome, and a lot more. It seems that when she talks about all the cool things she has done, he becomes quiet.*

When that happens, I try to steer the conversation into a neutral ground like movies or something to that effect. (Female, European American)

Additional information regarding the disclosure of information to clients and their families is provided in appendix C.

Exercising Patience

When it comes to building rapport and bonds of trust, it is important for you to exercise patience with yourself and the clients. Workers share their thoughts regarding the value of patience:

I realize that I am going to have to be patient. I can't expect that all the children will immediately trust me. (Female, European American)

One of the [elementary school] girls was reluctant to come to the art program today and was avoiding participating with the group. We tried to encourage her, but she preferred to sit alone. This withdrawal was not uncommon with children, so it didn't worry me. We decided to continue the project so that this may encourage her to participate. Just as we had planned, she joined in and took part later. She was probably having a bad day outside of the class, which is common. But her spirits were lifted in time. (Male, African)

One of the third-grade girls had math homework to do that she could not grasp. She did not understand the directions, so I tried to explain them to her. I sat with her for a while and tried to help her understand, being very patient and trying to explain in different ways. I could see that she was getting frustrated. Finally she got upset and said that she could not do it. I reassured her, telling her that I knew that she could but that maybe she just needed a little break. So we took a break and walked around the room for a little bit. When we sat back down together, I explained it again and she was able to do it, with help. I was so proud of her for trying so hard. The situation showed me that anything is possible with patience and determination. (Female, European American)

In summary, you should keep in mind that no single formula for building rapport works for everyone or for every community service situation. Building rapport requires time and sensitivity to the individual temperaments, styles, and circumstances present in the situation and in the clients' lives.

PRACTICAL TIPS

- Don't put pressure on yourself; keep an open mind. Be patient; give yourself and others time when trying to "break the ice" with them. Try to keep a positive attitude but do not nurture expectations before their time. Without creating a negative self-fulfilling prophecy, be realistic about the amount of time you will or will not have, and the kinds of bonding that may be likely or unlikely to occur during that time. You won't always create earth-shattering, intense relationships in a short period of time. Nevertheless, you can be confident you are doing important and significant work.

- Don't jump to conclusions about a client's attachment. Remember that a client's fondness for you (or seeming lack thereof) is not necessarily a statement of their relationship(s) at home. Appreciate bonds and attachments when they appear, but keep in mind that the development of rapport and trust can vary from person to person and site to site. Sometimes bonding occurs quickly, sometimes it occurs gradually, and sometimes it does not occur at all.

- Communicate appropriately with others. Don't use baby talk with children who are beyond toddlerhood. Talk in a clear, sincere voice. When necessary, be firm without being abrasive. Don't talk condescendingly to anyone in your community service environment, no matter what their age or physical condition. Professional, respectful communication is conducive to the building of rapport and trust.

- Appreciate your successes. No matter how small, whatever progress is made in terms of rapport and trust building should be considered an achievement during the relatively short periods typical for many forms of community learning. Do not discount the fact that significant connections, rapport, and trust can sometimes occur even in a short period of time.

- Observe others for cues. If you are still not sure how to respond, watch those around you for cues. If you are uncertain about the expectations and appropriate responses for your particular site, study the community learning environment as much as you can for additional ideas about building relationships. Remember, often the process is as important as the finished product when working with others. If permissible, work on "breaking the ice" before trying to accomplish large task demands.

FURTHER READING

Berne, P., and L. Savary. 1993. *Building self-esteem in children.* New York: Continuum.

Florida Co-op Extension Service, IFAS, University of Florida. n.d. *Winning ways to talk with young children.*

Galvin, K., and P. Cooper, eds. 1996. *Making connections: Readings in relational communication.* Los Angeles: Roxbury.

Ladson-Billings, G. 1994. *The dreamkeepers: Successful teachers of African-American children.* San Francisco: Jossey-Bass. Chapters 3 and 6.

Nunnally, E., and C. Moy. 1989. *Communication basics for human service professionals.* Newbury Park, Calif.: Sage.

White, J. D. 1976. *Talking with a child: What to say.* New York: Macmillan.

VIDEO RESOURCES

Hanna, S., and S. Wilford. 1990. *Floor time: Tuning in to each child.* New York: Scholastic.

Reader Notes

6

What Should I Do Now?

Addressing Issues, Behavior, and Limits

My classmate was sick today, and I was given the option of not going to [an inner-city middle school study hall program]. No one wanted to send me into the room alone. But I had to go. I had promised those kids that I would bring them a treat, and if I didn't show up I would have let them down and never gained their respect. As I walked into the classroom I saw the people from [another college] who were leaving. I told them I was going in alone, and the three of them looked terrified. They wished me the best of luck and said they would pray for me. I walked in determined. I had to send a few out to the dean, but fifteen made it all the way through. (Female, European American)

You who are engaged in community learning may be faced with having to discern the appropriate and inappropriate behavior of those in your community work environment. This is an important part of your development as a worker because you may be called on to respond to someone else's behavior, and you will want to respond appropriately. You may unexpectedly be faced with client behavior requiring an immediate response. You may be challenged with learning to set appropriate boundaries or limits while trying to make judgments about your own and others' behavior. This chapter will address some of the basic ways that you can begin to set boundaries or limits regarding individual client or group behavior.

THE ISSUE OF SETTING LIMITS

Three of the main issues related to setting limits are (1) you may be tested by clients with respect to your authority and role; (2) you may have a strong

81

desire to be appropriate in your reactions and extra careful to do the "right" thing; and, related to this, (3) you may struggle to find your "place" or your role, particularly with respect to being an authority at your placement site.

Being Tested by Clients

You may observe that clients, especially child clients, often begin their relationship with you by "testing" you to see if you will discipline them, set limits for them, be shocked by them, reject them, or accept them unconditionally. Workers share impressions and insights about the testing period:

> *When I first arrived at [a middle school], I did not know how the seventh graders would take to me. While I was supposed to be playing a role of authority, they knew I was only a twenty-year-old college student. The class became very disruptive when I first entered. (Male, European American)*

> *Today's experience at [a preschool] was not an especially positive one. Particularly difficult for me was nap time. The teacher left the room for a period of about ten or fifteen minutes to go take care of some errands in the building, so I was left with a room full of eight nursery school children who wanted to do anything but sleep. The children had, of course, been quiet and better behaved when the teacher was in the room, but when she left they did not recognize me as an authority figure and therefore they believed that they simply did not have to listen to what I had to say. (Female, European American)*

One worker solicited her younger sister for insight into how she might move beyond such initial testing with the adolescents who were not responding to the setting goals curriculum she designed for them. Her sister offered incisive advice that the worker found helpful:

> *I talked to my thirteen-year-old sister over the weekend about some techniques that she thought would work. She told me to let them know about the kinds of goals and dreams that I had at their age. She said to let them know that I hadn't always been an adult with adult goals and adult dreams. In talking to her, I was reminded of many issues. I went into the classroom with a new attitude and a new approach. I asked a few questions of the students about their early years and environments. Surprisingly, they were very open and eager to share, which sort of helped me to put things in perspective a little better. I cautioned myself against being biased toward these wonderful and deserving children. It was a very productive day! (Female, African American)*

Thus, consistent with the issues discussed in chapter 5, this worker realized that in order to move beyond the testing period, she had to ease away momentarily from her own goal orientation and gain the trust of the clients through the use of self-disclosure and some of the other techniques discussed in chapter 5. Notice that, paradoxically, the worker maintains her firmness and in a more gentle, seemingly less task-oriented fashion redirects the clients toward the task.

You may also find that clients are likely to engage in testing behavior in situations when regular staff are away and substitutes are present. You may notice that there is a tendency for clients to try to take advantage of substitutes, whether the substitute is you or someone else. However, the manner in which the substitute responds to the testing is significant, as illustrated by the following two examples from different classrooms in the same school:

> *[The teacher] was not in class today, and instead there was a substitute. She was being extremely passive, and they were taking advantage of not having the usual authority. I walked in and explained to her that I was a teacher's aide, and she told me to settle the class down. I was not prepared for this, but since the kids recognized me as a "friend," they listened to me when I told them to be quiet and do their quizzes. I had much difficulty keeping all the children quiet while I worked with one child in particular, and [the substitute] seemed flustered by the whole situation. This kind of responsibility made me realize the stress that [the regular teacher] usually deals with. (Female, European American)*

> *[The teacher] had to leave the room for roughly half an hour for a meeting, and a substitute was brought in. She did not know any of the children's names, so I was the "go-between" for her and the students. They seemed to listen more to my directions than hers, which I found interesting. The two of us were able to keep the classroom quite under control. [The substitute] still had some problems keeping a few of them focused, but she made the rules known from the moment she stepped into the room and did not give in to anyone. They knew that I was not going to let them get away with anything either. As a matter of fact, the children were quieter than I've ever seen them. (Female, European American)*

Desiring to Respond Appropriately

You may notice that you enter the community learning situation with your own individual expectations regarding client behavior, which may or may not match the expectation at your placement site. When behavior does not meet your expectations, you may become confused or puzzled and feel unsure about how you should respond. In the case of child-related placements, you may also enter the situation with different expectations about limits and discipline than those observed at the site. But more than anything, you may discover yourself feeling concern about the appropriateness of your own behavior with respect to clients. You may be concerned about properly redirecting clients' behavior when it has been inappropriate. In addition, as illustrated in chapter 5, you may frequently worry about clients' self-esteem and may want to support its healthy development. As an example, a worker shares the thoughtfulness that she puts into trying to respond appropriately:

> *To add to my list of fears, another worry of paramount importance is that I won't know what to do in a situation, or I'll do or say the wrong thing. I've always felt that I shouldn't worry so much about it, because I'll learn in my classes how to deal with them, but I realize now that I'm not always going to know the right thing to do in a specific situation—no one can just teach me that since every situation is different. Furthermore, there might not always be a right or correct way to act in a given situation. I've just always been terribly petrified that I might completely screw up. (Female, European American)*

Keep in mind that a certain degree of self-consciousness on your part is most likely normal for the process. With time, it will begin to subside. If it doesn't, seek support from your teaching or administrative staff.

Finding Your Place

Since teachers and agency personnel may be older and more experienced than you, with degrees and certifications that you may not yet have, you may feel that they have some degree of authority over you. Moreover, teachers and agency personnel are on "home" territory, whereas you may perceive yourself as more of a temporary "guest." Nonetheless, you will most likely find your "place" in time. Students discuss specific situations in which they felt their roles emerging:

> *It's kind of funny that I am a helper and I really have no clue as to what is going on just because I'm older [than the children in a dance program]. Actually there are some times when I have to take control and make sure the students do what they are supposed to even as they are telling me what to do. This may sound odd, but a good example of this is when they had already created choreography for a special dance, which I did not know, so they had to explain to me what they wanted me to do. But at the same time they were not focusing and wouldn't dance. They had just gotten into a disagreement. So I kind of had to take control of the situation by making them take control. (Female, European American)*

> *I decided to take some initiative in [a child care] classroom today. I have been considering for a long time that there really are not enough organized activities in the classroom. I assumed that maybe there were just too many behavior problems to sit down and do something together, but I figured I might as well give it a shot. I sat the children down and taught them a game I used to play with my campers this summer. I was amazed. The kids loved it. (Female, European American)*

Another worker shares a compelling incident in which her role as a community worker rather than a teacher worked to her advantage as she redirected the behavior of a middle school student in a classroom for the learning disabled:

> *For one [sixth-grade] young man, the fact that I am not a teacher turned out to be a really good thing. He is one of the students in a special program that requires a teacher's signature on a form that keeps track of his behavior in each class every day. I would watch him go to the teacher and get his paper signed, and return to his seat with an angry expression. One day I asked him if I could look at this form. I then looked at him and said, "Did you know that I don't fill out these forms?" He shook his head no. I then said, "Filling out this form is not my job. My job here is to help you with your work whenever you need me. As a matter of fact, I won't even ask to see that form again because it's not part of what I need to know to help you." The rest of that day he and I worked together. Since that time, he speaks to me more and more each day, seems less moody, and enthusiastically tells me about his work. I'm really happy to see him happy. (Female, African American)*

Related to the idea of finding your appropriate place, you may experience a great deal of concern about situations in which you are "on your own" with clients. There are instances when a teacher or agency staff person may ask you to be solely responsible for an activity or may ask you to supervise clients for several minutes. In these circumstances, you may perceive a significant degree of increased autonomy and responsibility, even if it is for a short period. At the same time, however, you may feel frightened. If you have had extensive orientation and preparation from teachers or agency staff concerning such responsibilities, you may not feel so overwhelmed. On the other hand, without such preparation, you may feel a bit panic-stricken. Students offer experiences and reactions to these kinds of situations. For example:

> *Today I had a more frustrating day than expected at [a child care center]. I felt frustrated toward the end of my visit when I was made responsible for organizing a game of concentration for a few of the kids. I sat at a table with four other kids and tried to teach them how to play concentration properly (and have some fun too). However, the kids have a very limited attention span and exhibit behaviors not so prominent in other preschool classrooms. While I was trying to facilitate the game, keep their attention, encourage them with positive reinforcement, and remind them to behave all at the same time, I was overwhelmed. (Female, European American)*

> *It was difficult to be in charge of four children [at community family support homework program] and have them listen to me. The hardest thing was trying to be in charge and tell them to behave when they were not. Maybe it*

is because I am only eighteen and haven't had to be in that position before that made it difficult. Kids aren't always good about listening, especially when the person telling them what to do is someone different than usual. They often try to test the new person in charge and see how far they can go. (Female, European American)

One of the four kids I was tutoring did not have her homework but had the audacity to lie and say she did (as she copied the girls next to her). Here's the thing that upset me the most (and I'm sure that I'll learn from it)—she explained to me that she couldn't do her homework last night because she needed to go somewhere with her mom. I couldn't think of a response, so she continued on and pleaded repeatedly that I not tell on her to the teacher. To make a long story short, I choked. The teacher asked me if everyone had done their homework, and I was about to say no, when out of the corner of my eye, I saw her looking up at me with these puppy eyes pleading desperately, and the words, "Yes, everyone did," suddenly escaped from my mouth. I sighed in disbelief at my own words. (Female, European American)

Nonetheless, as you gain more experience, you are likely to do just fine during these times, in spite of your initial anxiety and efforts to find your place.

CHALLENGES TO SETTING LIMITS

There are three major challenges to your setting limits with ease. For one, when you try to intervene and set limits, sometimes the behavior of clients appears to get worse before it gets better. Second, you may have somewhat idealistic expectations about how clients and their families should behave. Third, the most difficult challenge for you may arise when responding to apparently neglected or abused clients.

The Process of Change during Limit Setting

As you are attempting to redirect client behavior, particularly that of children, you may observe that initially their behavior actually appears to get worse. In part, this is because of the testing that some clients engage in as discussed above. Further, as discussed in chapters 3 and 5, when people enter new situations, it takes time for relationships and behavioral dynamics to develop. The same is true when setting limits and boundaries with clients; sometimes it takes time for that to work. With time, experience, appropriate limit setting, and patience, client behavior improves, and your ability to interpret behavior and to respond appropriately to it grows. A worker explains:

What surprised me is that at the beginning of my work, I would have been scared of how the [adolescents in an after-school program] were running around the building, throwing things, and pushing each other down. Tonight I have grown used to their hyperness because I have gotten to talk to them more, and I am no longer threatened by their liveliness. (Female, European American)

Notice that this worker draws on the fact that she has had the opportunity to talk to the students and get to know them better. She has learned to appreciate their energy level and not to see it strictly in negative terms. Time and experience can help you to interpret, improve upon, and build techniques for relating to others in the community service environment.

Unrealistic Expectations

Another challenge to addressing behavior and setting limits with clients is the fact that you may have unrealistic expectations regarding client behavior. Expectations can be too high or too low. Unrealistically high expectations sometimes result in your trying to achieve too much with clients too soon. On the other hand, expectations that are too low can be demoralizing for the client, especially if such expectations are accompanied by condescending behavior toward clients or their families. It is important that you keep an open mind and balance your expectations as much as possible. You will tend to fare better if you are open with respect to your expectations of clients and of yourself, are familiar with individual and cultural similarities and diversities across and within cultures (chapter 8), and talk regularly with supervisors and other community workers about your expectations, experiences, and concerns (Dunlap 1998b).

Behavior That Suggests Client Maltreatment

Finally, one of the most challenging situations in regard to behavior and limits arises when you suspect that a client has been neglected, abused, or mistreated at home, at the community site, or in other environments. When suspicions or knowledge of neglect or abuse have arisen, heroic desires and overcompensation may make it more difficult for you to set limits in the same manner that you would for any other client. Again, you will have to exercise the greatest sensitivity in terms of remaining supportive but also firm with clients who may have been maltreated.

In terms of making reports or sharing your concerns in these circumstances, you may feel that you are treading on uncertain and volatile territory. And you may be. In spite of the preparatory orientation you may have received, you may feel unclear about where to take your concerns or suspicions. The allaying of your uncertainty may depend on the degree of rapport you have established with teaching or agency supervisors, course professors, and college community learning facilitators. You may fear the possible fallout of taking your concerns to others, particularly when you are not absolutely certain about your suspicions. It is, therefore, important that you seek consultation with someone who can appropriately advise you, beginning with a trusted supervisor or staff member at the site, your professor, or an administrative facilitator. More specific guidance is provided in chapter 10 and sample guidelines in appendix H.

HOW TO SET LIMITS AND BOUNDARIES

In journal writings and during group reflection time in class, students mention a variety of approaches that seem to assist them in addressing issues, behavior, and limits. Students constantly add new skills to their repertoire of approaches that can help them succeed in their community service environments. As they do so, they generally try their best to draw upon a variety of resources to assist in their adjustment.

Approaches that you might consider include determining realistic expectations for the client and the situation, modeling appropriate behavior that clients can be invited to follow, providing positive reinforcement for appropriate behavior, managing and maintaining reasonable goals regarding limits and boundaries, and focusing on signs of incremental success.

Determining Reasonable Expectations

You will first want to attempt to assess what you should realistically expect from a client. To make a decision about the appropriateness of particular behaviors, you might consider the age appropriateness of the clients' behavior, their personality styles, their cultural styles, their communication dynamics, site or placement norms, and supervisor expectations. For example, it is unrealistic to expect preschool children to sit still for long periods of time, so you should set behavioral expectations and limits accordingly. With children of all ages, you want to be clear and concrete in your directions, without making them feel threatened or overwhelmed. Examples of students finding the right type and level of redirection or discipline for clients follow:

Now that we were aware of the stored energy in the [five- and six-year-old dancers], we decided to let them use it. Instead of having the children sit and listen to stories and participate in quiet activities, we had them engage in larger movement such as jumping, skipping, turning, and running. The [child] dancers had a great time exalting their energy in creative manners. (Female, European American)

One child, who is usually a well-behaved student, was extremely hyper today [in a middle school study hall]. I had to bring him outside and talk to him one-on-one. I explained to him that he needed to relax a little because the teacher was going to give him detention. He explained to me that he had eaten tons of sugar during lunch and that he could not control himself. I told him that every time he had an urge to blurt out, to write it down on paper instead. It seemed to work. While he still said things out of turn, his behavior improved. (Male, European American)

Students also speak to the need of getting child clients' attention before directing them to do something:

[The preschool boy] had a good day today, but it didn't seem to be as good as last week. He sat down when the teacher asked him to take off his shoes and socks. The teacher had to untie his shoes and then put the boy's hands on his shoe to get him to focus on them. Thus the teacher first got him to focus his attention on the task, and then she told him what he needed to do. He did the rest himself. (Female, European American)

When I first met [a particular elementary school boy], I thought that his body language was apathetic: he was usually frowning or hunched over a table, or he was fidgeting with something while staring off somewhere. I felt that I needed to touch him or direct his eyes to mine to even make eye contact with him. During a writing assignment, since he had nothing written, I asked him what state we lived in. He responded, "I don't know." That has been his famous reply signifying that he did not want to participate. I asked again and he finally replied, "Connecticut." This was when I felt like I was "pulling information like mining." Then I started a game: "for every state you think of, I'll give you a hint for another one." He became actively engaged after two or three minutes, and he thought of at least ten states (and their abbreviations!). This technique seemed to help motivate and support his effort. (Female, European American)

Unfortunately, however, there is no set, easy formula for determining realistic expectations for individual client behavior and the responses that will be appropriate for you and them. It is helpful to observe and consult with site supervisors when in doubt, and to ask questions even when it may seem awkward to do so. A student provides an example of how she found such consultation helpful:

It was not until we finished playing tag and started playing a game that involved half of the kids being rats and the other half being rabbits that the problems with [a first-grade boy] began. He was probably in Piaget's preoperational stage of development [Berger and Thompson 1998], considering he was actually acting like a rat, scratching people. The first boy that he scratched started crying and they started to argue, but I didn't interrupt them because I had been told by the teacher that it is best not to interfere unless the fight gets out of hand. Then suddenly [the scratching boy] stormed off saying that he hates me, that he is not my friend anymore, and that I hate him. Dumbfounded, I decided that it was best to leave him alone for a while because he wanted to get my attention and make a scene. I spoke to the teacher after class about this incident because I felt that maybe I didn't handle the situation as well as I could have. He told me that it was good that I didn't interfere with the original argument and that I handled the problem to the best of my ability. He also told me that things like this happen often with the child. This was unfortunate news, but I was greatly relieved to hear that his problem has been recognized and hopefully will be corrected. (Female, European American)

Thus this student benefitted from this challenging situation by trying to remain calm, consulting with her site supervisor, and trying not to take things personally.

Modeling Appropriate Behavior

When permitted, you may redirect client misbehavior by modeling appropriate behavior. Such modeling invites the client to participate and to behave appropriately. The following passage illustrates a challenging situation in which such modeling and invitation redirected a client toward appropriate behavior:

A small [preschool] girl with red hair gave me a glare and asked me to trace some hearts for her siblings. As I colored in the shape, she continuously looked over to check whether I was doing anything wrong. I carefully filled in the hearts. Nevertheless, she began to continuously insult me with rude remarks that I decided to ignore. But as I looked over, I was surprised to see that she was carefully coloring in her hearts in the same style as I. She had taken the style of my coloring as a model and copied it. She had taken me as an example and in the process her insults subsided. (Female, European American)

Workers offer other examples of inviting clients to behave appropriately by modeling appropriate behavior in a welcoming manner:

As we walked into the classroom, I heard one boy [from a middle school study hall program] say, "Let's give them hell." I made a decision right then and there. I had them all come in, and the first thing I said to them was, "Those of you who do not want to participate today bring your desks over here." About seven kids brought over their chairs. I put them in separate areas of the room with the circle of participants in the middle. I told them that to be in the circle was their choice, and they were welcome to leave at any point. We let the teacher discipline the students on the outside. I told them that anyone who stayed and paid attention the whole time would get a treat at the next class. They thought this was fair. I told them that "by choosing to be in the circle, you all automatically have my respect. I respect you, and I hope you all respect me." Something amazing happened. It was like lightbulbs started going on in their minds. By the end of the class, twelve kids had joined and stayed in the circle. It was the best class ever, by far. For once I felt that I had been successful and that I had actually reached the kids. (Female, European American)

The theme for this entry is confrontations. The activity for today was a trip to [a sports coliseum hockey rink with the children of an after-school crime reme-diation program]. There were two little dogs locked in an office near the rink barking through a window. The boys were teasing the dogs when a man yelled, "Get the f—— away from my dogs." I immediately approached the man and told him never to talk to the boys like that again. I told him to talk to them like people, not animals. My main goal was to show these boys how to handle situ-ations like this without resorting to violence. I feel that violence is a last resort, when everything else has failed. I explained to them that this man is used to dealing with rich people. So when he saw ten inner-city kids walk into the hockey rink, he felt threatened. His first reaction was to come off violently, hop-ing that the boys would be afraid and submissive. I explained to the boys that if they would have handled the situation differently and physically attacked this man, they would have ended up in jail. This would have made the man happy. Instead, they remained calm and allowed an adult to deal with the sit-uation. I told them they must quickly assess the situation and only use violence when they have no other choice, as in a life or death situation. They seemed to understand. (Male, Caribbean/Hispanic/African American)

Thus in both of these situations the workers tried to model the behavior that they felt would set a good example for their clients. In addition, they tried to verbally reinforce the clients for their appropriate behavior, which I dis-cuss next.

The Power of Positive Reinforcement

In chapter 5 we explored the effectiveness of encouragement with respect to building rapport and trust with clients. Encouragement is also extremely effective in setting limits or redirecting clients (Pasztor and Leighton 1993). Students frequently rely on the power of genuine encouragement for re-shaping or redirecting client behavior. However, it is important not to con-fuse genuine encouragement with condescension and patronization, which tend to produce distance rather than rapport and redirection. Students share how they use encouragement to help shape behavior:

Another issue I notice every week [at a preschool] is children's pride in their work at the art table. When I'm at the art table, I often get looks that say, "Am I doing OK?" or "Is this right?" Again, the children need positive affirmation. When I smile and tell the children that they're doing well, they often grin back with pride in what they've done. For some children it takes a lot of affirmation before they're convinced that what they've produced is great, but we keep at them. (Female, European American)

There was [an elementary school] student I had never seen before. He lasted about two minutes in his normal seat and then was moved to the back table because of behavior problems. He was very distracted by everything, refused to sit still, and was being really silly. I spent most of my time dealing with him. When he did the right thing, I praised him, and this positive reinforcement worked well. After I complimented his reading, he even raised his hand to answer the teacher's question. I told him what a good job he was doing, and he responded by concentrating better. (Female, European American)

Some community workers try not only to encourage their clients but also to inspire them by sharing their knowledge and philosophies. The appropriateness of such inspiration depends on the rapport and trust that has been established, the worker's familiarity with the clients' background and personal issues, the maturity of the worker and the clients, and the policies on personal sharing set at the placement site. For example, a student shares with clients her philosophy about survival:

I work with the females in the [middle school role-modeling program for at-risk girls] because it is very seldom that young black females are mentored by prosperous black college students. I want the girls to know about life and what they have to look forward to. I bestow upon my sisters the observation that there are various kinds of people—black, white, Haitian, Jamaican, West Indian, Hispanic, Latino(a), Pacific-Islander, Asian—just a whole bunch of people in this mixed-up society. I tell them that sometimes people will try their damnedest to hurt you and will break your back. And the funny thing about it is that sometimes it is your own kind that tear your world apart. I always tell them to be on their toes and stay determined in their goals no matter what. (Female, African American)

Setting, Managing, and Maintaining Reasonable Limits and Boundaries

Several themes emerge in students' writings regarding their attempts to manage themselves and their clients' behaviors. First, as mentioned in chapter 5, you may attempt to work on building rapport with clients before making heavy demands of them. It is helpful for you to attend your placement as consistently as possible, so that clients who may look forward to connecting with you can count on your being present on a regular basis.

Second, it is important that you maintain reasonable boundaries or limits with the clients. Without such boundaries, both you and the clients may become confused about appropriate behavior toward one another. Maintaining reasonable boundaries and limits may mean exercising firmness at times.

Firmer approaches must be used with careful discretion. Firm approaches can feel awkward for you at first but can be very effective when executed properly. Students provide examples:

I had to give some of the kids a lesson in manners. We were at the swings and each of the kids wanted all my attention and wanted to be pushed at the same time. One of them became very demanding saying things like, "push me now!!" I would say, "Wait your turn, please." Then he would say, "Push me!" I would go over to him and say, "Push me what?" He'd say, "Push me now!" And I'd say, "Push me now what?" And he'd say, "Push me now higher!" I'd reply, "Nope, what's the magic word?" He looked confused. So I'd say, "Please." He'd say, "Push me please." And I'd push him. Then later, when he asked again, I'd say, "What's the magic word?" And he'd say, "Please." Finally, most of the kids caught on. (Female, European American)

I have been having some trouble with the kids [in a preschool class] listening to me. I thought I would try the model you talked about in class [Nunnally and Moy 1989] and see how it went. A child was playing on the rocking horse and another child came up behind and grabbed on to the back of the horse, trying to lift herself off the ground. So I said, "[Her name] when you grab on to the back of the horse it upsets me because it can be dangerous if the horse tips over. I'd rather that you did not grab the horse like that." She looked at me and for a minute I thought she would laugh at me. But instead she just walked away from the horse. I couldn't believe it—it had worked! This is one tool I am definitely going to keep in my pocket from now on! (Female, European American)

I dealt with a tricky discipline problem on the playground [at a child care center]. Two little boys were running around tagging each other and playing quite innocently. One chased the other by me and I heard him say, "I'm gonna kick your a——." I caught up with the boy and explained that we couldn't use language like that on the playground. He looked at me as if he had no idea what I was talking about. I just explained that we don't use such words at school and he needs to watch what he says. I couldn't help it, and so I also asked him where he heard it. He told me his big brother says it to him all the time. I don't know if it was really appropriate, but I also told him, "Sometimes we shouldn't repeat what we hear grown-ups say if we don't know what it means." We left it like that and he continued playing. (Female, European American)

You may find it helpful to note that these students felt some uncertainty about the methods that they were trying, but they took small, calculated risks based on their curricular knowledge, their own past experiences, and their common sense. They tried to remain flexible, refrained from judging their clients, and attempted to strike an appropriate balance of firmness and supportiveness.

You are likely to find that maintaining boundaries with adolescent clients is more challenging, in part, because they are so close in age to you. Adolescents may tend to be very curious about you, particularly if you are just a few years older than they are. They see you as someone they can relate to, but you also have adult freedoms that they may admire. Adolescents may also ask you particularly "sticky" questions. This is, in part, a way of testing you, though it can pose questions and concerns for you regarding appropriate boundaries. Students share their insights about working with adolescents and maintaining appropriate boundaries:

> *Today's visit brought about embarrassment and the feeling of being uncomfortable. Today the issue of sex arose. This topic is a very sensitive one for me because I was never taught about it by my family. This was a topic that I learned through sex education class in elementary school. Talking to these [preadolescent and adolescent] girls was particularly difficult. The benefits of having three or four other volunteers is especially good in times like this. For this meeting I observed, inferred, and listened to how the more experienced volunteers handled this. (Female, African)*

> *I still feel as if I work much better with younger, preschool-age children than I do with preteens and teenagers. I do finally feel more comfortable working with adolescents as a result of my experience at [the teen support program]. But it is also a difficult situation at my age to be working with them because I am not that many years older than they. I think this is confusing for them. They do not know whether to think of me in a category with their other counselors or as being closer to their own age. This confuses the issue of respect, and the question of whether or not I am immediately respected for being an elder. There are many issues like these that forced me to do a lot of thinking and reworking of how I used to think. I think I have greatly benefited from it. (Female, European American)*

> *I had an interesting conversation with a few [high school] girls from the program in the library today. We were chatting, and we got onto the subject of drugs and alcohol. I drank a lot in the latter part of high school (arguably more than I do in college). It scared me a little that they were so into this as high school freshmen. I knew that it was not appropriate for me to talk about my experience, but I also knew that since they were being very candid with me, I couldn't be judgmental and I'd have to share a little to be accepted into the conversation fully. So when they told a story about being hung over or drinking too much, I would laugh and say "totally!" because in fact I did totally understand what they were talking about. I was careful, however, not to blatantly approve of what they were talking about. It was a tough spot. You can't advocate it, but you also want to be honest and have a real dialogue. However, when the conversation turned to marijuana, I was in a good position. I have honestly never smoked pot, and because I was now accepted as "cool" enough to talk with, I could say this and have it impact in a positive way. I was cool and I didn't smoke pot. At this point I tried to gently turn the conversation in a new direction. (Female, European American)*

You should not be surprised when such incidents occur and should be prepared to balance answers and comments in a neutral but nonevasive manner. You may want to consider how your comments and questions to clients may sound if quoted to parents and other authority figures, even if you have commented with an understanding of confidentiality. You should be quick to consult with your colleagues and staff for support and suggestions on balancing limits, but consult in a manner that does not violate the specific privacy and confidence of the clients who have put their trust in you (unless the client's health or safety is at risk, as explained in chapter 10).

Other Issues Related to Limits and Boundaries

Regardless of the age of the client, it is best that you not look too surprised by behavior that is inappropriate, disappointing, annoying, or surprising. You do not want a dramatic reaction from you to become discouraging or reinforcing. Students provide examples of maintaining their composure:

One [second-grade] girl did not know how to write a six, and as many times as I showed her, she still wrote it like a swirly two. It was as though she was just completely closed off to learning the correct way to form the number. She had taught herself this other way and was not willing to change that. I became frustrated but tried not to show it in front of her. (Female, European American)

A number of [elementary school children who speak a foreign language as their first language] spelled "this" as "dys." To me, that was shocking because these kids are in fourth grade. But I didn't show my surprise, and I just helped them formulate sentences and correct their spelling. (Female, African American)

Maintaining limits and boundaries may also mean that you allow clients, to whatever degree appropriate for the situation, to solve problems for themselves. When you are in "helper" mode, this can be a challenge. Workers provide examples that address this challenge:

[A girl and I at a middle school tutoring program] worked on the math problems. She answered my questions quietly and timidly. She just seems so unsure and reluctant to try. She seems scared to have anyone hear her say something wrong. A couple of times she would look hard at the paper and just sigh "I don't know" and give up. That was when I would make sure to tell her that she was close and encourage her to think about it another way. She would get it, and I really never gave her the answer. She did it, but I wonder if she ever really realizes that she is the one who completes all of her problems and that she is smart. (Female, European American)

I noticed that the [preschool dance program] staff would often get the children started on an activity, but as soon as the kids started taking over and working

*among themselves, the teachers would back away and let the children work.
They also suggested to the kids that they invite so-and-so over to play or that
they go play with the lonely kid in the corner. (Male, European American)*

Two important ways of gathering information about appropriate
boundaries within your community learning environment are referring to
orientation resources and observing other staff members' methods for setting limitations. This is important because in some placements it would be
considered inappropriate for you to set limits or to offer a response regarding clients' or staff members' behavior. In such cases you might cope
with your desires to respond or take a specific action by simply fantasiz-
ing about it in your journal, that is, by writing what you think you would
do in a given circumstance if you were in a position of greater authority.
Thus through your journal writing you may express how you would handle things differently if you were in a position to do so. During those
times, you might also make decisions about how you will engage with
others in your future career(s). Several students share examples of their
reflecting on how they would do things differently if they could:

*One girl, a five-year-old first grader, asked me if I had a boyfriend. I re-
sponded no. Then the assistant teacher told this girl that, as she says she always tells her, first a girl is supposed to have a boyfriend, then get married,
and then have a baby. I took great offense to this remark. Not only because
it is completely inaccurate but because it must have made this little girl feel
different from the other kids with two parents. My assumptions were proven
correct after the young girl said that her mother was not married. Unfortunately, probably out of shock of this woman's remark, all I could say to the
girl was "that's okay." I felt awful that I did not tell the girl that what the assistant teacher said was not true, but at least I reassured her that this was not
abnormal. (Female, European American)*

*All of the work that the children [at a middle school special education class]
do is a result of being "bribed." There is always an incentive to getting your
work done as quickly as possible. While the kids are working, the teacher
corrects the work from other classes so she won't have to take it home. During this time she is not to be bothered. Maybe I'm missing something, but
I have never seen her teach them anything. If they are learning anything,
(a) it's a miracle or (b) it's not from her. They have to learn everything on
their own, just like that. I know that is something that I could never do as a
teacher. These kids are not dumb; they just need special attention. (Female,
European American)*

*The adults [at the teen support program] discipline the kids very loosely. For ex-
ample, one girl was sleeping the whole time that I was there. Two of the boys
were throwing things at her and covering her head with a blanket. She simply
got up and removed the blanket. She told them to stop. I don't think they really*

stopped throwing stuff at her, though. It was frustrating. I wanted to stop them, but it is not my place. (Female, European American)

You may develop the techniques, by the end of the semester, for addressing in a more direct fashion your ongoing concerns about staff members' negative behavior. But when you do this, you must use discretion in how you approach the staff member(s), who may take offense. Until you have begun to master the art of doing this, you might want to consult with facilitators of your community service program first and test your skills gradually. Students who did, however, take their concerns about staff behavior directly to the staff members show how they carefully approached them:

Although the teacher's aide was not a particularly nice woman as far as treating the children in a negative manner in their presence, I think she improved as the semester went on. I did eventually comment to her that it made me feel a little uncomfortable when she said rude things about the children because I believe that their behavior will improve with time if we keep acting as good role models and refrain from comments that might hurt their self-esteem even when we are frustrated. (Female, European American)

[After an experience with a staff member in her thirties who has two children of her own, I have realized that] the way a suggestion or question is framed to a person can really affect the answer. If I had been rude and uppity about spouting off my human development knowledge to a woman who obviously had a lot more experience than I, she probably would have become cold pretty quickly. (Female, European American)

Focusing on Incremental Success and Reframing the Behavior

You may also experience great value in acknowledging to yourself the successes and strengths of the clients and the community learning environment. As noted in chapter 5, it is typically all too easy to notice and focus on weaknesses and shortcomings, and to get frustrated and overwhelmed by them. Those of you who observe the challenges and vulnerabilities, as well as the strengths, resiliency, resources, coping mechanisms, and incremental successes that exist among clients and staff in your placement environments, are likely to have a better experience than those who tend to obsess over the difficulties.

Focusing on strengths and success sometimes means analyzing more carefully (i.e., reframing) behaviors that at first glance appear negative. In the following examples, if students had not carefully analyzed the clients' behavior, they would have overlooked the positive characteristics that were also present:

One [first-grade boy] from the neighboring classroom was one of the five who chose to color in his lungs [diagram] differently. He had purples, blues, greens, yellows, and reds painted all over his lungs. I asked him why he did not make his lungs pink and his veins blue. He got very defensive and told me, "I can draw my lungs any way I want and you can draw your lungs the way you want. I like my lungs like this." At first I was shocked to see a child react in such a harsh way. It kind of intimidated me. But then I actually was amazed and impressed. This child had refused to follow directions but did so out of his own expression and uniqueness, not out of rebellion. He was able to express his own abilities in his own creative ways. (Female, European American)

I spent a lot of time with [a middle school–age boy] today. He is an excellent student, a dynamic thinker, and an emotionally turbulent individual in a class with a myriad of discipline problems. He is my favorite student in the class. I told him that if he wanted to, because of his status as a leader in the class, he could encourage the class to settle down, and he could learn more. Like all the kids, he is overcome by the media images, particularly those put out by MTV and rap music. Nearly every word out of his mouth is slang, and he is always looking for occasions to prove his worth in a fight. I like this kid a lot, but I worry about his future because of the peer pressure in his school environment. (Male, European American)

I then realized that all [a group of inner-city middle school students] need is just some individual attention and, more importantly, some confidence. All of these children were incredibly intelligent; they just put on this apathetic sort of facade to prevent themselves from caring, just in case they failed. (Female, European American)

Thus keeping an open mind and tuning in to strengths as well as weaknesses may assist you in perceiving strengths and resources that may be useful to you as you consider ways to set appropriate limits and boundaries in your community learning environment.

PRACTICAL TIPS

- Remember that there is not always a set response for every situation. Though guidelines are available and you should use them, each situation is unique and every element of a situation may not be addressed in the guidelines or other resources. In some instances you may have to rely on your common sense and good instincts.
- Do not hesitate to seek support. When necessary, draw upon the advice of your supervisory staff, administration, and faculty for support.
- Observe what others do. Decide with discretion what behavior is appropriate for you.
- Use discretion in all that you say and do. Also use common sense, sensitivity, site policy, and supervision as guides for appropriate behavior,

setting of limits, and redirection. If you would feel morally ashamed or embarrassed by something that you were to say or do to a client, then you are advised not to do it and to consult with support staff immediately. For additional guidelines governing on redirecting client behavior, see appendix E.

FURTHER READING

Hewitt, D. 1995. *So this is normal too?: Teachers and parents working out developmental issues in young children.* St. Paul, Minn.: Redleaf.

Kunjufu, J. 1984. *Developing positive self-images and discipline in black children.* Chicago: African-American Images.

National Association for the Education of Young Children. 1986. *Helping children to learn self-control: A guide to discipline.* Washington, D.C.: National Association for the Education of Young Children.

Nunnally, E., and C. Moy. 1989. Reassuring, advising, informing, directing, ordering, and closing. In *Communication basics for human service professionals.* Newbury Park, Calif.: Sage.

Saifer, S. 1990. *Practical solutions to practically every problem: The early childhood teacher's manual.* St. Paul, Minn.: Redleaf.

Sheridan, P., G. Foley, and S. Radlinski. 1995. *Using the supportive play model: Individualized intervention in early childhood practice.* New York: Teachers College Press.

Reader Notes

7

To Touch or Not to Touch

Affection and Gender-Related Issues

[The preschoolers] really look up to us and are constantly competing for our attention. Meanwhile, I don't really know how to respond to this affection. The teacher encourages the children to hug us good-bye at the end of each class. But, from my perspective, I'm not sure that I'm comfortable reciprocating this affection, with all the sexual harassment/ good touch/bad touch, etc., possibilities and all. (Male, European American)

In this chapter I discuss how you might encounter and handle hugs, kisses, flirtatious statements, and other affectionate behaviors that clients may direct at you. Workers' journals indicate that the issue of client affection may arise and may weigh heavily on you as you try to sort through appropriate and inappropriate responses. In this chapter we examine clients' affectionate behavior in light of developmental theories, and I present general guidance for handling client affection.

AFFECTION IN THE COMMUNITY SERVICE ENVIRONMENT

As you engage in your community work, you may find that clients, especially children, can be very affectionate toward one another and may also be affectionate toward you. During the course of a semester, you may be surprised to find that children sometimes try to hug you, kiss you on the cheek, hold your hand, stroke or play with your hair, or otherwise demand attention from you. Many of the student journals suggest that both men and women face this issue (Dunlap and Coughlin 1999). For example:

[A six-year-old girl at a soup kitchen community after-school program] imme-diately took "ownership" over me again and dragged me over so she could read a book to me. A boy also ran up and clung to my leg. At the same time, a girl started playing with my hair. [The first girl], upon seeing this, blew up. She pushed the other kids away and tried to cling to my leg and play with my hair simultaneously, indicating to her peers that she was the only one who had the right to do those types of things. The rest of the day pretty much followed that pattern. If I was left alone for a second, there would immediately be a child sit-ting in my lap, kissing my arm, holding my hand, playing with my hair, or anything else that requires some kind of contact with me. (Female, European American)

Today I was reunited with my old [first-grade] group. The kids were glad to see me because I'd been with other classes. One boy ran up to me and hugged my leg. I felt very awkward and didn't know how to react. So I let the boy finish hugging me. I went about my business and the boy came up and hugged me again, but this time he said he loved me. Once again I didn't know how to react, so I said that's nice. Nothing else happened that made me feel awkward, but I definitely felt like I didn't react in the right way. (Male, European American)

You might feel some awkwardness as you question the appropriateness of hugging, touching, and returning affection to clients. Even though clients are well-intentioned, you may feel uncomfortable when clients act in these ways. You may find yourself at a loss as to whether you should reciprocate a show of affection.

Today, with a greater awareness of sexual harassment, sexual abuse, and communicable diseases, you may feel somewhat self-conscious about phys-ical contact with clients and will want to ensure that you act appropriately at all times. It is necessary and important for you to think about these issues so that you will be prepared to respond in a manner that is appropriate, ethical, and considerate of the client's rights should such issues arise during your community learning. Community workers are confronted today with tough issues that were not thought about a generation ago. For example, two stu-dents discuss their concerns about HIV/AIDS and touching clients as they react to day-to-day situations at their site. The first reacts to a scuffle between two children, and the other discusses "universal precautions" (Elia 1995) that are often used today to prevent the spread of HIV and other diseases:

Another thing that happened today was two [child care center] kids fought over a book. The struggle continued until one of the boys decided to bite the other's hand to make him let go of the book. I was shocked when that happened be-cause I did not expect it from these two boys. Both the kids started crying and the teacher and I intervened to resolve the problem. The thought crossed my mind after I looked at his hand, which fortunately did not have broken skin, that AIDS could have been a problem in a circumstance like that. I don't remember in my childhood AIDS ever being a concern, but I suppose today that now it has become such an epidemic that it must have a lot of parents worried when kids seemingly do harmless things not knowing that they are risking their lives. (Female, European American)

There are things teachers can do to try to prepare for a child who has AIDS, whether they know of the child's illness or not. I think it's important to realize that the chances of contracting AIDS from a child in a classroom are very slim, but if circumstances are right it can happen. [At a preschool] the staff has very particular guidelines to follow to try to avoid the circumstances by which disease can be spread. For example, wet wipes are kept readily available in the classroom so that if a child is using a musical instrument like a recorder, it is cleaned with a wet wipe before another child uses it. At snack time, each child has a napkin with food on it, and they don't exchange any food. Throughout the site there are rubber gloves posted in certain areas, such as the backdoor to the playground so that in the event of an emergency they are readily available. (Female, European American)

In addition to concerns about HIV and communicable diseases, you might also experience preschool and elementary school–age clients who fashion you into their role model, hero or heroine, and therefore may display affection verbally or physically toward you. For example, student journals suggest that sometimes very young clients fantasize that service-learners are their love interest, their spouse, their ideal "mommy" or "daddy," their prince or princess, or their "knight in shining armor." Several students share their experiences in this regard:

[An elementary school–age boy at a soup kitchen community after-school program] asked me to be his girlfriend today, but he ran away before I could give him my answer. (Female, European American)

Several times this little fellow [an elementary school child] has asked me to come home with him and be his father. It seems like a reasonable request to him. (Male, European American)

One comment that I got the first day [at an after-school tutorial program] startled me a little. As I was leaving, a little girl came up to me and asked me if I could come home with her and be her "daddy." I didn't know how to react to that and didn't want to make any promises that I couldn't keep, so I just smiled at her and didn't say anything. (Male, European American)

There is no easy formula for responding to such situations. However, potential responses will be described later in this chapter.

In terms of older children, you may occasionally find that an adolescent client has expressed a romantic interest in you. To illustrate, in each of the following three examples, workers report that adolescent or preadolescent clients flirted with them:

One of the most interesting things about working at a high school is that I am often mistaken for a student by both students and faculty. Assumption and perception are very powerful things. So, it is possible that this guy at my table thought I was just another student. Anyway, a friend of this guy came over and chatted with him, looking over at me a few times. He saw me and said "hi," and we chatted a little. He came back a little while later, with a big grin on his face, and said to me, "My friend here wants to know if you'll go out with him." Not only was this extremely amusing, but it started off a conversation. I, of course, replied in the negative and joked around with them a little. (Female, European American)

The [high school] students in the class seemed happy to see me. But something happened that I need to talk about. When one of the girls saw me, she came over and kissed me on the cheek. Is this a problem? In the Latino community it is very common for people to kiss friends on the cheek. It is merely a sign of respect. But should I allow her to do it? Another thing that I have to get used to is all of the comments that the girls say concerning me being in the classroom. For example, a student who was not in the class came in to see the teacher and saw me sitting. She asked the teacher who I was and then she said, "Damn! Why am I not in this class." All of her friends laughed and I too laughed, but I felt a little embarrassed. (Male, Latino)

This day was the weirdest day because those little [middle school boys] tried to "hit" on [i.e., flirt with] me. They actually thought that they could get me to go out. One kept staring at me with that "I want you" look! I wanted to scream, but I had to play it cool around them. (Female, African American)

Thus you may find yourself in some distress over such interest and affection if it occurs. You may feel uncertain and hesitant about how you should respond to comments that are affectionate or seemingly flirtatious. As illustrated by the variety of descriptions presented thus far, you might initially respond in a variety of ways to a show of affection. You may choose to overlook it if, and only if, you feel that it is harmless; you may choose to avoid it by immediately redirecting the conversation; and/or you may provide very clear limits without humiliating the client, unless a strong defensive stance is warranted. Under no circumstances should you tolerate sexual harassment or other sexual inappropriateness if it occurs, and you should immediately report any instances that you feel are inappropriate to your supervisor, your professor, and/or your administrative facilitator so that they can support and advise you. You might also consult with your college or local women's or men's center for support and advice. Additional challenges, perspectives, and guidance are provided throughout the following sections.

CHALLENGES TO HANDLING AFFECTION

One indicator of how you might be predisposed to respond to issues of affection is how you were socialized during your own upbringing. College-age students tend to have firm notions of how boys, girls, and adults are supposed to display affection toward others. Traditionally, women have been socialized to be more nurturing than men (Gilligan 1982; Jensen 1998; Swann 1992). Therefore affectionate, nurturing behavior back and forth between clients, especially very young clients, and female workers may not seem as noteworthy as it does when men experience it. Student journals suggest that workers in general may be fearful of being accused of sexual inappropriateness such as fondling clients, especially child clients, but men express more anxiety about being wrongly accused of such behaviors (Dunlap and Coughlin 1999). In addition, heterosexism and homophobia within our culture may compound the fears of workers, especially men, when the affection is directed from or toward a same-sex client. Given the way boys and men are socialized to direct their affection in a *sexual* manner, men may feel more self-conscious about same-sex affection than women, who are permitted to be nurturing or affectionate in multiple ways, not primarily sexually (Dunlap and Coughlin 1999; Jensen 1998).

Another challenge to handling affection is that you may find yourself taking literally every comment made by clients. In some cases, it may be in your best interest to take them literally, as in the case of clients who may be a danger to themselves or to others. However, for the majority of clients, every declaration of love and affection does not need to be taken as a "fatal attraction." Clients, particularly children, may sometimes test you for signs of caring, rejection, and/or limits, or they may simply be infatuated with or in awe of you and other role models they admire. College students are not yet trained psychologists or other behavioral scientists, and therefore they cannot always ascertain whether a client is harmlessly testing or "acting out." At the same time, the client's behavior cannot be completely ignored in the event that it is inappropriate. With time and experience, you will become better able to discern the difference. In the meantime, you should observe the guidance that is provided in the next section, and you should not hesitate to consult with supervisors who can advise you on specific behaviors or circumstances.

As noted in chapter 5, another challenge related to the issue of affection involves the tendency for workers to erroneously assume that clients who attempt to display affection toward them verbally or physically are otherwise deprived of love and affection at home or in the placement environment. If you find yourself doing this, you may be trying to make sense of the client's behavior by attributing it to inaccurate stereotypes. This, in the long run, may do more harm than good because cultural misinformation may be reinforced in the process. In the following passages, workers make such assumptions:

While outside all of the [preschool dance program] girls lined up for hugs from any adult figure in sight. Two or three of them, after jumping on me, shouted out "I love you." That really caught me by surprise. I have never heard a five-, six-, or seven-year-old shout out "I love you" to a stranger. To me, that was always reserved for the mother and father or the familiar. I am not sure what to make of it. It seems to be a huge statement of their family instability and lack of attention. (Female, European American)

This common "clinginess" characteristic of many of the children at [a community after-school program] made me think that maybe at home, the children are getting inconsistent care giving. Most children come from very low income families, and this can put a lot of stress on their caregivers. Their caregivers might have to work all day, and when they finally arrive at home at night, they are simply too tired to pay attention to their children. It could be so little care that it is considered neglect. A youngster needs a proper amount of care to grow into a securely attached and consistent person. (Female, European American)

But such is not necessarily the case. While there are neglected and emotionally deprived children in all communities and from all socioeconomic backgrounds (Chideya 1995), it is not appropriate to assume neglect or deprivation based solely on one factor such as the way a client shows affection (Porter 1999). Clients' own personalities and temperament styles, as well as their cultural and familial styles with respect to touch, personal distance, and affection, can influence their affection behavior (Chao 1994; Gray and Cosgrove 1985; Shade 1989; Turner 1991).

Consequently, a show of affection, which might be seen as a sign of advanced emotional development in one context, might be taken as a signal of delayed emotional advancement within a context in which there is less familiarity with diverse cultural norms and expectations. A child or adult client who connects with you and treats you as affectionately as she or he would an extended family member (which would be normal and appropriate in their own cultural context), may strike you as starved for attention and affection.

On the other hand, a child or adult who has been socialized to be cautious of you if you are not from their referent group, until they get to know you and your intentions, may strike you as evasive and inappropriately withdrawn if you find the lack of bonding with them frustrating. If you can patiently get past the initial reservations of clients, and clients deem you "safe" or allow you "in," then at that point the client may treat you more along the lines of "family" or familiar community (Hale-Benson 1986; Shade 1989). In any case, you should observe the client carefully and try to respond in a manner that is ethical and as sensitive as possible to the client's pace, tempo, and style of interacting in new situations.

HELPFUL APPROACHES IN MANAGING AND RESPONDING TO CLIENT AFFECTION

Displaying both acceptance and limits when clients show harmless affection may be a challenging balance for you to strike, but it is of primary importance. In time, you will most likely strike the balance well, and you will more easily discern the appropriateness of displays of affection and make a suitable response to them. Usually the norms of your community service environment regarding affection will give you the best line to follow in order to meet this challenge successfully. The following two students provide examples. The first illustrates how she was assured that affection was appropriate, whereas the other was indirectly admonished that it was not. Incidentally, though neither worker provides details about the race or ethnicity of the clients, both illustrations also suggest that gender, ethnicity, and/or socioeconomic status may have combined to further complicate the issues of physical contact and affection. The first example was provided by an African American female service-learner working in a suburban, predominantly European American setting, while the second was offered by a European American worker in an ethnically diverse inner-city setting. Multicultural issues are discussed further in chapter 8. In each of these two examples, however, workers were directed by their supervisors on what was appropriate for their sites:

[One middle school student] likes to be hugged and will hug me when I arrive in the classroom. He is not atypical in that almost all of the students in the class greet me with a hug. When I first came to this site, I was very nervous about the students' affection toward me and others. I have been assured by the teaching staff that it is appropriate for me to give the students a quick hug when they ask for one. (Female, African American)

A little incident made me rather sad. There's one little boy [at a child care center] who always likes to sit on my lap while we play or read a story or something. Today he was on my lap and one of the teachers yelled at him, reminding him of what they told him about sitting on volunteers' laps. He reluctantly crawled off and sat next to me. I honestly saw no harm in his sitting on my lap, and I believe in the positive therapy of physical contact such as hugs and loving touches. (Female, European American)

Second, even if you are encouraged by staff to be affectionate, you still have to follow your own convictions, especially if those convictions call for greater caution than that observed among others in the community learning environment. It is better to be too conservative than not conservative enough when you are feeling uncertain about what is appropriate. Two students illustrate how they redirected or otherwise managed clients' affection in a manner that was developmentally appropriate and comfortable for them and the clients:

When we went inside, I observed something interesting about the kids [at a child care center]. First I felt a little weird when one of the students wanted to hold my hand whenever she did anything. I feel stupid that something as simple as hand holding, which all children do, made me feel uncomfortable. This girl, who was really attached to me, wanted all my attention, but all of the kids wanted to play with me so I suggested a game we all could play. (Male, European American)

The minute I sat down on the rug, [a little girl at a child care center] placed herself in my lap. Before long another girl was on the other side, and [a little boy] made room for himself on the very end of my leg. Then [a fourth child] came over only a minute later and sat on the rug right next to me. The children all seemed more affectionate than usual. [Two of them] almost became obsessed with giving me kisses on the cheek. I felt this was inappropriate. I said that only hugs would be allowed. (Female, European American)

Unfortunately, [a five-year-old elementary school child] told all of his classmates that I was his girlfriend. Besides being in shock, I did not know what to say to them. All of the other students were saying that was gross because I am eighteen and he is five. Then he started saying that he was six. I really did not know how to handle this problem without making him upset. I ended up telling them that he and I were friends, just as I was friends with all of them. (Female, European American)

A third element of value is for you to be familiar with basic developmental theories that can help to put child clients' affectionate behavior into a larger and less personal perspective when you are trying to respond to their affection. For example, according to classic developmental theorists such as Freud, children reach an age when they struggle with fantasies about marrying an opposite-sex parental figure, but they quickly grow out of it (see Berger and Thompson 1998).

Piaget's developmental theory suggests that young children become more cognitively aware of themselves as girls or boys, and therefore may display more curiosity and information seeking as they attempt to assimilate and accommodate new information about what it means to be a girl or a boy in our culture (see Berger and Thompson 1998). The expression of affinity, affection, infatuation, or sexual interest toward others may be a normal part of their emerging curiosity and understanding about themselves as boys or girls.

According to Erikson, as children work their way through adolescence and approach adulthood, they begin to struggle with their emerging hormonal changes and blossoming sexual interest, and their increasing need for displays of affection from others outside of their immediate familial context. At the same time, youngsters also continually try to prove themselves competent and capable at daily tasks, lest they feel guilty and inadequate (see Berger and Thompson 1998). Related to this, for adolescents in American culture, sex and sexuality are a significant part of the popular culture and media, both of which can influence their socialization and their identity development. Sometimes media and popular culture influences are healthy, but often they call for concern (Kilbourne 1987). Because of these media and popular culture influences, expressions of platonic affection and sexual prowess may play in some adolescent children's sense of personal competency (Jensen 1998).

When we examine affectionate behavior in light of developmental theories, we can realize that children's behavior may simply be a testing of their growth and new freedoms or limits. It can also be an expression of affinity or affection.

In any case, you should not ask for affection from clients but should be prepared to return affection in the form of a simple hug if the client initiates it or if the circumstances call for a hug of encouragement, celebration, or sympathy. This advice, however, is limited to those who are placed in settings that allow hugging and practice it. To simply ignore the affection may have the effect of rendering the client and his or her message invisible, which you may or may not want to do. Making the message invisible could also mean forfeiting opportunities to appropriately affirm and redirect the client. For example:

> As I was leaving [from today's visit, a boy at a child care center] came up to me and told me he loved me. This was not the first time, and it made me feel very uncomfortable, as well as unsure of what to say in response. I just smiled and pretended that nothing happened. (Male, European American)

With regard to this incident, through journal and in-class reflection time, this student was advised that if such an event were to occur again that he might try responding to the client with "thank you, I am very fond of you also" and keep moving along. Such a response affirms the client without reinforcing a level of affection that may be inappropriate for the situation.

In all circumstances, it is your responsibility to respond to affection in a manner that does not violate the rights or dignity of children who are to be considered naive and innocent, especially when prepubescent (Finkelhor 1994). It is advisable for you to first look beyond particular words and behaviors as acts of sexual interest or harassment and, without excusing inappropriate behavior, consider other possible explanations. It is important that children be redirected into appropriate behavior without being criminalized, especially if the child is prepubescent. Otherwise, excellent opportunities for mutual learning may be lost and, worse, the client could be traumatized.

PRACTICAL TIPS

- Observe placement norms. As a minimum, observe environmental norms regarding affection as you study and absorb the community site characteristics. Regardless of environmental norms, never abandon common sense and caution. Follow your instincts in favor of caution when uncertain.
- Watch for cues from the client. Be sensitive to a client's comfort level in terms of personal distance, touch, and affection, and adjust your behavior accordingly and within developmentally appropriate practice. If the client appears to be seeking more personal distance, then try not to crowd him or her. If the client appears to be seeking less personal distance, then negotiate or redirect that distance in a manner that is comfortable for both of you, within ethical and developmentally appropriate practice.
- Seek guidance regarding touch and other forms of affection. If affection becomes an issue or even could become one, seek understanding regarding the appropriateness of accepting and expressing affection. I encourage my students to consult with their site supervisor, the college community service administrator, and/or their course professor if they are uncertain about the appropriateness of receiving or returning affection.

FURTHER READING

Hewitt, D. 1995. *So this is normal too? Teachers and parents working out developmental issues in young children.* St. Paul, Minn.: Redleaf.

Levine, A., and J. Cureton. 1998. Personal life: Retreat from intimacy. In *When hope and fear collide: A portrait of today's college student.* San Francisco: Jossey-Bass.

Nunnally, E., and C. Moy. 1989. Nonverbal communication. In *Communication basics for human service professionals.* Newbury Park, Calif.: Sage.

Saifer, S. 1990. *Practical solutions to practically every problem: The early childhood teacher's manual.* St. Paul, Minn.: Redleaf.

Stewart, L., et al. 1996. Communication in cross-gender friendships. In K. Galvin and P. Cooper, eds., *Making connections: Readings in relational communication.* Los Angeles: Roxbury.

York, S. 1991. *Roots and wings: Affirming culture in early childhood programs.* St. Paul, Minn.: Redleaf.

Reader Notes

8

The Melting Pot and the Vegetable Stew

Multicultural Issues

When I entered [an inner-city child care center] classroom on my first day of active service, I was totally intimidated. The [exclusive suburb] where I live is very homogeneous, affluent, and white-bread. Most of the kids I have worked with come from towns that look like Norman Rockwell paintings. I was immediately taken by the sheer diversity of the kids. I don't know much about the socioeconomic makeup of the city, but these kids were every color, shape, and size. What if all my skills, experience, and tricks of the trade don't apply to kids who don't look like they are on Leave It to Beaver? *(Female, European American)*

In this chapter we examine the issues, feelings, and helpful resources that can accompany community work in environments where you might observe differing cultural styles, prejudice, institutional racism, and discrimination. The terms "melting pot" and "vegetable stew" refer to two different philosophies of multiculturalism. The melting pot philosophy is a traditional model suggesting that over the years cultures in America have come together and blended, and they should continue to melt into one huge common culture. Theoretically, under such a model, there is equal access to resources and privileges for everyone (Schofield 1986; Shujaa 1994; Tatum 1997). The melting pot philosophy is characterized by a color-blind approach and a belief in America as a just "meritocracy" that works the same for all people (Tatum 1992, 6), and theoretically everyone has an equal opportunity for advancement. Under this model racism, sexism, heterosexism, ableism, and other such issues no longer exert significant influence on an individual's success or failure.

The "vegetable stew" model challenges the "melting pot" philosophy and its view that all cultures within America should melt into one, namely, the mainstream culture. As immigrant, traditionally disempowered, disenfran-chised, and underserved groups are called to melt into the mainstream cul-ture and struggle to meet its cultural norms and expectations, they give up more and more of their own culture. The melting pot thereby maintains the status quo of historical power distribution and hegemony (Shujaa 1994). The vegetable stew, on the other hand, does not require a melting down or an abandonment of any culture into the norms and expectations of another. In a stew, each component can maintain its own essence and values while at the same time allowing a communion and mixing of diverse flavors in the stew. That is, the vegetable stew contains a broth that holds or binds its var-ious ingredients, which can both maintain their own flavors and contribute to making the combined stew all that it is.

The melting pot and vegetable stew philosophies of diversity underlie much of what many individuals struggle with concerning their work in multicultural environments. You may enter new environments with ideal-istic notions about race, culture, racism, cultural conflict and harmony, and discrimination. Or you may expect that by now American culture has blended into a huge harmonious meritocracy in which everyone is treated fairly or at least in accordance with the amount of work and effort that they have put forth. Some may expect that those who are struggling need only to assimilate or "melt down" into the mainstream cultural norms and behavior in order to be successful.

While many community workers have book knowledge about communi-ties that differ from their own, some may have limited practical or real-life experience with the personal and systematic realities that traditionally dis-enfranchised peoples have faced in the past and present. Once you have an opportunity to see for yourself and grapple with the fact that a meritocracy does not exist for everyone, then you may begin to approach your commu-nity work with greater humility, willingness to learn mutually, and an im-proved ability to relate to those who come from backgrounds that differ from your own (Berson 1997; Dunlap 1997, 1998b; Miller 1997).

The interplay of these multicultural issues in community service is not well documented or well understood (Damon-Moore 1997; Dunlap 1998b, 1998c; Ward 1997). Because of the demographics of college students, service-learning and other curriculum-based community service usually involves college students going out into challenged communities and en-vironments and learning to work with others who are relatively unfamil-iar to them. The same applies to graduating professional staff, who tend to be white and middle class and work with these same clients (e.g., Con-necticut Advisory Council for Teacher Professional Standards 1995; Ruiz 1990).

Often, when students first encounter environments that have been plagued by years of disenfranchisement and poverty, they experience "culture shock," a normal and universal response to unfamiliar cultures and their circumstances (Lynch and Hanson 1998, 29). In such environments, children and adults are less likely to have access to financial resources, medical resources, and a healthy physical development; adequate nutrition; quality education; access to play environments and peers; and positive and nonviolent images (Brooks-Gunn and Duncan 1997; Federal Interagency Forum on Child and Family Statistics 1997). This does not mean that every individual in those environments faces these challenges; however, they are more likely to. Negative media images that are prevalent in mainstream society concerning impoverished and ethnic environments may make it more difficult for workers to see the strength and resiliency of such individuals when they encounter them (Chideya 1995; Goodwin 1996; Porter 1999; Way 1998; West 1995). At times you may feel disappointment, sadness, and anger, particularly as you become more aware of historical and current structural inequities (e.g., Carnes 1995; Zinn 1980) that sometimes hinder human beings from moving beyond their current life and work conditions (Dunlap 1997, 1998b).

These are significant issues as community learning enters a new century. The demographics of our country are rapidly changing, and within the next few generations, people of color and mixed-race people from traditionally disenfranchised backgrounds will make up the majority of the U.S. population (Cushner, McClelland, and Safford 1996; DeGenova 1997; Wardle 2000). Given societal, historical, and current inequities, economically privileged community workers are frequently placed in a position to "serve" the traditionally disenfranchised. Sometimes they are ill prepared to understand and adequately meet the unique needs of the populations that they are serving (Barnes 1992; Canino and Spurlock 1994; Collins et al. 1990; Daniel 1994; Dwivedi and Varma 1996; Gibbs and Huang 1998; Ingoldsby and Smith 1995; Lynch and Hanson 1998; see also Connecticut Advisory Council for Teacher Professional Standards 1995).

In light of the intertwined nature of socioeconomic status and race in our society, not only is the socioeconomic status of the service provider and the client likely to be different, but their race and ethnicity are also likely to differ (Barnes 1992; Collins et al. 1990; Lynch and Hanson 1998; Ruiz 1990). Thus numerous issues related to unfamiliarity, trust, stereotypes, and prejudice often must be overcome in cross-cultural service-provision situations (Ruiz 1990).

European American service providers usually have had previous experience with people of color, but often it is not in-depth or long-term, nor is it of an equal-status nature (Barnes 1992). Long-term, equal-status experiences help reduce prejudice and increase cross-cultural understanding (Stephan and Brigham 1985). Since the client and service provider relationship and accompanying trust take time to develop, trust building can be painstakingly challenging even under the very best of circumstances. It can be even more challenging if the service provider holds negative, inaccurate stereotypes about the client or client's group membership(s). A cross-cultural relationship can also be challenged when either the service provider or the client is from a group that has traditionally held greater socioeconomic and networking privileges or is from a group that historically has been exploitative. In addition, the traditionally disenfranchised may have hesitations, past negative experiences, and/or stereotypes with respect to service providers and provider organizations that, understandably, can also challenge the trust-building process (Greene 1986; Phillips 1995; Turner 1994; West 1995). With all of this, you must be patient when trying to build bonds with clients who come from different racial, ethnic, socioeconomic, educational, historical, familial, religious, or sexual orientation group memberships than you do.

Therefore, as I suggested in chapter 4, when it comes to the community learning process it is important for you to realize that (1) you come to the community learning situation with your own cognitive filters or ideas and even "baggage" concerning those who are different from you; (2) those whom you encounter will also come to the situation with their own filters and "baggage"; and (3) some of what is experienced may have little to do with you personally but may reflect social and structural tensions that have existed long before the moment you are experiencing. Of course no particular interactions, thoughts, and feelings concerning multicultural and diversity issues should be trivialized. Rather, any single incident stands within the historical, cultural, and social contexts surrounding it. These important components should be included and examined, not overlooked, in work with children and families.

ISSUES FACED BY COMMUNITY LEARNERS
IN MULTICULTURAL SETTINGS

In their journals, workers reveal at least three major issues that may arise for you in multicultural settings. First, you may occasionally feel distrusted, isolated, and confused as you encounter environments and people who appear to be different from you. As part of the process of experiencing other cultures, you should examine and discover your philosophies regarding differences and diversity. Second, you may find yourself, from time to time, witnessing and confronting inaccurate and negative stereotypes firsthand, from both clients and staff. You will need to observe and think critically about the stereotypes and prejudices that you witness if you should encounter them. Third, you enter your community learning situations with a variety of skills, resources, personal strengths, and resilience for learning and growing in multicultural environments. You can best cope within and appreciate multicultural environments when you put all your skills and resources to effective use. Methods for doing so are presented throughout this chapter, with additional guidelines provided in appendix F.

Initial Reactions and Experiences within Multicultural Environments

My service-learning students comment from time to time that work in multicultural environments is a challenge to them because of their initial unfamiliarity with such environments. Nonetheless, they tend to enjoy the challenge and learn a great deal in the process. Two students articulate their struggle:

> *I enjoyed the service-learning project, though it was tough sometimes. I have worked with kids a lot before, so that was not a problem, for I am used to a lot of things kids do. I think it was just the physical setting, lack of structure, and the type of kids I worked with that was challenging for me. I had never worked with inner-city kids before and it was very new for me. (Female, European American)*

> *It was, and still is, quite different for me to be in such a diverse town. At home, there were only a couple of African Americans at my high school. It was a great opportunity at this service-learning site to see how different races interacted. I had never been exposed to such obvious differences in cultures before. Overall, I enjoyed my experience and was exposed to a great deal of new things. I plan to continue my service-learning next semester for my own sake. (Female, European American)*

Many parallels exist between initial adjustment processes in community learning and therapeutic counseling processes. In both community learning and counseling situations, it appears that time is required for cross-race service provider–client dyads to feel comfortable with and trusting of one another (Greene 1986). Trust cannot be assumed on either side. In both counseling and community learning, one person may assume a helping role while the other assumes a recipient role. In both situations, either a one-sided "I will teach you," "I will show you," or "I will reform you" model can be used; the alternative is a more equal, democratic, mutual learning model. Research shows that counseling programs that include mutual learning and client knowledge, goals, and perspective in the prescriptive process tend to be more successful than those that do not (Meier and Davis 1993; Ruiz 1990). The same may be true for community learning programs as well (Dunlap 1998c).

Regardless of the philosophy and approach that you use (i.e., teacher versus mutual learner model), the issues that arise for you in multicultural experiences may be varied and complex. To begin, you may fear noticing and acknowledging individual differences and cultural styles because you may not want to be mistaken as prejudiced or as attempting to stereotype others (Derman-Sparks and the A.B.C. Task Force 1989; Ramsey 1987). Students speak on this issue:

> *I think race is a subject no one wants to really get into because it leads to discomfort. I am reminded of a morning at my placement when a mother dropped off her [preschool European American] child. The mom and the teacher were talking. As they were talking, her child began to play with the white and black dolls. At one point the little boy made a reference to the different skin tones of the babies by saying, "this is a dark baby." Now maybe it was just me, but I felt a visible change in the demeanor of the [European American] teacher and mom. You could tell neither one of them really wanted to say anything, but they both thought they should. Their superficial comments were of little consequence, as the boy continued playing while they briefly addressed him. Perhaps, ideally that would have been an excellent time to address some multicultural issues with the child. It has been shown that children make racial inferences by the preschool age, so why not discuss it instead of avoiding it? (Male, European American)*

> *[A preschool dance program] girl befriended me right away. She told me she was from Puerto Rico, and she was fascinated by holding up her arm next to mine and comparing the skin tones, saying things like "Look! I'm darker!" I was so glad to hear her speak about race with such a carefree, even joyous attitude—it seems to be such an unspeakable topic in our society. The saying "the elephant in the middle of the room that no one talks about" expresses that so well. (Female, European American)*

The fear of sounding prejudiced, naive, or insensitive is a common concern. Such fear, while normal, can hinder you from moving beyond very superficial modes of communicating and learning about others (Greene 1986). It is important for you to try to overcome your fears and work toward communicating with those who seem different from you in a manner that is sensitive and considerate of whatever their struggles and issues may be. Attempting to understand and deal sensitively with others is an approach that some might trivialize as "political correctness." Barber argues that exercising genuine sensitivity toward those who have not had equal power in our society is an important and necessary task that goes beyond what conservatives call "political correctness" (1992, 91). He argues that we should not "dismiss those who worry about the ways in which speech [and behavior] reflect power relations" and that we should consider the "grim racist realities of a society in which [people of color, women, gays and lesbians, non-Christians, and other minorities] are largely powerless" (Barber 1992, 91). Many community workers, through their work and personal experiences, become more sensitive to the oppression and exclusion of people who hold minority status. One student discusses his views on the importance of being sensitive to the issues of traditionally excluded people, and the consequences of not doing so:

> *The struggles and triumphs of individuals belonging to minority groups living in American society are often ignored by members of the dominant culture because there is little appreciation of differences. Differences are usually considered deficiencies rather than positive attributes that enrich and diversify daily interactions. Oftentimes, it is the needs and voices of minority cultures that are not acknowledged and accepted because often they are the most powerless and voiceless of all individuals. These children have a higher risk of encountering both academic and social difficulties. On many occasions, these children are set on tracks for failure not just within the school system, but in society as well. Many parents are not socialized to deal with schools and their administrators. Many have other life stresses to deal with and are frequently misunderstood by the school system. With the lack of communication comes a discontinuity between what is taking place in the classroom and what is taking place at home. Children ultimately suffer the worst consequences that arise out of this huge misunderstanding. (Male, Hispanic)*

As Barber (1992) suggests, it is important for you to be sensitive to and nondismissive of the plight of others as you engage with them in community work. When handled properly, the respectful acknowledgment and exploration of differences can provide excellent opportunities for discussion, learning, and growth about others and about yourself (Derman-Sparks et al. 1989; Ramsey 1987). To illustrate this, several workers speak on the value of learning how to engage sensitively and compassionately in community learning environments, and how such engagement helped them grow:

> *I thought I would have an interesting and unique perspective working with [my service-learning partner who is European American] because we are different ethnicities. I am mixed race—a little of everything—and it is interesting to see how [kindergarten and first-grade] children react to us as individuals. One little European American girl looked up at me and said, "We've never had a black gym teacher before!" She was very excited about this. Then a little African American girl looked over and said to me in an almost accusatorial tone, "You're white!" I smiled because this was an obvious exploration of race, and I said, "I'm both!" The little girls both seemed to think that was okay. I was excited that young school-age children are still fairly uninhibited, willing to ask questions and explore new options and answers. (Female, biracial European American/African American)*

> *I sat down for a while on the ground, and some of the girls [at an inner-city child care center] started doing my hair. These girls are all of African American backgrounds and come in with braids and other styles that their mothers have done in their hair. We discussed how we each manage our hair differently. (Female, European American)*

Today we visited an art festival that featured a statue of an African-Caribbean woman looking at her baby. The [preadolescent African American] girls laughed at the woman. They called her clothes "rags" and made comments about the lady, calling her an "African bootie scratcher." I had heard these names growing up in the inner city. The girls noticed my displeasure. I was very angry because my whole family is from Africa with the exception of me and some of my siblings and cousins. I asked the girls if they saw all Africans as wearing "rags" and as being "bootie scratchers." They said, "Yes!" I then asked them if they saw me that way. They said, "No!" When I told them that I was African, they all seemed shocked that I did not fit their stereotype of Africans. I then asked the girls if the way they saw the exhibit was the way they saw themselves. They, of course, said no. But I told them that they should, because without that woman in the picture they would not be here. We stayed a while longer at the exhibit and they began to realize that what I had been saying was true. They apologized and I accepted. I later realized that all they have ever seen on TV was the typical stereotype of Africans as savage people. This example shows how the media influences the mind of children. (Female, African)

Each of these workers made good on the opportunity to explore differences, and they did so in an age- and culturally appropriate fashion.

Witnessing and Reacting to Inaccurate Stereotypes and Prejudice

As the previous experiences suggest, you may sometimes be caught by surprise when you hear clients, especially children, speaking on the issue of race. You may be especially bothered when client or staff comments are negative. If or when you hear negative comments involving race, gender, ableism, or sexual orientation, you may feel both amazed and saddened that children (and sometimes adults) could conjure such phrases. Further, because you sometimes do not expect children to be aware of differences, opinions, and concerns of a racial nature, you may sometimes automatically misinterpret any awareness as a sign of prejudice (Derman-Sparks et al. 1989; Ramsey 1987). The reality is that children are aware of gender differences before they reach their second birthday and are aware of racial differences, as they are constructed in our society, sometimes well before their third birthday (Aboud 1988; Berger and Thompson 1998; Clark 1988; Ramsey 1987; the Teaching Tolerance Project 1997). Even though you may not expect children to make racial comments, prejudicial insults and the like occur among children of all ages, particularly with respect to race, gender, and sexual orientation. Examples of racial prejudice follow:

One activity [with the elementary school children] was to mark their countries of origin on a map and notice any clustering. When the presenter spoke of Asians, one boy would push on his eyes to slant them and say "ching, chong." When Vietnam was mentioned he said, "Yeah, we killed those gooks." This makes me wonder what he hears at home. I was reminded of the article by Beverly Tatum, "Talking about Racism" [1992]. Perhaps that boy was in the "reintegration" phase of racial identity development [i.e., characterized by fear, anger, and blame toward minorities]. I hope he is able to progress to a more positive phase where he will accept himself and others. (Female, European American)

The [first-grade children in a special education class at an inner-city elementary school] were wonderful. They were so loving, hard-working, and full of vitality. The teacher really cared about them, and I thought she did a good job. However, things started to become strange when the teacher asked the children what they wanted to be when they grew up. She called on the first student, an African American girl, who replied, "I want to be a doctor." Then the teacher replied, "Well, maybe you could work in a hospital as a nurse or a receptionist." Then the teacher called on a little boy, who said he wanted to be a pilot, like his dad. The teacher responded by saying, "Well, I think you could find a job in an airport carrying luggage." This happened repeatedly. She basically told all of the students that she did not have very high expectations for them. These students were in the first grade! Where does she attain the right to put judgments and limitations on their capabilities? I was so angered that I wanted to set her straight, but I counted to ten and tried to control my rage. I guess she was trying to avoid setting up these students for dashed dreams. It just left me feeling sad that this teacher couldn't be supportive to these great children. (Female, European American)

Likewise, instances of gender stereotyping and sexism abound. For example:

I have to say that I was very surprised to find one [first-grade] girl displaying aggression toward another. In all honesty, I would not be so surprised if it was two boys acting in that manner, but the fact that these were two quiet, mild-mannered girls took me by surprise. I know I would not have been so quick to run over there if it had been two boys behaving that way. I guess that is just what society has instilled in me. (Female, European American)

I took an [elementary school–age after-school program] group of children to the infamous "toy room." This was a group of about five girls and one boy. The girls took great pleasure in dressing up the boy in girl's clothing. He didn't seem to mind and actually appeared to enjoy all of the attention. However, he made a point of telling me again and again that he was not gay, and when another group of boys came by the toy room he immediately tore off the shawl and skirt he had been wearing. This indicated to me that many cultural biases and expectations had been firmly implanted in this boy. (Female, European American)

Instances of sexual orientation stereotyping, heterosexism, and homophobia are plentiful as well. For example:

Today was also interesting because there was a newfound fascination with being "gay" [among a group of middle school children]. Everyone was comfortable

*yelling "faggot" and making many other derogatory comments about gay people.
The teacher was very embarrassed about her class's behavior and sent one of the
boys out of the room. She never went out to speak with him about his behavior,
and he therefore never understood why what he was saying was bad. He just
learned that he could not talk about any of his confusion or questions in class. (Female, European American)*

*Today in class one of the [sixth-grade] boys called one of the girls a lesbian. She
got extremely upset. I wonder if either of them have any idea what this means.
I also wonder how these kids have been educated on this topic. (Female, European American)*

You may find yourself viewing such childish behavior as prejudiced and
malicious, even though they may not fully understand the significance of
what they are saying. You may also feel disappointed that children have apparently been exposed to such prejudicial thinking. Also, you may not know
how to address such comments or issues for the benefit of all the children in
the situation (Derman-Sparks et al. 1989; The Teaching Tolerance Project
1997). Examples of students attempting to address or respond to such comments are provided in this chapter under the subheading "Helpful Approaches for Work in Multicultural Environments."

Another very important issue concerns whether educational settings in
which students are placed have a diverse staff and multicultural curriculum
materials. You may be pleased to find diversity within your placement's staff
and materials or you may observe that such diversity is absent. Often you
will feel concerned when you notice a lack of diversity among staff, toys,
dolls, and posters. Such absence may account, in part, for some of the stereotyping and prejudice illustrated above. The concern about media and other
surrounding images and environments may begin to develop as you consider, depending on your course curricula and personal interests, the role
that such images and environments play in the development of children's
self-concept, self-esteem, and ideas about others (e.g., Derman-Sparks et al.
1989; Hopson and Hopson 1993; Ladson-Billings 1994). Students placed in a
variety of different educational environments, from infant day care and up,
note the lack of diversity—in staff, materials, and curricula—that often exists.
With regard to staff, for example:

*All the [child care center] teachers are white, even though the majority of the
kids are African American. However, they all seem to be sensitive to race issues
and promote an antibias curriculum. (Female, European American)*

*I have been thinking about cultural constructs and their effect on children in
regard to my placement at [a child care center]. The children in my room are
almost all of color. I began to think about the fact that the caregivers are all
white, whereas the majority of the children are black, Hispanic and multira-*

cial. I am not saying this is in any way a negative situation, but I think it brings up many issues that are not often spoken about. (Female, European American)

I was speaking to one of the three African American girls [from the home for adolescent girls] and she told me how much she enjoyed speaking to me because she felt as though we connected. She couldn't talk about certain things with staff because she felt as though they wouldn't understand. The entire staff is composed of white women, which I consider to be somewhat of a problem (Female, Hispanic)

Students have similar reactions with regard to classroom curricula and materials that lack diversity, usually appreciating diversity when they see it and feeling disappointment when they don't. For example:

My service-learning partner and I decided to go to the library and investigate to learn more about the [elementary] school. We looked at the measly supply of books and found, to my dismay, that there was not one, not one, book that featured a story geared for marginalized children. All of the covers of the books showed white children. There were no books with a minority child as the main character. It made me question how a school with 40 percent minority children could omit minorities from their available literature. I came to the conclusion that because the librarians were all white, they just didn't think to purchase books about minorities. (Female, European American)

I am concerned because I have noticed that [an inner-city high school's] curriculum is not particularly connected to the lives of the kids. Even in geography, the perfect place for multicultural focus, there seems to have been very little discussion of different cultures. This problem is compounded by the fact that the teacher seems distanced from the students. The students say explicitly that they get the feeling that some of their teachers don't care about them, don't know them, and don't want to know them. In addition, they stated that they can concentrate better in those classes with teachers who do care and do make an effort to get to know them. Maybe it has to do with security. The more secure the students feel in their relationship with the teacher, the more relaxed and at ease they can be in the classroom. This is something that they could feel acutely. (Female, European American)

This was a very politically incorrect day for academic work [at an elementary school]. First, a girl with whom I was working had a worksheet on the topic of the letter I. It had a picture of an Indian with a headdress made of feathers as an example of a word that began with I. Then we did Columbus Day activities, making a necklace with the three ships and looking at a pop-up book. The book told the story of Columbus. I talked to her about the pictures, but she really just liked the pop-up pictures. I almost laughed at the irony of sitting with a non-English speaking Puerto Rican girl, who was one of the very few children of color in the entire school, and trying to explain why she did not have to come to school Monday and showing her a worksheet showing that "I is for Indian."

I did not put much effort into trying to explain Columbus Day, and I do not think she was connecting to what I was talking about anyway. (Female, European American)

As students reflect in their journals, they frequently ponder the role that available and/or missing media images play in children's development. For example:

[At a preschool] I feel that cultural diversity is not addressed enough. There should be role models and pictures available in the classroom for the children of color who are there. Besides themselves, they hardly have anything to identify with in the classroom. On the other hand, the white children are surrounded with an affirming environment. Why are children of color not given the same positive environment? Why don't they have more pictures of diverse cultures in the classroom? (Male, European American)

In today's [role model program for inner-city middle school girls] we looked at a video on body images. Afterward, the girls were asked to identify who they considered to be beautiful women in the entertainment industry. They all pointed out women who were either supermodels or [extremely slim] singers or models. All of the women pointed out by these African American and Hispanic girls were either white women or light-skinned African women. It sort of scared me to see that these young girls' definition of beauty was [exclusively] the European version of beauty. The girls in the group believed that you're not desirable to or accepted by the opposite sex if you do not fall into the majority's perception of beauty. These girls, at their young age, are actually looking for a way to be accepted among their peers. (Female, African)

Something really upset me. My friend and I both have [clients] as part of [a mentoring program for inner-city elementary school–aged girls] and we took them to the mall a couple of weekends ago. We separated and my friend took her [client] to the toy store. Her [Puerto Rican client] was immediately attracted to the Barbie dolls. Looking at the white Ken doll, she said, "Ooo, he looks good. He's so fine." Seeing a black Ken doll, my friend said, "What about him? He's just as good-looking, don't you think?" "No," she said firmly. "Why not?" Asked my friend. "Because he's black." This was the reply coming from a Latina with very dark skin. Who and what has instilled in her this idea that white men are superior? The fact that this seven-year-old girl, who has grown up in a housing project with mostly people of color and has gone to school with all different kinds of kids, thinks that white is more beautiful than black tells me something is terribly wrong. On television, black men are often shown in association with crime and violence. What kind of message does this send children, and how can these images be counteracted with positive ones? (Female, European American)

Related to this, sometimes workers consider how media socialization has affected their own development:

> *I think the media images I have been bombarded with since childhood have depicted black and Hispanic men as aggressive, violent, and threatening. Though I didn't know it at the time, those images were what shaped my perceptions of black people. I certainly never received any multicultural education, and I knew very few black people, so it wasn't like I had any other way of knowing that those messages were wrong. I am also noticing there really aren't any black superheroes. Rarely do you see black people portrayed in positions of strength, power, or authority. Stereotypes are very damaging because they can cause people to fear others they don't even know because of their race. I think that to be bombarded by these negative images every day must have an impact on children. As a prospective teacher (and a human being), I am sure I will have to deal with the pain that media images have caused children. (Female, European American)*

Occasionally workers express concern about the presence of diverse, multicultural materials and environments, perceiving such inclusion to exclude European American materials. They may perceive such "exclusion" because they are not consciously aware of the predominant presence of European American materials, media, role models, and perspectives in our everyday lives (McIntosh 1990; Shujaa 1994). For example:

> *[The resource room specializing in multicultural books and curriculum materials] is a library, a classroom, and an arts and crafts center for kids. It's an interesting place. It is full of nonfiction books: science, history, language, and biographies. They have lots of biographies. Most of them seem black-emphasized while the other books cover all sorts of cultures and religions. My personal thought is that if they're going to have a center like this, they should have some stuff on European cultures. It should all be balanced. (Male, European American)*

Noticing Differences and Similarities in Cultural Styles and Customs

While individual differences and diversity exist within any given culture, there are threads of common socialization that tend to flow throughout specific cultures. Individualistic cultures, such as mainstream America and other Western nations, tend to value independence, individual needs and goals, equal rights and responsibilities, privacy, competition, task completion, single or discrete categories of membership, personal control over the environment, time orientation, emphasis on youth and the future, individual and specific ownership, materialism ("newer, bigger, more"), independence in young children, and small nuclear families (Greenfield and Cocking 1994; Hale-Benson 1986; Hanson 1998; Lynch 1998, 53–54; Lynch and Hanson 1998; Okun 1996; Shade 1989). These kinds of characteristics are found among many postindustrialized, capitalistic cultures, even today, because of socialization styles that are carried from generation to generation (Dwivedi and Varma 1996; Galvin and Cooper 1996; Lynch and Hanson 1998; Shade 1989).

If you are more individualistic or mainstream American in your cultural orientation, you may initially have some difficulty relating to collectivist cultural practices. Collectivistic cultures tend to value interdependence over independence (which is often mistaken by outsiders as codependence), communal decision making and collaboration, process over end results, multiple categories of membership and tolerance for ambiguity, harmony with nature, ritual and tradition taking precedence over time, respect for elders and the aging process, shared ownership, spirituality, extended nurture of young children, and extended family and kinship networks (Greenfield and Cocking 1994; Hale-Benson 1986; Hanson 1998; Ingoldsby and Smith 1995; Lynch and Hanson 1998; Okun 1996; Shade 1989).

Children and adults of African American, Hispanic, Native American, and Asian cultures tend to be more collectivistic in their style of interacting with others, especially when interacting within their own culture (Shade 1989). This is not due in any manner to genetics but rather to differences in socialization styles that tend to exist for these groups (Greenfield and Cocking 1994; Hale-Benson 1986; Shade 1989). Collectivistic orientations are often characteristic of communities derived from agricultural cultures (Lynch and Hanson 1998).

Many factors play a role in the development of our cultural orientation or style. It is a combination of many influences, including an individual's personality; gender, ethnic, and racial socialization; degree of assimilation and acculturation within the mainstream culture; and familial reinforcement of behavior. Even within ethnic cultures that tend to be collectivistic there are individualistically oriented members, just as within individualistic cultures there are collectivistically oriented members. In addition, many members hold characteristics that are in various stages on the continuum between the two styles, depending on that multiplicity of factors (Lynch and Hanson 1998).

In collectivistic communities and cultures, people sometimes approach even strangers within their referent group as if they are family. For example, a teacher with a collectivistic orientation may treat the children in her classroom like part of her own extended family (Collins and Tamarkin 1990; Foster 1994). Studies have shown that some European American teachers tend to do this, depending on their own family and cultural styles, their experiences across cultures, and their willingness to learn about and adapt to cultures that differ from their own (Delpit 1995; Hale-Benson 1986; Hurd, Lerner, and Barton 1999; Ladson-Billings 1994). One worker describes the "we are family" approach (Ladson-Billings 1994) as she observes a seasoned teacher in action in an environment consisting of primarily children of color. The ethnicity of the teacher is not made clear by the writer, but her personal style appears very collectivistic in nature:

> *The "We are Family" approach to teaching really seems successful among the teachers [at an inner-city after-school tutoring program]. One teacher in particular embraces the children as if they were her own, and they really appear to love it. Often she hugs and touches them all. In fact, they run over to her for hugs. Also, she compliments them a lot. For instance, she'll compliment the girls' hairstyles and ask who did them, which they love so much. She is just incredibly warm and loving, which, in my opinion, has been extremely effective. (Female, European American)*

Your cultural socialization may influence how you interpret and respond to the people and events that occur in your community learning environment. For example, in the following passage, a student who appears to identify with collectivistic cultural practices provides an example of how his cultural expectations influenced his decision to intercede on behalf of two fighting children instead of letting them resolve their conflict on their own (which would have been consistent with individualistic cultural child-rearing practices):

> *At the end of [a visit at an after-school program] one of the boys I had worked with decided to fight with another kid. I was amazed to see these kids spitting at each other in the presence of a mother who had two younger children next to her. This mother stood right next to them and did nothing. She looked on as if this was not in her world and therefore it was not worth her time. So I jumped in before it got out of hand, but the lady's ignorance angered me more. I have never seen anyone back home in Africa sit and watch two kids fight in their presence without taking some sort of action. I was not impressed when I left today. (Male, African)*

There may also be instances in which you feel that your style and upbringing match that of clients, like the following worker, who senses a connection right away with a client because of their similar cultural backgrounds:

> *I was able to speak [with a young adolescent at a home for girls] for a short while, and she seemed quite friendly and easygoing, considering it was the first time she met me. We talked for a little while. On my way out, she asked me if I was Puerto Rican. I responded yes, and she told me that I reminded her of an old friend. I look at it as a good thing. In a way, it felt as though we had a sense of connection. I normally feel as though I can relate more with an African American or Hispanic, rather than with a Caucasian person. Perhaps it deals with the fact that we've been through so much more than they have, including the way we've been raised. (Female, Hispanic)*

But there may be other times when you will not feel this connection immediately, whether of the same cultural background or not, as described by many journal quotes in this chapter and chapter 4. In spite of matches or mismatches in gender, culture, personality, experiences, and so on, most workers try to enter the multicultural community learning environment with an open mind and an awareness of their own biases and preconceived notions. As workers share:

> *My interpretation of events [at a preschool] will be as objective as possible. I do, however, acknowledge that all my interpretations will not be completely objective because my view of social situations involving children are shaped by both familial and schooling influences that are exclusively mine. (Male, Hispanic)*

> *I am understanding more and more that I cannot impose my value system or ideas about what life ought to be on these children [at an inner-city after school tutorial program]. (Female, European American)*

In other words, it is difficult for people to be completely unbiased. We need to be aware of this and try to work toward objectivity as well as we can (Tatum 1997).

You may sometimes feel a great struggle as you try to keep an open mind and respond sensitively, yet appropriately, to initially perplexing situations or issues. For example, the following student describes how she had to listen carefully to the client that she was working with and learn more about his world when he was confrontational with his peers:

> *These [elementary school] children live in a low-income section of the city. They have been taught by their parents, as one child said to me, that "if you get pushed, then push the person back, do not let anyone hurt you." This comment was made by a young Puerto Rican boy aged nine. I get the impression that these children are taught from the very beginning that the world is a place of survival of the fittest. These children learn that if you don't fight for your rights and for yourself, people will just walk all over you. I don't know how to deal with this situation because I think the children have been taught this at an early age, and it is pretty hard to just teach them the opposite now. Their environment, I have to admit by seeing it, is a dangerous one, where they have to be very attentive to their surroundings and have to hurt whoever is attempting to hurt them. (Female, Hispanic)*

The above worker was advised to try to present this issue to the supervising teacher at the placement site, with the hope of finding a way to redirect the child without negating the important issues and concerns that exist within his family and community environment.

This next worker provides her intellectual reaction when a client's parent appears to panic about something that others at the site took for granted. Her attempt to remain calm and respectful of others' beliefs and customs are evident in her passage:

> *My fourth visit to [a child care center] was definitely an interesting one! I was assigned to one table and helped the kids with their ham and cheese sandwiches, peaches, and milk. Everything seemed fine until a mother who had just brought her two children in a few minutes before suddenly shouted, "What is he eating?!" and stared at one of her kids eating the sandwich. Apparently her family does not eat pork. It turned out okay. She was very nice about it. She understood that the teachers were just busy and forgot and that they did not mean any harm. (Female, European American)*

Even if you have difficulty initially connecting with clients based on cultural similarities, you can eventually make a connection in other ways (e.g., with respect to birth order, personality, family configuration, hobby similarities). As one student describes:

> *I really haven't had much experience with minority children because my home is predominantly a white area. Then when we talked about different methods to consider and use when working with African American children [appendix F] I found it very helpful to consider. The young girl that I worked with a lot was African American, and after we discussed the topic in class, I found myself paying more attention to how I interacted with this girl. I was very concerned about her because she is behind her classmates in her work. I saw all the difficulty that she was having, and I sympathized so much because I went through the exact same thing when I was in school, and it is so very frustrating. Keeping this in mind, I tried to offer lots of positive reinforcement and assurance to her. (Female, European American)*

Thus this worker, who did not feel that she was familiar with minority children, found herself initially relating to an African American client's personal situation more than to her cultural style, which allowed her to connect with the client more readily.

Many of the other issues that arise for workers center around perceived differences in child rearing and other family roles. For example, because of the greater emphasis on respect for age and elders, as well as the precariousness of life for children of color and less economically advantaged children in America, parental and staff discipline styles tend to be warm yet effectively more firm than middle-class European American styles (Deater-Deckard et al. 1996; Mosby et al. 1999). This becomes evident to some workers during their work with clients:

> *Today I discovered some things about the way authority is enforced and learning is fostered at [an inner-city after-school tutorial program]. In terms of a general style of care, the staff use a mix of the "harsh-warm" and "traditional"*

techniques [Deater-Deckard et al. 1996]. The teachers are firm and strict but also very warm, interested, and genuinely concerned about the well-being of the children. Although they do not at all expect any of the children to assume old-fashioned gender roles, they do feel very strongly about respecting elders and having good manners. This mix of approaches seems to work well for the children because the environment there is so chaotic and because many of them may come from homes where parents practice "authoritarian" or "permissive" styles of care. (Female, European American)

You may also have an opportunity to observe that not all families shelter their children from life's passages (e.g., births, weddings, parties, funerals, etc.). You may find to your surprise that some children are permitted to be involved with the birthing of siblings, family and community parties and celebrations, and funerals, and are encouraged to engage in the grieving process (Greenfield and Cocking 1994). Some of the children may have adult-like responsibilities (Hale-Benson 1986). As one student observes:

Many of the kids [who participate in the community after-school program sponsored by a soup kitchen] come from large families and therefore have many responsibilities. They must learn how to take care of themselves and, in some cases, their siblings as well. (Female, European American)

Those of you who were reared to view children as individuals who should be separated from adult activities may tend to expect children to be somewhat shielded from such events and responsibilities. Those of you reared in more communal or collectivistic cultures may relate better to the extended family networking and the child inclusiveness of most of the activities within the family or community (Shade 1989). One Jewish worker shares her perspectives on similarities between her culture and African American culture on dimensions such as communality after attending a community Kwanzaa celebration:

The stress that the African culture places on tradition, family, and unity filled me with many strong emotions. I still cannot get over the similarities between African culture and Jewish culture. I am not insinuating that they are the same; however, there are a great many parallels. The Kwanzaa principles of unity, self-determination, collective work and responsibility, cooperative economics, purpose, creativity, and faith should be the base of anyone's philosophy. When people work together and help one another collectively, the world will be a much better place in which to live. One must continue to have faith that the state the world is in right now is temporary. We must have faith that to some capacity the world will improve. (Female, European American)

In noting similarities and differences between yourself and those with whom you work, you may also be surprised by the age of parents and caregivers. You may discover parents to be much younger than you expected. Likewise, you may come upon parents and caregivers who are much older than you expected, as when grandparents or older extended family members rear children they themselves did not birth. For example:

Today I learned [an eighteen-month-old girl at a child care center has] parents who are still in high school, and they planned to have her. They have been working with her, and she has been progressing quite well. I think it is great that these parents are breaking the stereotype that teenage parents are inadequate and unfit parents. (Female, European American)

[A thirteen-month-old baby at a child care center] is out today, and one of the workers told me a bit of his history. First, his mother, at age nineteen, is pregnant again. I am upset that she is pregnant. She consistently seems to be forgetting to send his bottles, long-sleeved shirts, etc. How much attention is he going to get with another baby in the house? (Female, European American)

[An inner-city middle school-age boy] lives with his grandparents. I can tell that all of the children in this class have much more complicated lives than most give them credit for. (Female, European American)

You may also notice that children from collectivistic cultures tend to talk a great deal about their immediate and extended families, including their siblings and grandparents. Frequently, some of their extended family members are neither blood kin nor related by marriage, but rather are members informally adopted into their families. Siblings and extended family members play a greater role in their care taking and daily lives than in families who are more nuclear in their orientation (Hanson 1998; Willis 1998). Workers share a variety of their insights gained about the collectivistic family configurations of their clients:

This afternoon I learned a lot [about the children at an inner-city after-school tutorial program]. I was working with a group of four girls and one boy and they were discussing what they called "telenovelas." Apparently, a telenovela is a show much like a soap opera. At first I assumed that they were all watching the same television show in their respective houses but then, after further discussion, I realized that they all live together. When I asked them if they lived together, they began listing the people they lived with. The other noteworthy thing was that they were calling people who live with them "Aunt" and "Uncle." The girls also cited as part of their family several other children who usually attend the center. (Female, European American)

[An eight-year-old] little boy asked me lots of questions about my family. Throughout my work with him, he has brought up family matters numerous times. Today he asked me how old I was and when I told him, he said that he had a brother my age. Then he told me of six other brothers and sisters, and

this is when I realized the importance of family to him and also the support and love that he must receive at home. The children at [an elementary] school, for the most part, seem to come from close-knit families. Children rely heavily on their families for almost everything. They value the family above all else, and if one of their family members were leaving, I think they would have a tougher time dealing with the move. (Female, European American)

[An after-school program boy's] self-confidence stems from his supportive family. He is the third child, and his older siblings are both in high school. When I was working with him, he continually made references to his sisters and his parents. He told me the tricks that they had been teaching him to help him remember his multiplication tables. It sounds like the whole family practices the tables with him and tries to help him understand. (Female, European American)

Related to this issue of the extended family, you may also witness diversity among those who drop off and pick up children from the various programs. For example:

[At an inner-city elementary school] a lot of people who picked up the children were not mothers and fathers. They were grandmothers, aunts, uncles, or just a friend of the family. I grew up in a small suburban town, and I never dealt with multicultures. Their world seems completely different from mine. I came from a family that had the traditional mother, father, brothers, cats, and dogs, but these kids come from a completely different array of environments. (Male, European American)

Thus the basic ways that multicultural issues may arise for you can include your experiencing culture shock, witnessing and reacting to stereotypes and prejudice, and gaining an awareness of cultural similarities and differences. The issues that arise are variable, challenging, and sometimes distressing. We will explore some of the reasons that this is so as we examine the challenges to this part of the community learning process.

CHALLENGES TO WORKING IN MULTICULTURAL ENVIRONMENTS

There may be at least three challenges to your work in multicultural environments. The first is the fact that many of us have been bombarded, throughout the course of our lives, with negative media images and ideas about members of challenged communities (Goodwin 1996; Porter 1999; West 1995; Wilson and Gutierrez 1995). The second is that when we do have an opportunity to reeducate ourselves about challenged communities, often the new models that we are exposed to are themselves simplistic and outdated. The third is that many of us have not yet learned how to explore our own ideas about others in a manner that will give us practical insight into our day-to-day work in challenged communities.

Negative Media Images and Socialization

In our society, we are constantly bombarded with negative or inaccurate images of people of color and other people who hold "minority" status. These images portray minorities as troublesome, unintelligent, threatening, dangerous, and lazy (Wilson and Gutierrez 1995). The failures of people in communities that are suffering economically and in other ways are promoted so frequently that the strivings, sacrifices, and successes that exist within those same communities are frequently overlooked (Belle 1982; Blake 1997; Bullock 1995; Coll, Surrey, and Weingarten 1998; Cooper 1991; Edwards and Polite 1992; Hrabowski, Maton, and Greif 1998; Phillips 1995; Rose 1989; Scott 1991). With some assistance from course curricula (Derman-Sparks et al. 1989), students often become better equipped to perceive the inaccuracy of media images or the absence of positive media images concerning challenged communities, enabling them to become more critical of these kinds of media images.

Also as discussed earlier, students note the fact that negative media images concerning people of color, women, gays, and lesbians are so prevalent that they are reflected even in young children's comments to one another in community service environments. Appreciation of racial, ethnic, socioeconomic, gender, sexual orientation, and other differences and similarities is difficult because it is challenged by media and other socialization processes that promote negative stereotypes about those who do not correspond to "ideal" mainstream American cultural conceptions.

Simplistic Multicultural and Diversity Models

There is yet another challenge to gaining a better understanding of other communities and cultures. When we do attempt to reeducate ourselves in order to acquire unstereotyped notions regarding diversity, the available educational opportunities often take a simplistic, superficial, or patronizing approach to understanding others. This approach is known as the touristic model. It scratches the surface of other cultures by focusing on traditional foods and regalia while overlooking important age-appropriate versions of the structural issues of privilege and oppression that impact cultures (Shujaa 1994; Thompson and Tyagi 1993). For example, a student articulates her criticism of a child care center's sensitivity training program that she considers somewhat superficial:

> *I found through my work at [a child care center] that the activities developed for multicultural awareness and self-awareness were lacking and rarely practiced.*

The program uses activities like storytelling, face painting, stringing beads, as-
sisting in food preparation, dance, cutting, bingo games, dramatic play, wash-
ing hands, and so on, to accomplish this. I felt that their approach would be de-
scribed as touristic by those who have the antibiased curriculums we studied
[Derman-Sparks et al. 1989]. The teachers definitely try, but there are instances
where "Indians" were described as people who wear feathers, while the teachers
pointed to stereotypical images in outdated books. (Female, Hispanic)

Community learning, when accompanied by critical reflection in courses, does provide opportunities to observe beyond superficial levels, and even beyond what can be learned in books, in order to gain a better understanding of diverse others (see Berson 1997; Dunlap 1998c; Eyler et al. 1997; Mabry 1998). Community learning can also help decrease rigid notions about one's power or privilege in this society (Dunlap 1997, 1998b; Miller 1997). In other words, hands-on work in economically and otherwise challenged communities can help you develop a better understanding of the forces outside of people, such as poverty, discrimination, and glass ceilings, that act to hinder and sometimes prevent advancement. In doing so, you can become more aware of your own privilege and vulnerability, which can be both humbling and compassion enhancing. Hopefully such experiences will eventually challenge you to a social commitment and activism that will enable you to work in greater partnership with community members to improve conditions.

Fear of Exploring Diversity Issues

A final, related challenge to this process is that sometimes we have little awareness of the cultural histories of those with whom we work. Moreover, we may have not been encouraged to explore these issues in the past. In addition, we may have little understanding of our own ideas on cultures and cultural difference and may feel little comfort in exploring our own socialization regarding diversity issues. It may be crucial for you to explore your own socialization with regard to race, culture, gender, and sexual orientation, and so on, so that you understand how your perspectives have evolved and how your perspectives are similar and different from others who have developed through different socialization and experiential processes. Some of the approaches presented in the next section may be helpful in that regard.

HELPFUL APPROACHES FOR WORK
IN MULTICULTURAL ENVIRONMENTS

There are three approaches and resources that will be most helpful as you work in multicultural environments. The first is your being aware of your own racial identity, its development, and its impact on your style of relating to cultures and cultural differences. The second is having an awareness of other models or frameworks regarding culture to help you put your observations and evaluations into additional cultural contexts. The third is developing strategies that permit you to speak more comfortably on issues of race, culture, and forms of oppression when they arise during your work.

Gaining Knowledge of Oneself as a Cultural Being

Resources you may find extremely helpful include Tatum's (1992) article addressing students' reactions to the inclusion of multicultural material in the curriculum. Such resources may assist you in understanding your own feelings regarding racial and other multicultural issues. Tatum (1992) outlines Helms's (1990) stages of racial identity and illustrates the association between racial developmental stages and students' feelings and reactions to multicultural course curricula and experiences. She notes that if you have not had much experience in the past dealing with racial issues, then you might initially react with more resistance than those who have been exploring these issues for some time. It is also important for you to move through the process of exploring such issues so that you can grow beyond the resistance stage (Williams et al. 1999). I have found resources such as Tatum (1992, 1997) and others (listed at the end of this chapter) to be extremely helpful to my students. When uncomfortable feelings and emotions arise centering around racial and multicultural issues, students then have a theoretical and developmental framework for understanding those feelings as a normal part of the process of encountering new paradigms that are unfamiliar (Williams et al. 1999). A student explains how she found curriculum resources helpful for exploring her own ideas and behaviors with respect to issues of diversity:

> *I was very moved by the Tatum [1992] article and was compelled to take out my journal before I had even finished. I was aware of racism, but I hadn't looked at my own whiteness and the advantages that come with that, unknown to me because I take them for granted and assume it is the same for everyone else. Also, I had never thought about it in the sense of a process of racial identity, something we all go through. My initial reaction was as follows: "I feel a pit of fear in the bottom of my stomach, questioning myself as I have before on how do I figure out if it is a gender thing, a racial thing, a culture thing, or a me thing. What lens am I looking through? I feel guilty about injustices and my naiveté. This is hard, but hard is good." (Female, European American)*

Many European American students believe that because they have been socialized as "white" that they have no ethnic culture (Fine et al. 1997). They do not realize that life in America for a white person in itself has provided a culture that is considered to be the "norm." This norm is so prevalent that, without close and critical examination of it, it is hardly detectable to those who hold membership in it (Dovidio and Gaertner 1986; Feagin and Vera 1995; Fine et al. 1997; Harris 1993; McMillen 1995). The worker quoted above, who discussed the development of her racial identity, continues:

> *I also really liked the [Tatum 1992] article because I felt validated in a lot of ways. I have been feeling very lost and without a culture or identity and without a "race." I have felt unable to relate to the "kinds" of people I was raised around and found myself more comfortable around people with differences. It just helped to read that it is a process, a continual one. (Female, European American)*

Whites in America often are not used to critically examining their own culture and their own place within that culture. Thus they find it more challenging to consider the everyday cultures of people of color who, in contrast, are accustomed to engaging in such analyses on a daily basis (Feagin 1998; Feagin and Sikes 1994; Feagin and Vera 1995; Fine et al. 1997; Fiske 1993; Hale-Benson 1986; McIntosh 1990). It can be particularly difficult to consider other cultures by any framework other than one's own when it has been the norm (Fine et al. 1997; McIntosh 1990). Further, people from more privileged socioeconomic backgrounds traditionally have not shared this same requirement for moving among other cultures. People from less privileged backgrounds and people of color are usually quite adept at switching perspectives as they move in and out of their own and others' cultures, since life and success in America have always required that they do so. Several workers make note of this issue as they encounter race-related events in their community settings:

> *Tonight we watched a very scary horror movie [at a teen support program]. The kids were not scared by it at all, but I was terrified. At some moments I couldn't even watch it. At one part, a boy said, "What happened to all the black people in this town?" The movie had all Caucasians. What scared me is that I didn't even think of that. The supervisor said, "They were smart, they got out of that town earlier." This was meant to make them feel better. I didn't realize that there were no African Americans in the movie. This makes me angry at society and the way people so easily conform to it without even knowing it. (Female, European American)*

> *During "work period" today, the [elementary school] children were coloring worksheets. I observed that the African American children colored the characters' skin brown where the other children left the characters' skin the color of the paper, not coloring it peach or another lighter color that was available among the vast number of crayons. Many people of color are very "aware" of their heritage and ethnicity, whereas it seems that not so many European*

Americans notice their ethnic background. Is this generalization already show-
ing at this young age? It could be. (Female, European American)

One boy [at an after-school program] had a shirt on that said, "Yes, I am black;
No, I am not a criminal." That made me think because obviously race is a se-
rious issue these kids face every day. I started thinking about the race issues
these kids face every day. (Female, European American)

The above quotes illustrate a range of thoughts and emotions you may encounter during work in multicultural environments. In many of my courses,
I ask students to list the range of emotions that they feel when encountering
or discussing issues of culture, race, sexism, and other issues of oppression
(see Williams et al. 1999). Students from a variety of racial and ethnic backgrounds have reported emotions such as anger, fear, guilt, blame, anxiety,
regret, shame, disgust, disbelief, shock, betrayal, persecution, hurt, pain, relief, validation, connection, frustration, tentativeness, confusion, disequilib-
rium, comfort, encouragement, insight, pressure, responsibility, enlightenment, and feelings of being overwhelmed. The range of emotions that can
be experienced may affect your comfort when approaching multicultural
topics. When you know that you may experience many emotions and allow
yourself to confront your feelings, you can then appropriately acknowledge
your emotions when they occur, work on your issues, move on, and
progress toward greater understanding and personal growth.

Gaining Knowledge of Other Cultural Models and Paradigms

It is important for all of us to gain an improved awareness of cultural socialization and its influence on us and others. Knowledge of basic cultural
socialization processes such as those described earlier in this chapter are
useful resources when we are engaged in work in multicultural communities. For example, because of a greater "process" focus and cautionary style
when outside of their referent group (appendix F), children of traditionally
disenfranchised cultures may first tune in to the tone or psychosocial aspects of a situation and then to the actual task that they have been called
to perform after becoming comfortable with the psychosocial aspects. You
can fare better when you understand that if children from these cultures
appear withdrawn or inattentive initially, they may need a little extra time
to get psychosocially comfortable with you if they perceive you as someone outside of their culture or community, or if you seem unfamiliar to
them. You should spend your first moments and even days with hesitant
children just allowing the children to get comfortable with you while gradually moving them toward larger task demands. In the meantime, for example, clients whom you are tutoring may spend extra time sharpening
pencils, shuffling papers, and observing others in the environment, and

you may have to exercise both patience and limits when they do so (Shade 1989). As two workers explain:

> *It was amazing [during my first visit at an after-school tutoring program] how the attention of [a particular boy] just swung from one thing to the next. Every five minutes he had to get up and sharpen his pencil. (Female, European American)*

> *It was even more difficult for me to keep the attention of a boy at an after-school tutorial program] and get him to do his work. He was distracted and kept running out of the room to get another book, to sharpen his pencil, to go to the bathroom, to talk to his teacher, and so on. Instead of constantly telling him to sit down, I let him get up after sitting for a while and let him run around for a minute, and then told him to sit down again. This seemed to keep his attention, possibly because he realized that I would let him get up if he had been sitting for a few minutes. (Female, European American)*

As noted in chapter 7, once bonds of trust are established, you may find clients from cultures that differ from your own to be surprisingly responsive to you and the task demands. In some circumstances this may occur quickly, whereas in other circumstances it may take longer, if it happens at all. The following journal excerpts demonstrate how students were particularly sensitive to the reactions, pace, and tempo of clients in multicultural environments:

> *I have developed a strong kinship with a little [European American girl at a preschool]. At first this concerned me because when I examined my feelings, it occurred to me that I had developed a strong kinship for the only white girl in the class. I thought about what we recently talked about in class, how some African Americans can be more reserved when first meeting someone because they are unsure of how they will be received [appendix F]. The white child was immediately comfortable with me and affectionate, but the two children of color were more reserved. I think that I responded more to the white child at first because of this, and now that I am aware, I realize that I am going to have to be patient. I can't expect that all the children will immediately trust me, and in the future I am going to be careful to not always do what is most comfortable for me. (Female, European American)*

> *The [preschool supervising] teacher was asking a Latino boy something about snack, and he got this look on his face that I know I get when somebody says something to me that I don't understand—kind of a blank stare. At times like these, all the child needs is a translation from the bilingual assistant. I can just imagine how his actions (the blank stare) might have been interpreted if someone with a limited view had been there. In a less understanding setting, he probably would have gotten labeled as a lazy, apathetic Hispanic kid. He is lucky to be in a school environment where people don't reject his ability to*

speak Spanish. I hope that when he gets to elementary school, his ability is seen for the gift it is rather than a hindrance. (Female, European American)

Research literature on children from collectivistic cultures has also suggested that they often have high energy, which is sometimes confused with hyperactivity or out-of-control behavior (Hale-Benson 1986; Kunjufu 1984; Shade 1989). In these cultures, children may be accustomed to experiencing multiple stimulation at the same time, for example, musical, visual, auditory, and physical (Allen and Butler 1996; Boykin and Toms 1985; Hale-Benson 1986; Kunjufu 1984; Shade 1989; Willis 1998). In one study, for example, African American children were found to perform better on math problems when they worked on them accompanied by music and motion, while for European American children, such music and movement hindered math performance (Allen and Butler 1996). Thus stimulation that may help facilitate cognitive functioning among one group may tend to serve as a distraction among another group, depending on how the members have been socialized. Students speak on the high energy that they observed in some children:

I was particularly struck by the numerous times the [first-grade] teacher complained that the class was fidgeting. Although the children were not sitting as still as stones, I thought that their behavior was exceptional, so I could not understand why the teacher was finding fault. I remember reading that African American children are more active, by socialization [Kunjufu 1984]. Maybe this teacher, like so many others, doesn't respect this quality and therefore her classroom is not conducive to it. Most of the children in the room were African American, so if the teacher had previously taught an all-white class at another school, it is possible that the comparison made these children seem rambunctious. I thought this could lead to a self-fulfilling prophecy as the children singled out as "bad kids" might try to play the role. (Female, European American)

The students at my site are all Hispanic and African American, or from biracial backgrounds. Many of them have a resiliency that outshines their deficits. They all try extremely hard in their academic projects. They come to [the after-school enrichment program] as a voluntary extracurricular activity to better themselves and to be constructive. It is not a requirement of their schools. I love working with children of color because they have this energy that is wonderful. They are full of ideas, laughter, and suggestions, and they never hold their tongues. I know that this specific experience is going to be challenging. I must possess great patience because I have to deal with these children and all of the energy. But it is worth it. (Female, African American)

I spend most of the gym class at [an inner-city elementary school] keeping an eye on [a particular boy] and his best friend. The two of them rule the class. What is surprising is that both of the children are more mature than the other children, but they never pick on anyone smaller. The only people they wrestle is each other. I think teachers might feel intimidated by their quick wit and good looks. These two children have social skills that many adults are lacking. For this very reason, unlike [the staff] I find it difficult to believe that either of them has ADHD. Actually it seems ludicrous. (Male, European American)

Sometimes workers interpret client high energy negatively. For example:

There is always a great deal of chaos in [an inner-city elementary school] classroom, mostly the kids shouting out questions to us and trying to show us their drawings. There is a very obvious lack of discipline. This is a big difference from the [predominantly white, middle-class children at another school with the same art program]. In that program, the room in the beginning is usually very quiet, or filled only with small side conversation. Once the teacher gives the instructions, the children follow without too many reminders. Generally, they are fairly intent on the task at hand, and therefore the class runs smoothly; there is clear structure. (Female, European American)

It is noteworthy that in the last passage, the immediate focus on the task that is associated with individualistically oriented cultures is evident. Students who are familiar with alternative frameworks for evaluating children and the meaning of their behavior may not be so quick to judge or misjudge the high energy of their clients, regardless of their ethnicity or socioeconomic status. As examples, students share their efforts to examine energetic behavior through multiple lenses:

Most of all, I was able to make quite a few connections between my [child care center] experiences and what I have read and learned in class. Because the class was so diverse, I could easily make comparisons to what I have learned. I noted collective play and children devising their own schemes and games. I observed a lot of body language and rhythm in the African American children. There was a lot of back-and-forth conversation, and many of the African American children were able to be tuned in to many stimuli at once. They were also able to use a lot more body language, touch, and facial expressions to communicate. (Female, European American)

Today there was another child in the class. He is a three-year-old African American boy. What struck me most about him was his great "verve" [or high energy; Hale-Benson 1986]. My concern is that some of his future teachers will not recognize his great spirit and may not work with him to channel his energy constructively. I know from my own educational experience that teachers sometimes tend to consider the quiet children as "good" or "cooperative." Spirited children can be labeled as "difficult" or "disruptive." This is probably why so many black children are misdiagnosed with ADD, or being hyperactive or having a learning disability. Of course, this problem is not just limited to African Americans but can effect any child regardless of race or culture. (Female, European American)

You may observe that not only do the children often have high energy, but children and staff who are collectivistically oriented are more likely to come into physical contact with others and touch them in the community service environment once they become familiar with them: Two workers explain:

> *I would like to note that the African American children in [a child care center] classroom are much more likely to come into physical contact with me on a daily basis. These children are more likely to jump on me or hug me or even cling to me than the white children in the classroom. I really do not know why that is the case, but it is very noticeable. (Female, European American)*

> *I keep noticing that the Spanish-speaking teacher aides [at a preschool] offer more physical contact to the children during group time. It's not necessarily that [the head teacher, who is European American] rejects physical contact with the children or lacks "body comfort"; it just seems that more children climb into [the two aides'] laps and seek physical comfort from them. It is usually two or three of the several Spanish-speaking children who seek them out. [The two aides] are perhaps the ones with whom some Spanish-speaking children may feel most confident, literally because they speak their language. (Female, European American)*

Although it may be easy to be put off by what at first glance appears to be chaos, you are advised to appreciate the energy, vitality, inspiration, and affection of children from all cultures when it is present. You are also advised to be as sensitive as possible to any cultural or personal norms that you notice, regarding eye contact, social distance, emotional vitality, assertiveness, and verbal and nonverbal gestures and customs (Fiedler et al. 1971; Hecht, Collier, and Ribeau 1993; Triandis and Triandis 1960; Wardle 2000).

Talking about Similarities and Differences

As noted earlier, clients, even very young ones, do ask questions and make comments about color, race, ethnicity, gender, sexual orientation, and the like. Service-learner journals strongly suggest that you should not overreact when responding to such questions, comments, and even apparent insults. Workers discuss a plethora of incidents, several of which are represented below. In each situation, the worker set appropriate boundaries and limits while also trying to provide an environment for mutual learning and growth—despite feeling insulted. Examples of worker responses to racial, sexist, and homophobic responses are provided, respectively. Notice that the first two accounts carry both racist and sexist overtones:

> *Today was a really hard day [at an elementary school where a young European American boy] was acting up. He has a lot of problems with anger. It seems all stored up in him from something—maybe his parents are divorced. Anyway,*

today he really was out of control and decided to break away from the group, a deliberate disobedience of the rules. The teacher looked at me and asked me if I wanted to give it a try, and I said sure, having some idea of how to approach him. I did just as I thought I should, walking up to him, getting on eye level, and being generally friendly but firm in asking him to rejoin the group; but he quickly got angry and said that I hated him and ran farther away. When I approached him the second time, he looked up at me and said to my complete surprise; "Well you're nothing but a . . . a . . . a brown lady!" I smiled and said, "Yes, I am a brown lady, but that's not an insult," and then I walked away. It seemed to me that it was turning into a game and he was just getting what he wanted, which was attention from me. I was a little disgusted with his remark, though. I will investigate the school's approach to these kinds of matters so that I can reinforce what they've been teaching. (Female, biracial African American/European American)

I am attached to all the students [in a first-grade elementary school class]. There is [a six-year-old boy] in particular, whom I adore. Many times he holds my hand or sits on my lap and pals around with me. Today, he seemed tired and refused to go to recess with the class. I finally set an ultimatum and said that I would tell the teacher when he got back from lunch that he wasn't listening. He didn't care one bit. He said to me, "S——! you ain't my motha! You just a white b——!" I was stunned. This came out of the mouth of one of the cutest little six-year-olds I've ever seen. I didn't know what to say, so I said, "What did you say to me?" and he repeated that I was "a white b——." I said, "Why would you say that to me when I'm asking you to do what you're supposed to?" I was angry and hurt, and the illusion of this special relationship with a secret handshake and everything had been shattered with this one remark. Reflecting on the situation, I think he was testing me to see if I'd like him no matter what, even if he wasn't being cute. (Female, European American)

I discovered something today that I found very disturbing. I learned that many children at this age do not really understand what it is to be homosexual, as a group of them were making fun of each other today and calling each other "gay." Then one girl asked me if I was gay. I told her that I wasn't, but if I were that wouldn't be a bad thing. In my opinion, it is unfortunate that with all the things there are for children to learn, they are being taught intolerance by our society. (Female, European American)

In terms of responding to racist, sexist, and heterosexist comments and behavior, you are advised to balance your responses carefully as the students above attempted to do, so that you neither reinforce inaccurate stereotypes and philosophies nor promote any one particular group as better than another. Failing to strike this balance could put you in a rough spot with the client, the staff, and the parents, depending on their discussion policies and beliefs. You should keep in mind that families are incredibly diverse in terms of characteristics such as ethnicity, gender roles, sexual orientation, socioeconomic status, and occupations (Coontz 1992, 1997; Okun 1996). For example, many children are reared in gay and lesbian households, and whether or not you believe that such relationships are appropriate, you should be sure that the children with whom you work are not made to feel that there is something wrong with them or their family (Chasnoff and Cohen 1996; Gillis 1998; Hybrid Productions 1997). In addition, research literature suggests that children reared in gay and lesbian households are as well adjusted as children reared in heterosexual households. Therefore it is important that you try not to view children being reared in gay and lesbian households as necessarily handicapped, underprivileged, or needing rescue or reform (Patterson 1994; Tasker and Golombok 1995).

To summarize, many techniques and resources are available for assisting you in your work in multicultural environments. There is no single approach or method that will work at all times or in all locations. When referring to the material in this chapter (and appendix F), it will be helpful for you to keep in mind that as much or more diversity exists within any one culture than between cultures. However, we can think of cultural styles such as those presented here as threads that may flow throughout cultures. These frameworks for thinking about cultures and our work within various cultures are not to be used to promote stereotypes but to provide additional methods and resources for working with children and families. As in all learning, finding the approaches that work best for you requires time, dedication, research, study, open-mindedness, communication, flexibility, optimism, and patience. Multicultural awareness and understanding is not a destination to be reached all at once, but rather a lifelong journey of learning to be enjoyed and incorporated in our day-to-day lives if we are to live successfully in a diverse and ever-changing world (Dunlap 1999a,b).

PRACTICAL TIPS

- Do not expect community learning environments to be completely free of racism, sexism, heterosexism, homophobia, classism, and other forms of oppression. Be grateful when environments are free of the social problems that exist in our society today, but remember that totally bias-free environments are rare. Most environments are works "in progress" and are continuing to evolve in a positive direction in this respect. It is also a pleasure to see environments that express an appreciation for equality and diversity by reflecting those values in terms of the diversity of their personnel, clientele, books, toys, materials, and other resources. However, when your placement does not provide such an atmosphere, allow yourself to learn as much from what an environment does not offer as from what it does offer. Allow what you perceive as weaknesses and flaws in the environment to motivate you toward social and community activism against oppression in the years to come.

- Do not expect clients, even child clients, to be completely free of bias. Everyone has expectations, biases, conceptions, misconceptions, and comfort zones regarding others. Communication and experience can change that, but it can be a time-consuming process. Note the process of change as you observe people in various stages of their work on issues of race, sex, class, and sexual orientation. Focus on ways that you can appropriately model bias-free behavior for them.

- Enter the multicultural community learning setting with a well-informed and open mind. Familiarize yourself as much as possible with the communities and cultures that are represented in your community learning setting. What are the historical, political, and sociological issues that the community has faced? Who are the community leaders? What are the concerns of many of the members of the community? What are the negative and stereotypical images that are associated with the community? How can you critically reevaluate and critique those images? Consider familiarizing yourself with the local, community, and public interest newspapers that are valued by constituents of the community. Be familiar with some of the local churches, synagogues, or mosques that are rich sources of history and culture.

- Commit to learning more about other communities and cultures beyond the one(s) represented in your community learning environment. The more you learn about other cultures and communities, the more you will appreciate the strengths and resiliency of every community. Also, the more comfortable you will feel within your community learning environment or other environments that initially may seem unfamiliar. Part of your learning about other communities should involve your examining your own development, beliefs, and behavior concerning those from that community. You should think critically about how your own and others' beliefs and behaviors might contribute to, or might help alleviate, the challenges of the community. In doing so, strive to work in better partnership with the community for both your and their improvement.

- Seek models and approaches that go beyond the superficial. Challenge yourself not to adopt a superficial or simple touristic method of learning about others; instead, take a more in-depth approach.

- Be aware of your own racial and cultural development. Consider your own racial identity stages of development and how they may influence your ideas about race, socioeconomic status, and meritocracy. Try to look at things from more than one cultural perspective, and from more than one stage of racial identity, as you try to make sense of your observations and experiences in the community learning environment.

- Be patient with yourself. Give yourself time to become comfortable and to build relationships in your community learning environment. Even under the very best circumstances, gaining comfort takes time.
- Do not hesitate to seek support when you feel you need it. Consult with your community learning administrators, professors, and/or agency staff when you feel that a situation has arisen that is beyond the scope of the basic issues that have been addressed here. Talking and brainstorming with others is usually very helpful in the community learning process.

FURTHER READING

Chideya, F. 1995. *Don't believe the hype: Fighting cultural misinformation about African Americans.* New York: Plume/Penguin.

Hale-Benson, J. 1986. *Black children: Their roots, culture, and learning styles.* Baltimore: John Hopkins University Press.

Lynch, E., and M. Hanson. 1998, *Developing cross-cultural competence: A guide for working with children and their families.* 2d ed. Baltimore: Brookes.

Okun, B. 1996. *Understanding diverse families: What practitioners need to know.* New York: Guilford.

Rose, M. 1989. *Lives on the boundary: The struggles and achievements of America's underprepared.* New York: Free Press.

Tatum, B. 1992. Talking about race: The application of racial identity development theory in the classroom. *Harvard educational review* 62, no. 1: 1–24.

Tatum, B. 1997. *"Why are all the black kids sitting together in the cafeteria?" And other conversations about race.* New York: Basic.

VIDEO RESOURCES

Chasnoff, D., and H. Cohen. 1996. *It's elementary: Talking about gay issues in school.* Hohokus, N.J.: New Day Films.

Guggenheim, C. 1995. *The shadow of hate: A history of intolerance.* Montgomery, Ala.: Southern Poverty Law Center, Teaching Tolerance Project.

Hybrid Productions. 1997. *Camp Lavender Hill: A short documentary about the first summer camp for children of gay, lesbian, and bisexual parents.* San Francisco: Hybrid Productions.

Kilbourne, J. 1987. *Still killing us softly: Advertising's image of women.* Cambridge, Mass.: Cambridge Documentary Films.

Peters, W. 1985. *A class divided—Jane Elliott's Blue Eyes and Brown Eyes.* New Haven, Conn.: Yale University Films.

Riggs, M., V. Kleiniman, and Signifying Works. 1991. *Color Adjustment.* San Francisco, CA: California Newsreel.

Wah, L. M. 1994. *The color of fear.* Oakland, Calif.: Stir Fry Productions.

Reader Notes

9

Expanding Horizons

*Working with Individuals
Who Have Special Needs*

> *I found it so incredibly sad that all three of these [preschool children with special needs] are not always able to communicate what they want to say or how they feel. Imagine seeing mouths moving but having no way of being able to understand. Imagine not being able to finish a puzzle and getting so frustrated that the only way you can communicate is through physical violence. There are so many little things that people take for granted in their lives. The ability to walk, to listen, to sing, to write, to smile, to be loved, or even to be able to physically do whatever it is you want to do. These children don't necessarily know that other people don't have the same daily struggles that they do, but the fact that they live with these problems is so amazing. (Female, European American)*

You may be working with children, adults, and/or families who have a diverse range of physical, cognitive, and psychosocial abilities and limitations. Some or all of your clients may have specific sensory impairments (e.g., blindness), illnesses (e.g., HIV infection), physical disabilities (e.g., cerebral palsy), learning disabilities (e.g., dyslexia), or social/emotional disabilities (e.g., autism). For the purpose of this chapter, people who have developmental challenges or disabilities of these types are referred to as individuals with special needs. This chapter will introduce you to reactions that you may experience and suggest helpful approaches for your work with clients who have special needs.

WORKING WITH INDIVIDUALS WITH SPECIAL NEEDS

Students who work with individuals having special needs commonly experience initial apprehension and then surprise at the capabilities of the clients;

adjustment in communication because of client and worker sensory, physical, emotional, or language challenges; and disappointment when workers witness clients being negatively stereotyped and socially maltreated.

Initial Apprehension

Students who work with clients having special needs, like learners in any environment, may well feel apprehensive and confused in the beginning. Above all, you may find yourself struggling with existing stereotypes about those who have special needs. You may find yourself conjuring up a variety of very dramatic stereotypical images of people who have an array of abilities and disabilities. Because of absent and inaccurate depictions of people with handicaps and special needs in the popular culture media, you may expect to find clients who are severely challenged and have a sensational appearance. Many students brace themselves for their first encounter. Yet you may be surprised to find that it is sometimes initially difficult to distinguish clients with special needs from other clients. You may discover that your stereotypes of what it means to have special needs do not fit the reality. Students share their initial expectations and the reality of their experience:

> *Many of the children [at a preschool swimming program for children with special needs] do not look "retarded." I think that some of my nerves about my experience were coming through when I looked at the kids this way and expected them to appear deformed. I feel stupid now admitting to this, but that was my approach. (Female, European American)*

> *The children [at my preschool site] are four years old and have developmental concerns ranging from speech and behavior to substance abuse and poverty. Frankly, it was very hard for me to notice any problems in the children. They all seemed like normal, happy children to me. (Female, European American)*

You may also be surprised when you observe many of the capabilities of individuals with special needs. You could find yourself amazed by clients with paralyzed limbs who are very adept in swimming pools or at riding horses, for example. Several students describe some of the many skills that they notice among clients with special needs:

> *This was the first day that I [and a fellow service-learner] met with [a young man with muscular dystrophy]. I think we were both a bit nervous because we didn't know what to expect. [When we finally met him], he was very different looking than I expected mostly because he looked normal. I guess I was expecting him to look a bit retarded and to talk with a slur, but this was not the case. So far the only physical difference between him and me is that he can't walk easily but relies on a wheelchair. He seems like a smart and talented young man. (Female, European American)*

[At a preschool] I thought the two children who were deaf were the only ones with problems because I couldn't see any physical problem with the third child. I later realized that is a horrible generalization for me to make because it became very clear very quickly that this [third child] becomes frustrated too easily and as a result often became violent. On the other hand, [this same boy] appeared to be incredibly smart to me. At one point he began talking about DNA and the double helix. I was shocked that he even knew the names of those things but then he went on to explain the shape of the double helix to me and I was stunned. I also spent half an hour outside with a little girl who is for the most part deaf. She is able to understand and even talk, although she is almost completely deaf. She seemed willing to repeat things so that I could understand what she was saying. She is an incredible little girl because she seems so willing to learn. (Female, European American)

I found out about [a therapeutic horse riding program] at the college volunteer fair. It amazes me the effect that the touch of an animal can have on a person. The [clients] range in age from two to eighty years old. They have either physical or mental disabilities. Their faces light up when they are riding a horse. The act of riding stimulates walking and for people who can't walk on their own, it stimulates muscles that they haven't been able to use. They come from a wide variety of backgrounds. Their disabilities range from behavioral problems to M.S. [multiple sclerosis] or blindness. Everyone seems to have a positive attitude and to be improving their lives. One person has Down's syndrome and when I saw him ride, he seemed like a different person. He takes charge and is much more composed with his movements. (Female, European American)

You may also be impressed by the family support that you witness. A student notes:

Today in the after-school homework club, I worked extensively with two [middle school-aged] brothers. The elder child was disabled. He used a walker on wheels to move around and had considerable difficulty articulating his demands and concerns. His younger brother was very responsive and extremely mature when handling his brother's situation. He listened patiently and aided him with his difficulties. I was extremely impressed with his maturity in defending his brother to his friends. Together they waited to be picked up from school. (Female, European American)

There are also instances however, where working with clients with special needs turns out to be more difficult than you anticipated. Your expectations and initial impressions can depend on the severity of the client's condition and your previous experiences concerning such conditions. For some of you, visits might continue to be overwhelming for some time before you feel more comfortable. Two students explain in the following examples:

I was very upset watching this group of children with pervasive developmental disorder [PDD, also referred to as autism]. I found it hard to remain at this site for the entire time allocated. I would have left early if I possibly could. My shock over the behaviors of almost all the children was overwhelming. I have worked as a substitute teacher's assistant in a special needs class in [a different city] where one boy in the class had PDD, and I did not do well in that atmosphere. I do not think that I have that inner strength to work with this special group of children. I become too emotional. (Female, European American)

Today [a second-grade boy with ADHD] was at it again. He started picking on a girl and she said stop it, and he wouldn't listen to her. I then warned him to slow down, at which point he said "shut up" and proceeded to make fun of her some more. Finally she lost it and said, "I hate you and I am going to get my brother to beat you up!" He then started to cry and said, "I am in trouble. I am always in trouble. Its all because of my stupid brain. My brain always gets me in trouble!" It was very hard for me to hear him say this. (Male, European American)

Those of you who find yourselves in situations such as this can be further supported through group reflection and supervisory consultation, and by going to the site or college library to research information about the disability.

Communication Issues

You may experience some surprise at how well clients with special needs communicate, albeit in their own way. For example, clients also have disagreements with others now and then just like anyone else. You may begin to see individuals with special needs as less fragile emotionally and physically than you once assumed they were. Your fear of accidentally hurting or, in a sense, "breaking" them may begin to decrease a bit. Workers share how their particular clients express themselves and interact with others:

The children [at a preschool for children of diverse backgrounds and abilities] use pretty well articulated words. One child doesn't seem to be able to form words so she uses gestures with her hands. She may grunt and throw her arms in the direction of an area where there is a toy that she wants to play with. The other children frequently demand "look at me" to the teachers. When the children are upset and can't seem to think of the words fast enough to tell the teacher, they get even more frustrated. The instructor tells the child to slow down so that they may be able to think of what they want to say. (Female, European American)

At my service-learning site today a four-year-old African American female child with hearing and speech impairments came into our classroom during activity time. Her speech barrier was difficult at times, but I usually could tell what she wanted to say to me by the expression on her face or her hand motions. I was very happy to see that the children in the room paid little attention to her disability and even helped to decipher what she was trying to express. The children played together well, although they did have some disagreements (Female, European American)

You may also have the opportunity to work with clients who have severe physical or mental disabilities that make communication seem nearly impossible. In some of these cases, you may find it difficult to work with the client(s) and may seek additional support and training in order to feel comfortable enough to really be an asset to the client(s).

Reactions to Patronizing Behavior

You may also feel frustrated by the condescending and patronizing manner in which clients with special needs are sometimes treated. For example, the two following students share their disappointment:

Today was the first day of working with a young man with muscular dystrophy. Although his social worker is really nice, she kind of treats him like an old man. I can tell by the tone of voice she uses. It is kind of babyish and high-pitched when she talks to him, but when she talks to us, it sounds regular. I want to treat him as a twenty-two-year-old man because that's what he is. If I were in his situation, I would not like to be treated as if I were an old cripple. I think he will enjoy talking and being exposed to people of similar age because most people treat him like an old man just because he is in a wheelchair. (Female, European American)

First of all, a few weeks ago I had an automatic sort of dislike for the aide who is in the [special needs classroom at an inner-city elementary school]. The first day, she had informed me that these kids were disgusting and were never going to amount to anything. I was shocked. She has admitted many more cold opinions to me since then. She is so inappropriate it shocks me every visit. Probably, four out of my five visits she says she can't wait until 2:30, so she can go home. Finally, I asked her why she works here, and she said she's a single parent who needs to put food on the table. I feel badly for her in a way, but she doesn't need to add herself to the long list of people who probably already hate these kids. I too could be reeling off a long list of my problems instead of helping the children, but I choose to serve the right purpose. (Female, European American)

Fortunately, you can learn as much from the negative behaviors of staff as you can from favorable behavior. Negative behavior, as difficult as it can be to tolerate, can help you determine your own expectations and limits for your future professional behavior. Hopefully you will not engage in similar behavior in your own career.

CHALLENGES WHEN WORKING WITH INDIVIDUALS WITH SPECIAL NEEDS

Working with individuals who have special needs may include confronting your own stereotypical and absent images of individuals with special needs. You may also be confronted by your own sense of self, privilege, and heroic desires.

Stereotypical and Absent Images

One of the major obstacles to your beginning to work with clients with special needs is that, as a culture, we do not have enough mainstream media images of people with special needs integrated into our images of people in general. This is improving somewhat, but images that focus on the humanity, skills, and diversity of people with special needs are relatively far and few between.

Therefore, when you anticipate working with clients with special needs, you may experience a great deal of worry or concern about your ability to relate to them and to do a good job. However, once you actually take on the task, you are likely to quickly learn and become aware of some of the similarities and differences between the individual(s) with special needs with whom you work and people who are considered "typically developing." You will learn to distinguish negative stereotypes from the real special needs for help and support that the clients have. As an illustration, some of my students discover that making the transition from school to home or from home back to school can be even more difficult and may require more support and time for children with special needs than it does for other children. For example:

> *When the [preschool] kids were getting on their buses, something very interesting happened. The one girl in the class who is blind and deaf was ready to get on her bus. She put on her backpack and even went outside with the teacher, but as soon as she [perceived the presence of the] bus, she began to scream and cry and throw her body. When I got outside, she was kicking and screaming and the teachers had to leave her lying there until she was ready to get up. Apparently she loves school so much that she hates the idea of leaving. I think that has a lot to do with the supports available at [the preschool] where she is able to communicate and be understood. I am sure it is very difficult to live in a house where she can't be understood as easily. (Female, European American)*

Heroic Desires and Related Emotions

The normal heroic desire to help and save others who are less fortunate (discussed in chapter 4) also applies to your work with individuals with special needs. If you work with individuals with special needs, like the students in chapter 4, you may discover yourself coming face-to-face with your own background, privileges, emotions, expectations, and desires to make a difference. As noted in chapter 4, these emotions can prove debilitating if they are not understood. Conversely, when appropriately supported, these emotions can give you a greater appreciation for the struggles and strengths of the clients. In many cases, these opportunities also have the power to help motivate you to social action. Several students share their desires, emotions, and experiences with regard to their work with clients who have special needs:

> *[The second-grade teacher at an elementary school] pulled me aside and told me my job is to work with [a particular] young boy. He is a young African American boy about seven or eight years old. The teacher informed me that he was diagnosed with Attention Deficit Hyperactivity Disorder. As soon as she told me this, my eyes lit up. ADHD is something that has always interested me, well, at least since I was diagnosed with it in tenth grade. I had suffered through many years of confusion about my behavior and my lack of ability to concentrate, so having the opportunity to help someone who is going through what I went through is just what I was hoping for. I left the school thinking about how much there was that I could do to help him and knowing that he and I will develop a relationship that will benefit us both. (Male, European American)*

> *[My service-learning partner and] I went to visit [a young adult man with muscular dystrophy]. He was very excited because he told us that he had been inside all day, mostly watching television. I noticed that every time we come he is sitting in the same seat and never moves. We also talked about our classes we are taking and the ones we plan to take next semester. He seems very interested in our schedule. I think this is because he never went to college so he is trying to find out what he missed. He repeatedly said, "Oh, I would love to take that class." When he said this, I began to feel sorry for him because he isn't given the same opportunity I am given. But it also made me realize how lucky I am to have the opportunity to take these classes. When we left today, I looked through the car window and saw him getting up from his seat. As he stood up, his face looked like he was in horrible pain. He held on to the wall with both hands while he held himself up. Then he slowly attempted to walk to the other room. Even watching something so small heavily impacted me. (Female, European American)*

HELPFUL APPROACHES IN WORKING
WITH INDIVIDUALS WITH SPECIAL NEEDS

Student journals suggest that those of you who are engaged with individuals with special needs can be supported in at least three ways. First, by realizing that your adjustment is a process that will take time. Second, by setting limits and boundaries that are appropriate for the special needs that the client has. Third, by utilizing available resources to familiarize yourself with the specific special needs that the client(s) has.

The Adjustment Process

The journals of students whose clients have special needs suggest that the adjustment processes are similar to those of other students. There is the initial apprehension and the occasional feelings of awkwardness, followed within the first several visits by the development of greater comfort. You who realize that adjusting to new situations takes time will enjoy greater comfort and ease as you gradually unfold and develop within your placement setting.

Setting Appropriate Boundaries and Limits

You may find in your work with clients with special needs that verbal limit setting alone may not be as effective as it is in other settings. Therefore, it may be necessary for limits to be set in additional ways or in a manner that is understandable or clear to the client. For example, it may be necessary to slow the speed of communication so that the client has more time to process the limits that are being set. This does not mean talking "baby talk" to clients but simply taking extra time to be sure that you have the client's attention. The limit-setting approaches will vary, depending on the individual capacities and needs of the clients and the policies and procedures that are set in place at the site. Workers illustrate how they get the attention of their clients with special needs when redirecting them:

[A preschool boy] seemed to have trouble understanding me. One of the teachers informed me that he may have either a hearing impairment or perhaps a learning disorder. Apparently it is necessary to look him straight in the eye when speaking to him or it is near impossible to get him to understand your words. (Female, European American)

[Some of the preschool] children who really have special needs can be entertained and amused by a smile or a touch, which makes them happy. The teacher and the assistants use a lot of praises and touches to comfort them. When they start to get out of hand, the teacher and the assistants hold them, hug them, and rub them gently to calm them down. The children respond really well to this. I would also like to add that it is very interesting to watch children with special needs, but it is also very sad. "Please" and "thank you" are used a lot so the children get accustomed to using them. "Lights off" helps calm the children down and gets them to clean up after playtime is over. They then sing songs like, "Clean up, clean up everybody everywhere. Clean up, clean up, everybody do your share," to a snappy tune. (Male, African American)

Using Resources

Frequently, students seek resources about specific disabilities so that they can gain greater understanding about them. You may find such information extremely enlightening. Accessing and reviewing these resources can help you feel more empowered and competent in your work with clients with special needs. For example:

> *I realize that [a boy and a girl in the first grade] have learning problems, or developmental deficits, and they may overcome these problems when they get older, or they may not. The possibility of overcoming a developmental deficit is directly linked to the students' attitude, self-esteem, and support in their microsystem [or immediate environment]. I learned from the reading that if the child compensates for a developmental problem through physical, psychosocial, emotional, or spiritual advancement, the child's self-esteem is likely not to drop. (Female, European American)*

> *I came across a book called Working Together against AIDS, by Barbara Hermie Draimin, DSW [1994]. The book focuses on two main topics: working toward prevention of the AIDS virus and helping those people who are living with AIDS. The book did a very good job of describing what kids could do to help others with HIV and AIDS and where they could go for more information. The book also tells the reader that by speaking up to other kids who treat people wrong because they are living with AIDS, they are helping to end the prejudice against people with AIDS. The book points out that people with AIDS can teach you about life as well as death and, therefore, they do not like to think of themselves as dying from AIDS but rather as living with AIDS. (Female, European American)*

In sum, as you gain more experience and seek and rely upon resources when needed, you can make the most of your community work with clients with special needs. Again, as with the other areas of diversity discussed in this book, the process will not result in an easy-to-find destination but rather a journey that will take some time, patience, and experience.

PRACTICAL TIPS

- Expect diversity among those with special needs. The stereotypical images held by many in our society concerning children and adults with special needs may not match the reality of the diversity and range of abilities that actually exist among them.
- Do not panic over normal first-visit jitters. Just as with other community learning placements, it is common to have previsit and first-visit jitters and anxiety.
- Research information about clients' needs and abilities. Be sure to read appropriate resource materials to familiarize yourself with the specific challenges or conditions that the clients at your site face so that you can better understand the meaning, scope, and research findings concerning their particular developmental challenges or disabilities.

- Reach out for support when needed. Do not hesitate to seek support from the appropriate staff, professors, and/or administrators.

FURTHER READING

Batshaw, M. 1997. *Children with disabilities.* Baltimore: Brookes.

Hallahan, D., J. Kauffman, and J. Lloyd. 1995. *Introduction to learning disabilities.* Needham Heights, Mass.: Allyn & Bacon.

Hardman, M., C. Drew, and M. Egan. 1998. *Human exceptionality: Society, school, and family.* Needham Heights, Mass.: Allyn & Bacon.

Marschark, M. 1997. *Raising and educating a deaf child: A comprehensive guide to the choices, controversies, and decisions faced by parents and educators.* New York: Oxford University Press.

Mercugliano, M., T. Power, and N. Blum. 1999. *A clinician's practical guide to attention-deficit/ hyperactivity disorder.* Baltimore: Brookes.

Ploch, D. 1996. *What do you mean, my child's not perfect? A reference manual and guide for parents and families of children with disabilities or special needs.* Uncasville, Conn.: Easter Seal Rehabilitation Center of Southeastern Connecticut.

Sheridan, P., G. Foley, and S. Radlinski. 1995. *Using the supportive play model: Individualized intervention in early childhood practice.* New York: Teachers College Press.

Reader Notes

10

Did She Really Say *That?*

Shocking Statements and Other Traumas

> *[One particular fifth-grade girl at a soup kitchen's community after-school program] is one of the more mature kids. I had an opportunity to talk with her a little bit while making sparkly glitter glue drawings at the art and crafts table. Just as I sat down, she out-front told me that she got her period today. I was shocked at her bold, immodest statement, so all I said was, "How do you feel about that?" She said she had a big tummy ache but she was pretty happy that she finally got it. Finally got it, in the fifth grade?! I thought. I didn't even get mine until a couple years later. And when I did get it, I was so embarrassed that I didn't tell my mom until a couple months later, let alone an almost complete stranger helping out at a soup kitchen! So I asked her if she had told her mom yet, and she said "of course." I bet she has an older sister she really looks up to and imitates, which is the reason for her anticipation and pride when she finally got her period. (Female, European American)*

Almost every person who has ever engaged in community work can attest to moments that left them confused, stunned, or shocked. It may have been an unexpected comment, a gesture, a behavior, or an embarrassing mishap. Whatever the situation, many past community workers can relate to such moments, and you, as a future or current worker, should know that such moments occur from time to time.

I do not want you to expect such events to the degree that you create a self-fulfilling prophecy. At the same time, however, I do not want you to overpersonalize such events and think that you are the first and only community worker to experience such moments if they occur. I also do not want to portray agency staff, community members, and clientele in a negative manner. I suspect that if clients and staff kept journals regarding their

experiences with community learners, they would have just as many surprising reactions to you, and they would not find everything about community learners to be pleasant or appropriate in their eyes. It is important
to remember that the comments made by the workers provide the students'
perception of and reaction to those with whom they work. Their interpre-
tations are not necessarily accurate. Nevertheless, the fact that students
have recounted, without solicitation, such events in their journals suggests
that at the time they made a significant impression upon them.

The things that seem to catch workers off guard are plentiful and diverse.
When such comments and events actually occur, learners understandably
often see no humor in the situation. Many workers are able to look back on
such events with humor, whereas some are not.

SHOCKING STATEMENTS AND TRAUMAS

Workers find themselves caught off guard by a variety of things seen, heard,
or experienced. For example, one worker describes a harrowing experience
that was reported to her at the site where she worked and another discusses
a situation reported by a child:

> *I volunteer at [a center for battered women]. Just the other week they had a
> problem and had to evacuate the shelter because some husband who was look-
> ing for his wife had weapons. But now everything is back to normal. (Female,
> European American)*

> *I was playing on [a child care center] playground with a little boy, and we were
> sitting down. He began to play with my hair and became very imaginative, pre-
> tending that he was shampooing it. Then he said something startling that
> caught me off guard, and I did not know how to handle it. He told me that one
> day his mommy brought home a new daddy, and the new daddy used to put
> soap in his eyes and it hurt. I said to him something along the lines of that it
> was probably an accident. The boy responded by saying that it wasn't an ac-
> cident and that now the new daddy is in jail, so he doesn't see him anymore.
> Then the boy changed the subject. I will mention it to the teachers at my next
> visit. It just caught me off guard and put me in an uncomfortable position. Al-
> though this has never happened in my life, unfortunately some children expe-
> rience a great deal of pain at home. (Female, European American)*

Suggestions for responding to these kind of heart-wrenching events and
comments are provided in the following pages.

One worker was surprised to find out that she contracted a mild but con-
tagious virus most likely from a client at her placement:

> *I was extremely sick and didn't go to [my service-learning site]. Actually, the
> virus I have in my throat, the Coxsackie virus, is supposedly common among*

children, and the doctor told me it was very likely that I caught it from the children at the site. Even if I did not catch it from them, children are very susceptible to this, and I am sure the teacher doesn't want a classroom full of sore throats! (Male, European American)

Another worker describes an incident in which one of his young clients with ADHD, in a moment of frustration, begins to eat his art project, much to the surprise and dismay of the worker:

We worked on art together, making a food object out of homemade clay. [A second-grade boy with ADHD] found so many other uses for the clay, but not the one it was intended for. He finally made a cookie and a hot dog. About a half an hour later, I was looking for him and saw him standing over the mini–food sculptures again. I went over to talk to him and noticed that he was eating them. I couldn't believe it. Why would he do this? How could he do this? It was not because he was hungry, that's for sure. I then asked him to stop, but he wouldn't. I told him that it wasn't nice to do that to someone else's work. So he started to eat his own. Finally the teacher came by and told him to go sit down. (Male, European American)

Thus a range of surprising, shocking, and sometimes inappropriate events can occur. These events may include humorous incidents, client diversity, upset clients, name-calling and insults, client and family circumstances, client maltreatment, and staff behavior. We will consider each of these briefly.

Humorous Events

Incidents may occur that are surprising or even shocking and yet exceedingly funny to you. For example:

Today was one of the funniest service-learning days that I have experienced thus far at [a middle school]. A boy who sits in the back of the classroom was leaning back in his chair and reading over his paper when the inevitable happened. The entire room had been silent and then he fell and went crashing backward into the row of computers. He took down a keyboard while waving his hands wildly and kicking all of the books and papers off his desk before landing on the floor in a mess. The room was then in an uproar. The teacher rushed over to help him and to pick up the fallen computer and papers. The entire class was laughing out of control. For a moment I lost my dignity and sense of "adultness" as I tried to hide my face. (Female, European American)

[A boy at a middle school] was sent to the dean's office for violation of the dress code. He was wearing a T-shirt that depicted Calvin (of Calvin and Hobbes) peeing into a Nike sneaker. He had turned the shirt inside out after one teacher reprimanded him for wearing it, but another teacher thought that it was still inappropriate (you could still see the image) and sent him to the dean so they

could determine if he needed to be punished. When he returned from the of-
fice, they'd given him a shirt to wear over it that said, "I'm talking and I can't
shut up." (Female, European American)

[A child care center girl] came over to me and told me she had to go to the bath-
room. So I took her inside and waited outside the door while she went. I could
hear her in there, singing about Jello. Finally, I hear, "Can you come in here
an' wipe my butt?" Yee-hah! I walk into the bathroom and there she is, bent
over and waiting for me. Oh well, I'm used to baby-sitting and someone had to
do this for me at one time, so I can deal with it. Then she says, "I'm only three,
but when I'm four I'm gonna learn how to wipe my own butt." I didn't know
what else to say because I thought she was so funny, so I just said, "Well, that
will be very exciting!" (Female, European American)

Reactions to Client Demographics and Diversity

As discussed in Chapters 4 and 8, you may meet with initial surprise at
your perceptions of differences between yourself and the clients with whom
you work, for example, with respect to client age. You may be surprised to
find out that clients or family members are older or younger than you expected. Two workers describe such instances:

The kids at [an after-school program] pretty much range from about six to ten
years old. However, when I first arrived and took a look at the kids, I would have
guessed more like three to thirteen years old. I cannot believe the different speeds
of development kids go through. I thought this one girl was also a volunteer like
me, until I soon discovered that she was only ten years old! I didn't act surprised
when I found out, even though I was. I also noticed that she seemed to act like a
"mother" to all the rest of the kids, which probably was a result of her greater
physical maturity compared to the others. (Female, European American)

During the time that I was there [today at a child care center] one mother came
over to pick up her child. She couldn't have been any older than sixteen. It re-
ally shocked me. I mean, I know that a huge number of young girls have chil-
dren, and I have known teenagers with babies, but seeing this young mother
scared me into seeing how much [this child care center] does for the commu-
nity. They feed the children breakfast and lunch, presumably because many of
the parents cannot afford it. It makes me feel guilty that I thought [the child
care center] was crazy and disorganized at first and that I didn't see what an
important program it is. (Female, European American)

Upset Clients

You may also experience surprise when clients, staff members, or others
involved in the community learning setting express anger or frustration to-

ward someone at the site. You may become extremely self-conscious if you feel that the frustration is directed toward you because of your desire to "do a good job" in your work. Workers describe examples of overwhelming incidents in which clients seemed upset with them:

> *I was playing with one of the [child care center] boys and he kept on touching me. I really didn't know how to react, but he kept jumping on me and trying to hit me in the face. I told him to stop, but he kept doing it. I finally said, "Let's play with the dinosaurs." Then when we were playing with the dinosaurs, he began to smash his into mine. He lunged forward and hit his head on my dinosaur. He then started to cry and would not talk or even look at me. When I tried to comfort him, he became violent and tried to push me away. I felt bad but I didn't do anything to him. Even though I knew that, I continued to apologize. His father walked in while he was crying and asked, "What is wrong?" The boy then told his father that I had hit him in the face with the dinosaur. I was really embarrassed and I did not know how the father was going to react. I remembered that when I was younger I would exaggerate things that happened to me. I apologized again and his father said, "He apologized, now make up." He came over and slapped my hand and I felt great. He was really a sweet little boy. He gave his teacher a hug and a kiss when it was time to leave. (Male, European American)*

> *Today I was a bit shocked by one girl in particular. She was sitting on the windowsill, which is quite dangerous. I asked her to get down. I remembered as soon as the words were out of my mouth that we are not supposed to give them an option by making a command a question. She said no to me, and I said in a firmer manner that she had to get down. She got down, but when I tried to explain to her why she could not sit there, she put out her hand and said, "Talk to the hand" [in other words, I am completely ignoring you and do not want to hear anything that you have to say]. I was taken aback. No adult I knew would say something like that, so I was shocked to hear it from the adorable four-year-old in front of me. I realize that she has probably heard the expression from an older sibling, family member, or just simply from a passerby. I wonder if she knew what it meant, but I think she was probably imitating someone she had heard. (Female, European American)*

Name-Calling

You may find yourself surprised by name-calling when it occurs in community learning environments. Workers share examples:

> *I was thrilled yesterday when a huge group of young people came to [a youth-oriented museum]. Members of the first group to come were probably around fourteen or fifteen years old. They all, particularly the girls, seemed to take great joy in two things: regressing and recalling childhood as they saw the toys and games, and being verbally very sharp and rough with each other. They weren't necessarily mean to each other, but I think "challenging"*

is a better way to describe it. One girl, for instance, kept explaining things to other people using phrases like "you dummy" and "you're so stupid, that's not how you do that," but nobody really seemed to take any offense. Two minutes later she would turn around and coo at the baby turtles (Female, European American)

One problem I cannot seem to resolve, and maybe I am just trying too hard to stop the name-calling. Children [at an elementary school] call each other too many names, and a lot of times they mention each other's mother and they have been about to fight, and I have to intervene. I just tell them to stop and even though they do, they continue to give each other mean looks. I do not know how to stop them. These children are already close to twelve—almost teenagers. Whatever they are used to doing is pretty hard to stop. I told a few kids that if they did not keep their hands to themselves they would have to go home for the day because I was not a referee for wrestling. They just laughed. They actually did keep their hands to themselves, but I don't know what to do about the name-calling. The children from my other volunteer program [in the suburbs] also engage in a lot of name-calling, which, however, does not include each other's mothers and does not seem quite as aggressive (Female, Hispanic)

As noted in chapter 8, students also express surprise at seemingly racist, sexist, and heterosexist comments. Students provide examples of these additional kinds of unfortunate name-calling that they find shocking and that often pose dilemmas for them as they ponder appropriate responses:

Tutoring today [at a middle school] was rather frustrating. It turns out that a child [race not specified] got hit because he had called another child a "chink" and a "homo." The teacher implied to me that this is a common occurrence. It's sad that the racial sensitivity and racial differentiation is so emphasized in peer-to-peer relations so young. (Female, European American)

Today [at a middle school] I overheard a boy, who couldn't have been older than twelve, say to a girl, "Why are you dressed like a hooker? Are you like sleeping around or something?" It was something about how the boy said it that made the phrase remain in my head for the remainder of the day. There was not only a degradation of the female gender in his statement but also a lack of respect for his peer. (Female, European American)

The biggest incident that happened today blew my mind. I was sitting at one of the [child care center] tables talking with a three-year-old boy while everyone was eating. All of a sudden, the boy turned to me and told me that the kid sitting next to him was a "gay lover." My mind went blank and my mouth dropped. I did not know what to say to the kid and I was hoping that I heard him wrong. So I asked him to repeat what he had said. Once again, this time very clearly, he told me the same thing. I did not know how to respond to this kid. I didn't want to tell him that he had said something bad because what he had said wasn't bad, but the way he said the word, he meant it to be bad. The next thing I did was ask him what he meant by that. Through his food chewing, I heard the word "sex." Even after having a couple of hours to think about this incident, I still do not know what I should have said. It boggles my mind that a three-year-old knows these words. (Female, European American)

The history of name-calling and of racist, sexist, and heterosexist remarks, as well as their social function, is sad and complex indeed (Foster 1986; MacLeod 1995). Such name-calling, in part, grows out of a society that was founded on racism, sexism, and heterosexism (Barber 1992; Carnes 1995; Zinn 1980). As noted in chapter 8, although such comments are disturbing, many workers find that they can provide opportunities for discussion and learning (Derman-Sparks et al. 1989). Related to this, one worker speaks on the surprise and frustration that he felt about the way that staff responded, or failed to respond, to certain types of name-calling, thus losing moments that could have been transformed into opportunities for learning:

These kids [at an after-school tutorial program] can't get enough of wrestling and play fighting. They also threaten each other. They never swear, and if they do, the other children cry out "he said the s-word" or "she said the a-word." But they don't hesitate to say "I'll kill you" or "I hate you" or "I'll shoot you." Also, teachers seldom reprimand them for saying these things, and not nearly as much as they would if they heard a swear word. It's strange how in our society swearing is so much more taboo than threats of violence. Their parents and teachers should scold them just as much when they make these threats as when they swear! (Male, European American)

Client Circumstances

You may also find yourself caught by surprise by the personal circumstances of some clients and their families. You may be surprised by the tragic experiences that some children face. For example, children may be challenged by the substance abuse of their parents, severe illness of family members, and loss of their parents due to incarceration. Students share examples:

On the way from [picking up boys from a middle school, one boy] noted for the second time that we passed the hospital where his dad did drug rehabilitation. He said he used to visit him every weekend while he was straightening out. I shudder to think that this is a fond memory that he has of his dad, but he talks about it with such spirit that I am afraid that it is. I hope that he is just happy that his dad was saved and got a chance to straighten out before anything truly drastic happened. (Male, European American)

It hurts me to see little children like a five-year-old [preschool girl] in a foster home with nine other children. Nobody knows where her mother or father is, and she is hungry for attention and affection. I'm hoping to work with more children in the future. I want to be able to understand the needs of the children and learn the ways to help them overcome some of life's difficulties. I understand that being a teacher is preparing the children to face the world, give them the knowledge, and most of all self-esteem. (Female, Lebanese)

[One of the first-grade] girls brought out two photo albums from her cubby and asked me to look at them with her. In the pictures her father was obviously extremely ill and very emaciated. Her English is limited, and she can often be difficult to understand. Unfortunately I was not able to catch what she said, and while I was attempting to decode, she continued talking about the next picture. She has obviously experienced great emotional stress at a very young age, having to personally deal with his illness and being a part of a family coping with an illness. I wonder whether her showing the pictures is a way of reaching out to people. (Female, European American)

In such circumstances, you may find that clients, especially child clients (because of their age-appropriate egocentrism), spend a great deal of time blaming themselves for the challenges that their families face. One worker discusses a child client who blames himself for his family's circumstance:

I spent today getting to know [a second-grade boy's] background. He told me that his father is in prison in [another state] and that it was his fault that his father is there. The discussion ended there, and I did not want to push him to tell me about it. (Male, European American)

Child clients in such circumstances can benefit a great deal from professional support (e.g., a play therapist, social worker, or child counselor) so that they do not internalize the challenging events that are surrounding their families. You may or may not be privy to information about the services that clients are receiving due to the privacy or confidentiality of such information.

Even so, there are ways that you can be supportive to children when they say, do, or experience things that you find overwhelming. Those methods are presented in the latter part of the chapter.

Client Maltreatment

As noted in chapter 6, the situations that may cause the most stress are those in which you suspect that individuals in the community service environment have been abused, neglected, or otherwise mistreated at home, at the site, or elsewhere. My students have indicated that most caregivers they meet appear loving and supportive, and they obviously care a great deal about their child or adult dependents. However, occasionally workers encounter apparently abusive situations, which is quite distressing for them.

If you chance upon unexplained bruises or marks on clients, or hear comments that suggest that clients have been exposed to age-inappropriate violence or sex (beyond what they might absorb from watching network TV), you may feel extremely overwhelmed. First, you will rightfully feel unsure of whether or not your suspicions are valid. Second, you may not be certain about the proper protocol for addressing such concerns at your particular site. At most sites the reporting of suspected abuse and neglect to site superiors or law enforcement agencies is mandatory. However, specific reporting protocols can vary from placement to placement. I advise my students to take these concerns to their site supervisors for discussion immediately, and of course I continue to monitor the situation through follow-up discussions with the service-learner(s). Along these lines, an example of one site's community worker reporting procedures is provided in appendix H. Examples of workers who found themselves suspecting abuse follow:

Although most of the day went incredibly smoothly [at a preschool] there was one incident that caught my attention and disrupted my thoughts. I believe that one girl in the class may be emotionally maltreated or neglected. The child always comes to school wearing clothing that apparently has not been washed for some time, and she always refuses to take her shoes off at nap time. Today her socks were gray and very dirty, and the teacher found worms in them. We were all a little bit shocked. Emotionally, the child is very passive, rarely saying a word and always saying yes when asked a question. During my first encounters with the child, I thought that she might have some kind of learning disability or auditory impairment. She often plays alone yet she appears to be extremely happy and always smiles. I know that the other adults in the classroom are also beginning to wonder, and I am sure that they will act appropriately according to their own findings and beliefs. I cannot jump to conclusions; however, I will be observing this child more closely in my visits to follow. (Female, European American)

A few of the children reveal less than ideal homes through play. When I listen to conversations on the [child care center] playground or in housekeeping, comments like "make that dog shut up or I'll kick it across the yard," "shut your mouth before I slap you silly," and "get your butt into the kitchen and start cleaning" make me cringe. (Female, European American)

There may be instances in which you not only suspect that clients have been abused but are given confirmation to one degree or another that they have been maltreated. These instances can be very disturbing and challenging for you when they occur. Several workers share their reactions in this regard:

Something happened today that I found to be very troubling. One of the girls in [a high school] class came into class with a black eye. Of course, everyone in the class stopped what they were doing to look at her, even the teacher. The student approached the teacher and asked if she could talk privately with her. I overheard her talking, and what had happened was that her father struck her. She was describing how he had hit her, and when the teacher asked her why, the student only said that he wanted to kill her. The police had just taken her father away. I don't know how anyone can hit their children. What could have come over him that made him want to punch her? I think about this and I get so upset. Why do adults hit children? This girl is his daughter, for Christ's sake. This issue brings about so much anger that it is difficult for me to talk about it (Male, Hispanic)

This week was like no other! It began as usual with the children [at an after-school enrichment program] being very attentive and responsive to how they should work. However I was disturbed by the news that one of the girls had been molested by some boys or possibly an adult. I was very sensitive and aware now of how I should treat this girl. What I am really trying to say is, after I know something like this, I can't help but to act differently toward her. Throughout the class she behaved normally, but the way I viewed her now had changed. I was more aware of things people do and say to her. I was furious but calm. I was in a state of mixed emotions. (Male, African)

One [elementary school boy] who has been known to act out in class was found to have been sexually abused and had to be taken away from his home. Usually dealing with him is not too hard because my supervising teacher takes over when it seems that I'm having a hard time. But today, he and I were left alone together because he was talking while everyone was lining up and the teacher asked him to sit down and wait with me for a few minutes. When she left, he began spurting out scary phrases like, "just what do you think you're doing, kid?" and "oh, you're not going anywhere." I thought back to his sexual abuse and felt a horrible sadness for him. Then he got up and I told him to sit down. He proceeded to throw his chair across the floor and flip his desk over. It was at that point that the teacher came back in and took care of the situation. It was time for me to leave and, to tell the truth, I was glad to leave. I wasn't ready for that. (Female, European American)

Because of the overwhelming nature of such incidents, you should not hesitate to seek support from academic or agency staff to assist you in processing such events and in responding appropriately. They should be able to listen to your concerns and direct you to helpful responses, resources, or support.

Staff Behavior

Occasionally you might be surprised, or even shocked, by the manner in which staff in the placement environments treat clients. Negative staff behavior does not seem to be the norm; however, from time to time staff behavior is less than desirable. Several students offer examples:

Today I noticed an interaction between [a child at a preschool] and one of the aides that rather disturbed me. It was snack time and the teacher decided to try a new strawberry-flavored cream cheese. [The child] is usually a good eater but today he was not very hungry and only sampled a few bites of the food. The aide kept trying to interest him in tasting the cream cheese. He kept refusing and she persisted, saying to him that he would not know if he liked it if he did not try it. Finally, after he refused several times, she put her finger up to his mouth and tried to force his lips open to make him try the cheese on her finger. He would not open his mouth so she then took his finger, put some cheese on it, and put his finger up to his mouth. I sat and watched this interaction and felt myself becoming very agitated. I felt that she was not only invading his personal space but also denying his right to choose his own food and control his body. (Female, European American)

I'm still a bit skeptical about the way [an elementary school teacher] conducts the class. Today she returned some quizzes the students had taken last week. She has a system whereby the students who get perfect scores on their quizzes are given a piece of candy. Each student is called up to the front of the class and given his or her quiz. Before calling out one of the names, [the teacher] said to her aide, "You won't believe this one," and then called out the name of a girl who had gotten a perfect score. I thought that was very inappropriate. I looked at the student as she walked to the back of the classroom with her quiz and candy. Instead of looking proud and happy, she looked ashamed and embarrassed. It seemed to me that she was picking up on the fact that the teacher had held low expectations of her and that her success resulted in shock and surprise. This student definitely deserved praise, but not accompanied by the comment. (Female, European American)

Today I visited [a middle school] social studies class that I found quite disturbing. The teacher was a middle-aged man who totally dominated the class. He was very flippant and shot out questions to the entire class. The room structure was set up so that the "quiet" girls sat in the front row, the white boys sat together on the side of the room, and the minority boys sat in the back row, next to what appeared to be the "popular girls." Throughout the class the teacher seemed to pick on the back row. He constantly jumped down the throats of the energetic, fervent African American boys. The teacher was threatening and even rude at times. He said to a blond girl in the back row, "Maybe if you hold your hand over one ear all the knowledge won't all pass through you!" (Female, European American)

You might expect that simply reporting such incidents to supervisors and administration would result in the immediate correction of staff behavior. But recall my experience of almost getting dismissed from my own volunteer position. Addressing staff behavior is not always that simple. I am not suggesting that such behavior go unreported. To the contrary, it assuredly should be reported for the clients' sake. But I am suggesting that you proceed tactfully and strategically when trying to address staff behavior. There is no one recommended route for you to take, but you might begin with the facilitators of your community learning experience whom you trust the most (e.g., your professor, your site supervisor, the site volunteer coordinator, the college community service administrator). If nothing else, they can listen and brainstorm possible responses with you or can decide if a staff member's behavior warrants reporting on more official levels. Also, do not forget to include such negative experiences as part of your learning and decision making about your own standards of professional behavior for now and for the future. Again, so that you do not become disillusioned when such events occur, keep in mind that most staff do not behave this way; fortunately, such instances seem to be the exception rather than the rule.

CHALLENGES THAT SHOCK OR SURPRISE

One of the greatest challenges you will face as a community worker is dealing with the reality that neither you nor those with whom you work live in an ideal world. We would all rather that people not suffer, that people not face crises, that people—especially children—not be used and abused, that they not be exploited, and that they not be exposed to things that are inappropriate for their age. We cannot overlook the fact that, unfortunately, these things do sometimes happen and may sometimes be reflected in the day-to-day conversations that you overhear or the things that you observe when you interact with others (Children's Defense Fund 1995; Edelman 1992; Erikson 1976, 1994; Federal Interagency Forum on Child and Family Statistics 1997; Good 1996). Through community learning, many workers eventually commit their lives to improving the educational and psychosocial lives of children and families.

Another challenge to shocking or surprising parts of the process is that, when you are engaging in community work, the last thing that you want to have happen is something that might make you feel embarrassed, unqualified, or incompetent. When things happen unexpectedly or surprisingly, we can be caught off guard. Under such circumstances it is easy for us to feel embarrassed or even responsible for what occurred, even if it was totally out of our control. As noted in chapter 3, there is a normal self-consciousness that occurs in any new situation until we become better acquainted and more comfortable in the environment. As you become more familiar with an environment and more "expert" at what you do within that environment, you relax more and feel more in control (Charness 1989; Weinman 1990; Wong and Wong 1998).

An additional challenge to this process involves the great influence of television and other forms of media on children. You will sometimes observe clients mimicking things that they have seen on television. Two workers describe surprising incidents that they think may have been motivated in part by television, movies, or radio:

Today I realized how easily children are influenced at this age. Whether it is television or radio or anything else, kids absorb more than most people think. For example, there is a wrestler by the name of X-Pac in the World Wrestling Federation. After every interview, he crosses his arms toward his waist in a X shape and tells all around him to "suck it!" Now, a ten-year-old who sees this over and over again will repeat it—and that is exactly what happened as [an elementary] boy told a girl to "suck it" during recess. I was immediately irate but had to take into consideration that this kid had no malicious intent. Instead, he was repeating what he had seen on TV. I pulled him away from the girl and told him not to do that again. He couldn't understand what was bad about it, and I explained until it finally made sense. But it is hard battling images that kids see every day when they only see you a couple of hours a week. (Male, African American)

[A six-year-old boy] said, "I have a date tonight and I bet she is hot." I looked at him and I was so shocked. I said, "How old are you?" He said he was six, and I couldn't believe he was just six and was able to talk about having a date. He then started singing, "I want to freak you in the morning, freak you in the evening just like that," [a song] by Adina Howard. Now this time my mouth dropped open. I asked him where he learned the song and he told me he heard it on the radio. Sometimes you think that children don't understand what is going on, but you'll be surprised at the things they know. All I could think about was the media, *and how certain things they do and say corrupts the minds of young people. (Female, European American)*

APPROACHES THAT ARE HELPFUL
WHEN YOU ARE SHOCKED OR SURPRISED

Whether you are working in economically challenged communities or in more privileged communities, if you participate in the community long enough, something eventually will be said or will happen that you will find surprising and/or extremely disappointing. Thus it is important to realize that all communities have their challenges, even if those challenges aren't at first obvious. As an example, Chideya (1995) points out that the use and marketing of cocaine among members of affluent communities often goes unnoticed and unpunished because of greater privacy and easier access to legal defense resources. In general, problems may take longer to manifest in more privileged environments because such difficulties may be easier to conceal on a surface level (Briere and Elliott 1994; Chideya 1995; Coontz 1992, 1997; Finkelhor 1994; Jenny et al. 1999; Sleek 1998).

Therefore, wherever you are placed, when you witness shocking, surprising, or disappointing events, you need to respond as appropriately as possible and direct your energies in a manner that is helpful and appropriate for the situation. When you feel uncertain about the appropriate response, consulting with your immediate supervisors and others involved in the community learning process is the best tack to take.

Try to Stay Calm

But what about the uncomfortable time period between the shocking event itself and your consultation with someone who can assist you? The most helpful strategy is to stay as calm as you can and try not to panic right away, at least not outwardly. Try to focus on the needs of the client(s) rather than on your own feelings of embarrassment and self-consciousness (which you can deal with later). Again, studying and absorbing the norms of your particular work environment may provide you with additional clues concerning how unexpected events are handled in the environment. It helps to defer making emotional judgments or jumping to stereotypical conclusions when the surprising event occurs. Two workers provide examples of how they stayed calm outwardly and focused on the needs of the clients:

This morning I was greeted with tears from one of the [kindergarten] children. She approached me the minute I walked through the door and said, "I want to go home." Quietly I walked into the hallway with her. I knelt down, gently put my arm around her, and asked her what was wrong. She told me that her stomach felt funny and that she had diarrhea and hadn't been able to make it to the bathroom. Apparently she had messed up her panties and was very embarrassed by the whole experience. The teacher asked me to walk her to the bathroom and then up to the nurse's office. I held her hand as we walked together and talked together. Eventually the tears subsided and a small smile crept over her face. We talked about her feelings and about different embarrassing things that had happened to each of us. She looked at me with amazement as though she could not believe things like this could have ever happened to me. In supporting her through what I'm sure was a very traumatic moment we were able to connect and share experiences. (Female, European American)

A very interesting and different (for me, anyway) topic came up today. A first-grade girl with whom I have been working closely [in a special needs classroom] told me she was going to visit her father. So I asked where he was, thinking of a divorce or the like. She told me he was in jail, which came as a complete shock to me. As I said, I come from a very small, suburban, un-diverse town, where people keep to themselves quite a bit, and for a first grader to suddenly announce that her father was in jail, it surprised me. I tried my best not to show that, and I treated it as if she was going to see him anywhere else. (Female, European American)

Thus I advise my students to try to take several approaches when they are faced with surprising and shocking circumstances. First, be as nonjudgmental of the clients, families, and staff as possible while collecting additional data. Second, avoid overreacting but respond as effectively and appropriately as possible. Third, avoid invalidating the client's experience when he or she shares it with you. Even in cases where clients may be exercising their imaginations, they are entitled to be gently redirected without being stripped of their defenses, creativity, and dignity.

Consult with Supervisors

Community workers who are provided opportunities for consulting honestly and genuinely with supervisory staff and who take advantage of such opportunities seem to fare well as they try to make sense of unexpected situations and handle such events appropriately. Students who need support benefit when they seek it through communicating in their journals, participating in class discussions, and/or making individual visits with supervisory staff, administrators, or faculty. It is important to realize that you are not alone in your experiences and that you should seek support when you feel you need it. A student shares an example of how she sought support from supervisory staff and found it helpful:

One of the major things I have learned from the [battered women's center children's tutorial program] is that children are in fact sometimes abused and they do show signs through pretend play and their interactions with others. There was an incident that I mentioned in my journal earlier about a three-year-old girl who got mad at her doll for going to the bathroom. Then she said that her daddy hit the doll. When I turned around to see what was going on, I noticed that she was under the table hiding [and trembling]. I just sat there amazed and clueless through the whole incident. I had never realized that a child would act out this type of scene in play. I later talked to the supervisor and she explained to me the procedures the center goes through to deal with children and cases like hers. She told me about an incident in which another three-year-old girl showed extremely clear signs of suspected sexual abuse. (Female, European American)

You should keep in mind that as a representative of your college and of the agency for whom you work, you should try to respond to unexpected events in a manner that is first and foremost ethically appropriate with respect to the clients. You also should try to respond in a manner that supports good relations among your academic program, the community, and the college. For this reason, you may fare better when you have very clear guidelines regarding the reporting of incidents and concerns. As I mentioned earlier, I advise my students to consult immediately with their site supervisors if they have any concerns, rather than make a report directly to the investigative arm of social services without consulting the supervisors who are responsible for the clients at the particular agency. However, each community learning program or placement site may have different guidelines and expectations for making such reports. Whatever the guidelines are, you should have a clear understanding of them and should inquire about them if they have not been made explicit.

Responding to Name-Calling

In terms of the client bantering and insults already discussed, you might also consider that not every comment has to be taken literally (Cooper 1996; Foster 1986; Hecht et al. 1993; MacLeod 1995; Wiley 1991). Among some individuals, verbal banter and threats may serve as a way of testing others within and outside of a culture. In some instances, the bantering may even border on humor (Foster 1986; Hale-Benson 1986; Hecht et al. 1993; Wiley 1991). Nonetheless, do not take harmful insults lightly. When you are trying to assess the meaning and seriousness of verbal statements made by clients, it is important to take verbal comments seriously while simultaneously observing the nonverbal behavior, context, body language, and reactions of the parties who are present.

If you do observe one child insulting another and elect to intervene, you might say, "I think that you are hurting her or his feelings with your words." If that does not work, you might ask the child how he would feel if someone were to hurt him with words like that. Such a question may engage the child's empathy, which might assist him in managing his behavior. If those techniques do not work, turn to the helpful resources available to you (e.g., your site supervisor). Also note that with adult clients you have to proceed much more cautiously because they may not see you in an authority role that warrants your redirecting their verbal behavior. Here again, consultations with supervisors would be key.

PRACTICAL TIPS

- Stay as calm as possible and do not overreact to surprising comments and behavior. Clients, especially child clients, could find overreactions to their comments and behavior to be reinforcing or frightening. On the other hand, do set appropriate limits when needed and redirect behavior appropriately (as discussed in chapter 6).

- Don't take everything literally. Sometimes clients may test you or seek attention, and they may do so by trying to unnerve you with words. In all circumstances, however, listen to your gut instincts. If you feel concerned, seek support immediately and as calmly as possible.
- Be prepared for the fact that clients often disclose genuine information. Sometimes when clients say things, they are sharing their reality with you and not trying to shock or unnerve you. It does not necessarily mean that they are unduly dependent on you or that they are devoid of support from others, but rather that they include you in their conversation from time to time. Again, when you are not certain about the appropriate response, seek support from supervisors or others involved in the community learning process.
- Do not stereotype. Realize that whatever the statement, problem, or trauma that is shared with you or observed by you, it is an issue that is most likely occurring in every community. Many issues appear more overt or more obvious in some communities, whereas the same issues are better camouflaged in other communities.
- Seek guidelines (e.g., appendix H) for reporting suspected abuse, neglect, or other maltreatment. Seek the procedures that apply to your site and consult with supervising staff, agency personnel, and/or professors—whoever seems most appropriate. Consult with someone who can evaluate the situation and possibly take action if necessary.
- Remember that as much can be learned from challenging situations as from easy situations. Workers can learn as much from experiences that they consider difficult, confusing, and ambiguous as they can from easy, straightforward situations. This is where journaling, discussing, and critically processing your experiences can help you connect your challenging experiences to your overall learning and curriculum.

FURTHER READING

Channing L. Bete Company. 1999. *About emotional abuse and neglect of children.* South Deerfield, Mass.: Channing L. Bete Company.

Channing L. Bete Company 1993. *What you should know about stress and your child.* South Deerfield, Mass.: Channing L. Bete Company.

Erikson, K. 1994. *A new species of trouble: Explorations in disaster, trauma, and community.* New York: Norton.

Furman, R. 1995. Helping children cope with stress and deal with feelings. *Young children* 50, no. 2: 33–41.

Good, L. 1996. When a child has been sexually abused: Several resources for parents and early childhood professionals. *Young children* 51, no. 5: 84–85.

Nunnally, E., and C. Moy. 1989. "Communicating on sensitive topics: Sex, money, and death." In *Communication basics for human service professionals*. Newbury Park, Calif.: Sage.

Pasztor, E., and M. Leighton. 1993. *Helping children and youth manage separation and loss*. Washington, D.C.: Child Welfare League of America.

Reader Notes

III

ENDINGS

11

Is It Time to Say Good-Bye?

Arranging Successful Closure

> *Today was my last day at [a child care center]. I was a little worried with how I was going to tell the children that I wouldn't be coming back. It even crossed my mind that maybe it would be easier if I just didn't tell them at all, but I decided it would only be easier for me and just harder on the children. I didn't tell all of the children that I wouldn't be coming back. Instead I just told the children with whom I had worked closely and had developed a real relationship. Some of them took it in stride, but others were very upset and begged me to come back again. I told them that I might return next semester (which I have been considering), but it wasn't definite. This calmed them down a little bit. I had anticipated this reaction because often some of the children even ask me to come over to their houses. (Female, European American)*

I hope you have had a rich and fulfilling community learning experience by the time you reach the point of leaving your placement and saying good-bye. The issue of saying good-bye to those with whom you have worked within your community learning environment is an important one (Dunlap 1998a). For a large proportion of community learners, saying good-bye comes as somewhat of a relief at the end of a busy semester, but at the same time, it weighs heavily on their minds and hearts. Many students are just beginning to feel a sense of attachment and embeddedness within the community learning environment when the semester comes to an end and it is time to ponder leaving. But this period of closure can provide a wonderful opportunity not only for making the transition away from the community work site to other future opportunities but also for reflecting on the overall community learning experience and its value. It is also a time to set goals for future community work and/or social activism.

Preparing for closure in advance serves several functions. First, it helps clients cope with losing people who have been working with them but are now moving out of their lives. This can be a significant issue for many clients, especially child clients, particularly if they are dealing with issues of loss, trauma, and change or if they have difficulty with transitions in general. Second, it helps everyone in the community learning environment to put the "saying good-bye" issue on the table for discussion and planning so that support can be provided for community workers, clients, and staff. Third, preparing for closure helps to prevent last-minute "closure disasters," as I call them. Such disasters might take the form of your suddenly developing a mysterious illness on the very last day of work, preventing you from attending on your last day, or your arriving on your last day to find that the clients are away on a field trip. Such "closure disasters" can leave both you and the client(s) feeling a sense of what might be called "closure frustration." Clients, likewise, can also miss out on the last visit when closure has not been attended to adequately.

Thus considering the closure process in advance helps everyone involved in the community learning process to prepare for an effective good-bye.

THE ISSUE OF CLOSURE

For a community worker, saying good-bye or making transitions away from situations in which attachments or bonds have been formed with others may not be easy. Several workers offer a range of emotions and experiences with respect to saying good-bye:

> *Today was my last day with the [elementary school] kids. It was hard for me to go in there knowing that I had only two hours left with them. Today was routine, however. At the end of the class, I took a few minutes to say good-bye and to thank them. I told [a little boy whom I had grown particularly attached] to never stop trying because you can see in his face when he's about to give up. I said my good-byes and gave my hugs. Overall it was an enjoyable experience. I may even spend next semester there. (Female, European American)*

> *During lunch I decided to sit somewhat more removed from the [first-grade] children. It seemed like a way to make the good-bye a little easier. I also wanted to watch and memorize each and every one of them. (Female, European American)*

Then it was time for me to leave [the preschool] for good. Ask me how easy this was! I said good-bye to [two of the children]. I kneeled down and put my arms out and [the first] ran over and gave me a hug. [The second] asked me if he could get a hug too and I said sure. So he jumped off the ramp he was on and came over and gave me a hug. [The first then] said to [a third child], "We are not going to see him anymore." And I said, "Sure you will. I'll come and visit." That made them happy. It made me happy because I felt that the kids really liked me and enjoyed my presence around them. It also made it even harder to leave. I left with a sad smile on my face. This concluded my service-learning and my day. (Male, African American)

Clients and staff are also affected by the closure process:

Today was the last day that I would visit [a child care center] classroom. I didn't quite know what to expect from the children. I wasn't sure if they would understand that I wasn't coming back or if they would even care. The teacher mentioned to the class that it was the last day that I would be visiting with them. A few of the children that I was close with were very sad. When we went outside, they wouldn't leave my side as if they thought I wouldn't leave if they stayed with me. When it came time to leave, they tried to block the door so that I couldn't leave the playground. I felt much more sad than I thought I would when I left. (Female, Hispanic)

I think that some of the [adolescent] kids really do enjoy my presence because when they heard that tonight was my last night, they were sad. They kept asking me why this was my last night. I told them [I may be] back next year. (Female, European American)

When I had to leave, I made a point of saying good-bye and thank-you to [staff members A and B at a youth-oriented museum] because I don't know if I'll be able to continue volunteering next semester. I was really pleased when [staff member B] said to me, "Come back! We need you, we love you," and some other complimentary phrases that made me feel good. (Female, European American)

Closure Circumstances Vary

Nevertheless, closure may not be much of an issue for some clients. As two workers explain:

Today was my last day, and although I was a bit sad, the [third-grade] children didn't seem to care so much! I can understand that, though. I was only there once a week for a couple of hours at a time. The children only seemed to be dependent on me and not attached to me. I would talk with them and they would ask me to do certain things like help them with their math problems, but they would have been just as happy having someone else help them. Therefore they were not attached to me and who I am but rather dependent on my actions or what I could help them with. That is to be expected, though, since I spent so little time with them. (Female, European American)

Today was the last time I would be going to the [child care center] and I felt really sad. However, when I arrived everyone was off in their own little worlds and no one paid me much mind. For the first half an hour none of the children wanted to play with me, so I just sat and observed. I think I had been expecting a grand finale for my last day. (Female, European American)

Likewise, closure may not be much of an issue for some of you because of the way that your community learning environment is structured. For example:

Today was my last class with the two-year-olds and their mothers. I wasn't as attached to this class as I was to the other class with older children. I feel this way because these younger children had their mothers with them and they very rarely interacted with the volunteers in the class. I learned through helping this class that I enjoy teaching older children. (Female, European American)

Postponing Closure

Some of you may opt to "postpone" the closure process by committing to your community work for an additional semester, or longer, on your own. Your desire to continue your placement assignment will most likely be welcomed by those with whom you are working, but do not take that for granted. So you need to discuss your ideas and intentions about continuing with the appropriate supervisory and administrative staff and negotiate the situation with them. Students explain how they arrived at their decision to continue an additional semester:

I have grown quite attached to these children. I thought about how I would say good-bye to all of them. Should I tell them I would not be returning, or not say anything at all? I did not know how other volunteers had handled saying good-bye. I walked into the recreation room, thinking that I would talk to my supervisor about it, but the minute I looked around the room, I knew my mind was made up. For now, I will not have to deal with saying good-bye because I have decided to continue volunteering at the [center for battered women] next semester. (Female, European American)

The day before my second-to-last day I wondered how I would say good-bye to the [elementary school] students. But after being confronted by their teacher about coming back, I accepted. I didn't think about it, I just blurted "yes." Now that I think about it, I am glad that I said yes to her. I have grown to really like the kids in the class; even though this course is over, I am glad that I am going to keep going and help these kids out. (Male, European American)

Last Thursday was supposed to be my last day, but I couldn't bear it. I love being with the kids way too much. I came back Thursday because I wanted to. (Female, European American)

Closure Reflection

During the closure process you may find yourself looking back and reflecting on your community learning experiences. For example, you may look introspectively to evaluate the experience and consider whether it was worthwhile. This is also a time when you may express growth in your understanding of the world, its diversity, and the higher good that exists beyond your own front door. For example:

Overall, I think that my volunteer experience was an extremely positive one. I got to know a bunch of wonderful [child care center] children and see both good and bad teachers in action. Throughout, I was able to make exciting connections between my experiences and my child development class work. I think that I have a lot more theoretical and practical tools and a little more experience for my future. (Female, European American)

Career Choices and Social Activism

During the closure period, you may also commit to future careers and/or social activism. You may also make a transition from desiring to engage in community service for the purpose of "giving" or for the purpose of fulfilling your course requirement to the purpose of engaging in social activism for structural change. The newer goal involves your helping to make significant, more realistic, long-term differences in the lives of others (Foos 1998). Several students provide examples:

I am hoping to work with more children in the future. I want to be able to understand the needs of children and learn the ways to help them overcome some of life's difficulties. I understand that being a teacher is preparing children to face the world, give them the knowledge, and most of all self-esteem. (Female, Lebanese)

This experience [at an inner-city child care center] is shaping my ideas about the future. I am beginning to see myself in an urban setting practicing pediatric dentistry with less fortunate children. (Male, European American)

I wish there were more I could do [to help a particular girl at a child care center]. I wish I could be there for her more to help her grow up with a healthy self esteem. Ultimately, that is what I want to do when I leave college, I want to find a career in which I will be able to impact neglected and abused children positively, and help them grow and develop into happy and successful adults. (Female, European American)

CHALLENGES TO THE CLOSURE PROCESS

The closure process within community learning can be challenging in several nonexclusive ways. For one, as a culture, we tend not to handle transitions well. Second, the need for closure is often ignored or overlooked in the community learning setting. Third, the short duration of many community learning placements makes the issue of closure somewhat ambiguous and awkward. And finally, unexpected events and illness can exacerbate the challenge of saying good-bye.

Transitions Are Difficult

Saying good-bye and making transitions in general can be a challenging (yet an often very rewarding) part of our life experience. We live in a culture that does not handle transitions involving closure very well. For example, we tend to deny loss, illness, and death, and we tend to keep the mourning process, when we do experience loss, as brief and covert as possible (Bridges 1991; Hardgrove and Warrick 1974; Kubler-Ross 1974, 1981; Waterman 1996). One student relates to this tendency as she reflects on her community learning closure experience:

> *A comment I would like to make relates to the death and dying chapters. Not really about it, but the idea that children need to be well-informed when a change has occurred or is going to occur. [The first-grade teacher] spent a lot of time explaining to the children why it was my last day. She explained clearly the situation, and it reminded me of my reading [Berger and Thompson 1998] recently of how grown-ups try to hide facts about friends moving or leaving or dying, so that children will not be upset. What we learned is that if children aren't informed, that is when they are most upset. When I saw the teacher's and the children's reaction to this being my last day, it made me feel really good—as if I had really affected them and helped them out. (Female, European American)*

Some students find closure so challenging that they opt to not tell their clients that they will be leaving. For example:

> *I chose not to tell the [first-grade] children it was my last day. I did not want to see their reaction, bad or good, and also my reaction could have been very dramatic. It is just easier than saying good-bye. Half of me regrets not saying anything, but the other half still believes it was easier this way. (Female, European American)*

Although you may feel inclined to proceed in this fashion yourself, it is not advisable to do so. Instead, you might try some of the methods presented later in this chapter.

The Need for Closure Is Often Overlooked

In the case of community learning programs, the closure process may frequently be overlooked altogether, not only by the students but also by the agency staff and the administrators who assist in facilitating the community learning process. Within many programs, the focus may be on initial logistical arrangements and worker adjustment into the programs, with less attention on the closure process. As an example of this, one student discusses her disappointment when staff and students failed to acknowledge her departure:

> *I felt the need to let [the child care center staff and children] know that this would be my last day with them, rather than disappear out of their lives. However, the teacher did not really seem to think anything of this and didn't even tell the children that I wouldn't be with them anymore. In fact, at the end of the day when it was time for the children to be picked up by their parents, she had me go inside and sweep the floors and wash the tables. I didn't even get the chance to say good-bye to the children and they had no idea that this was my last day. This bothered me because I felt that I had formed a relationship with each of the children and with the class as a whole. I wanted to say good-bye not only for the children to understand that I would be leaving but for myself as well. I learned a lot from the [child care center] class, and I wanted to thank each of them, in a way, for making me feel so comfortable and for allowing me to become part of the group. (Female, European American)*

This quote illustrates the need for community workers and staff to address the closure issue in advance.

Duration of Placements Is Sometimes Frustrating

As already noted, another challenge to the closure process is that just as workers and clients are experiencing greater comfort and stronger bonds, the semester comes to an end. Workers explain:

> *I would like to continue volunteering at [a soup kitchen community after-school program] when the semester has finished. Right when I start really getting to know all the kids, and they finally become comfortable talking to me about anything, the semester ends. (Female, European American)*

> *Last Day! I can't believe it. Time has flown by so quickly. It seems like it was only last week when I first stepped into the [first-grade] class and there were eighteen six-year-olds giving me the strangest looks. Now, when I step into the classroom, the first one to see me always gasps to the others "she's here!" The teacher told the class it was my last day and they all made pouting faces. I promised them that I would come back in the spring and visit them. (Female, European American)*

Even though curriculum-based community learning programs tend not to extend for more than a semester or year, you should not discount the impact that the program can have on you, your learning and emotional growth, and your clients (Delve, Mintz, and Stewart 1990; McCarthy 1996). Even though there is some frustration in bringing your program to an end after a short period of time, there may also be some relief as you look ahead to the next semester. As you will see again later in this chapter, many students also opt to continue their community work, on their own, and thus provide for themselves an extended period of engagement in the setting.

Closure "Disasters"

Unexpected closure disasters, which were briefly mentioned in the first section of this chapter, can exacerbate the challenge of closure (Dunlap 1998a). For example, you may brace yourself emotionally for that final visit then find, upon arriving, that the clients are away on a field trip. Such disasters can be minimized by planning ahead. But even the best planning cannot always prevent unexpected events from occurring. Students describe situations in which closure was made worse by the fact that some of the clients with whom they usually worked were missing on their last day:

> Today was the last class at [a children's art program]. It made me a little sad to go today. The class was very, very good today, but there were a few kids missing. This made me especially upset because I won't see them again. (Female, European American)

> This is kind of a sad day, since this is the last day I will be here with the [preschool] children. Today only some of the children came to school. How inconvenient. This means that I will not be able to say good-bye to a few of the children with whom I had grown attached. (Male, African American)

Closure Illness

Legitimate illness may prevent accomplishing closure for workers who desire it. For example:

> Today was supposed to be my last day at [a child care center], but because I had the flu, I was unable to attend. The infirmary said this epidemic of the flu was the most contagious they had seen in a long time, so I felt it would be best not to go. (Female, European American)

Student journals suggest that, unfortunately and preventably, workers are absent more frequently on the last day of their community learning than any other day during their assignment. This could be in part because most service-learning assignments tend to end during a high-stress period in the se-mester, when students are preparing for the end of the semester, final exams, term papers, and sometimes graduation. They are also often trying to make travel preparations for winter or summer break. Thus you may be more sus-ceptible to feeling overwhelmed by schedules and may have more stresses on your health during this time. Dealing with community learning attach-ments and closure issues may be more challenging than usual during this pe-riod, and therefore you may feel inclined, or at least tempted, to miss your last day(s). I strongly recommend, however, that you remain as reliable and consistent as possible throughout the duration of your community learning assignment. Many students report that although they are tempted to abandon the last day because they feel ill, once they actually get started, they feel much better.

If you do have to miss that final day, however, you need to give as much advance warning as possible to your site supervisor or course professor and try to arrange an alternate visit to make up for the one missed. You also have to be prepared for whatever consequences, if any, your faculty, administra-tion, or site supervisors impose upon you for unexcused missed visits.

HELPFUL APPROACHES DURING THE CLOSURE PROCESS

There are at least three approaches that you may find helpful as you bring your community service to an end. First, planning ahead is the best tack to take. Second, you might also provide small handmade or low-cost gifts or ac-tivities to help facilitate the ending process. And finally, you might reflect on your community learning experience and look ahead to how you might apply or continue your work in the future. Each of these approaches may help you develop a healthier attitude toward bringing closure to your community work.

Planning Ahead

One of the most helpful approaches that you can take is to consider the closure process well before the semester ends. In that regard, you may find it helpful to communicate with clients and staff in the weeks prior to the end-ing of your assignment to let them know when your visits will come to an end. This may be especially helpful for workers who are engaged with chil-dren who may have difficulty making transitions in their day-to-day lives. To let them know that, saying something like "this is the second-to-the-last time that I will be visiting the center" may be very helpful. However, it is most helpful for the worker to consult with the relevant staff or administration per-sons before following any course of action regarding the closure process (Dunlap 1998a).

Closure Gifts and Activities

As a way of acknowledging your departure, you might consider giving appropriate little "closure" gifts to clients, if the authorized staff member(s) at your site approve. In the case of child clients, these gifts might include, for example, crayons, books, coloring books, a musical tape, a letter, a snapshot. In the case of adolescent or adult clients, the gifts might include, for example, a small plant or seedling, a card, a note, or an inspirational poem. Workers explain:

> *I brought cookies to [the second-grade class of an elementary] school today since it was my last day. (Female, European American)*

> *As [a middle school boy] was leaving the car after our final visit, he told me for the fifth time (at least) that he liked my hat. It was a blue Nike hat, and I took it off my head and put it on his and told him to keep it. His eyes lit up and he was speechless. I won't ever forget the expression on his face. I know that it meant a lot to him and that it was something he wouldn't soon forget. It's amazing how something that means so little to me personally can mean so much to someone else. (Male, European American)*

You might also, in conjunction with the staff with whom you work, opt for a little "closure activity" of sorts, which might include a short period of celebration, cookies, juice, games, and/or other activities. For example:

> *Today was my last day at [a child care center]. The other volunteer and I decided to do something special today with the children, since it was our last day. I brought in a nicely illustrated book of nursery rhymes, and we chose three to do with the children. We first read the rhyme, and then we asked them which parts should get acted out in the story. We then chose children to act out the various parts, and the class recited the rhyme with us as the children acted out the story. We did this as many times as was necessary for the children to get a chance to act out all of the roles that they wanted. The children really seemed to enjoy this activity. (Female, European American)*

Workers have also reported instances of staff and clients creating thank-you cards and posters for them, much to their delight. For example:

> *Before I left, the teacher and the [second-grade] children presented me with a book of pictures and words that they put together thanking me for coming to the classroom every week and working with them. It was really nice, and to tell you the truth, I was sad to leave them. But I am planning to go back and do an internship with this teacher next year. (Female, European American)*

> *I've enjoyed working here [in a seventh-grade classroom] so much that I want to continue it. Since today was my last day, the teacher gave me a big*

tin of cookies for Christmas. She has been so nice, and I love talking to her. (Female, European American)

A few of the kids [from an after-school tutorial program] went out of their way to say good-bye to us today. One girl even gave me a small bead when I left. I put it in a small box on my desk, and I treasure it. (Male, European American)

Some workers bring closure to their experience by overcompensating. Their overcompensation may come in the form of buying expensive gifts or facilitating expensive and very time-consuming activities. While closure gifts and activities are nice, it is important that your gifts are not overdone so that the gifts do not overshadow remembrance of the relationships and experiences that were shared. Also, a closure gift or activity does not have to occur on the last day, when you may be vulnerable to overcompensation. With approval from staff, you can plan your closure activity or gifts for a later time (e.g., early in the next semester), giving yourself, the clients, and the staff more time to adjust to the change before saying a final good-bye.

Other Approaches

There are other approaches that seem to be helpful in the closure process. As mentioned earlier, if you feel that you will greatly miss your community service when it ends, or if you have found your work particularly rewarding, you may opt to continue your work in the next or a subsequent semester. It is important that you negotiate a continuation with the appropriate staff first, only promising to clients and staff that which you can reasonably carry out. Thus you should negotiate and promise to continue working only if you will be able to follow through so that children and staff are not let down by unfulfilled promises.

If you are not sure that you can commit to a volunteer assignment, then you should try to negotiate with the staff something less time-consuming, such as a follow-up visit. You may mention that you would be interested in continuing the work without making a firm promise to do so, which would allow you to spend more time deciding. Whatever the case, any promise that you make must be sincere, genuine, and reliable.

Nevertheless, if you make arrangements that later cannot be carried out, it is important for you to communicate with the staff and/or children and try to negotiate whatever substitute accommodations you can. For example, if you originally intended to serve the following semester once a week for two hours a week and find that you cannot do that because of, for example, an unexpected change in your schedule, then you might try to renegotiate with the staff a schedule of once every two weeks instead. Again, it is important for you to keep the lines of communication open about your scheduling limitations, and keep your attendance as reliable and consistent as possible.

You may also find it helpful to look toward the future and to think of ways to relate or transform your energy for community learning into activities and causes that go beyond your current and next-semester placement obligations. You might think in terms of connecting your community learning experiences to your own career interests and professional development, or to activism for community and world change in the future, if you have not already begun to do so. A student provides some of her final reflections as she brings her community learning assignment to an end by reflecting on her future and deciding to move more toward social activism:

> *Today, on my last day, I was playing with [one preschool girl in particular] in the dramatic play area, and she was feeding her "baby" a bottle. She is an African American girl whose hair is always "done up" with fancy clips, barrettes, and bows. She is always smiling. I often have the urge to take her home with me and buy her lots of gifts and toys. She often talks about how she's going to move away, and that "you might never see me no more." I watched her look at her "baby" and how she gently held its head up as she fed it. "What's your baby's name?" I asked. She seemed to think about it for a few seconds and then replied, "Justice." I got goose bumps all over my body. What three-and-a-half-year-old smiling girl, who makes her own breakfast and worries that she will have to move out of her house, names her doll "Justice"? It just seemed so all-encompassing—why should one child have to share a room with three people and live in poverty, while another child plays Super Nintendo all day, goes to Chucky Cheese for dinner, and then stops at Block Buster to rent a Ninja Turtle movie. Where is justice? As I reflect on my experience, I find that these children are just like any other children—they are bright, inquisitive, and thirsty for knowledge. I am more determined than ever to teach in inner-city schools and make a difference. (Female, European American)*

To summarize, even though saying good-bye is not always an easy process, it can be made easier by planning ahead, reflecting on the past, and looking to the future—toward your social concerns and future goals for making a difference.

PRACTICAL TIPS

- Consider and prepare for closure without obsessing over it or overdoing it. Accept closure as a normal part of the community learning process. It deserves as much attention as the initial adjustment process. However, do not let the closure process overtake you and cause you to feel that you have to "do" something, particularly in an overcompensatory manner.
- Consult with supervisors regarding closure. Let supervisors and other community learning colleagues know that you are thinking about the

issues involved in the closure process. Ask them how the closure process has been handled in the past, and ask them for their advice regarding your closure. Do not be discouraged if they initially seem surprised by your questions.

- Brief the client(s) on your departure several visits prior to your last. If appropriate for your assignment, and if approved by supervisors, you should acknowledge your final visits to the staff and clients with whom you work.
- Be gentle but firm with yourself. Don't be surprised if you feel overwhelmed or ill on the last day. Many students feel this way on their last day. However, try to fulfill your responsibilities if you are able. Once you actually get started, you will probably feel better. If you are truly ill, advise the staff and reschedule your visit as soon as possible.
- Be sure that all documents related to your community work have been filed. If final attendance sheets, supervisor evaluation forms (e.g., appendix G), class reports, or other documents relative to your work are due to your course professors or administrators, be sure that they are appropriately filed. If your community learning supervisors are required to file an evaluation of your work, they may find it helpful if you provide them with a stamped, addressed envelope for easy mailing.
- Be as certain as possible when committing to serve in the future. If you decide to announce that you will continue your community work, be prepared to follow through on that commitment. Also understand that recommitting is a process that must be negotiated with the staff. If you are not certain about recommitting, with the staff's approval, you can agree to at least later write a letter to the clients, send them a postcard, or pay them a visit.
- Include a focus beyond your current community learning. Consider new goals for your future learning, service, and community activism as you move beyond your current community learning placement.

FURTHER READING

Bridges, W. 1991. *Managing transitions: Making the most of change*. Reading, Mass.: Addison-Wesley.

Channing L. Bete Company. 1992. *About grief*. South Deerfield, Mass.: Channing L. Bete Company.

Chickering, A., and N. Schlossberg. 1995. Where are you going from here? Taking it with you. In *Getting the most out of college*. Boston: Allyn & Bacon.

Driscoll, A., et al. 1997. *Assessing the impact of service-learning: A workbook of strategies and methods*. Portland, Ore.: Portland State University Press.

Pasztor, E., and M. Leighton. 1993. *Helping children and youth manage separation and loss*. Washington, D.C.: Child Welfare League of America.

Waterman, F. 1996. Great good-byes. In K. Galvin and P. Cooper, eds., *Making connections: Readings in relational communication*. Los Angeles: Roxbury.

Reader Notes

Afterword

Reviewing the Community Service and Learning Adjustment Process

In this afterword I tie together and summarize the community learning process as considered in the critical reflection work of past service-learners. My examination of student journals suggests that community learners often experience uncomfortable emotions as they enter environments that are unfamiliar to them. After the first few visits, however, their discomfort significantly wanes, and with each visit they begin to feel more comfortable, more welcomed, and more connected to those with whom they work. They begin to build rapport and trust with the clients and staff, and they may test their skills at redirecting clients when the need arises.

As workers experience these new environments, their own self-concepts and self-definitions may be challenged, even if momentarily. They may begin to observe firsthand the structural hindrances that exist in many communities. As they come face-to-face with such new revelations, they may experience a range of emotions from anger and guilt to relief and enlightenment. They learn to reach out to trusted others for support and advice, and they find their own strength, creativity, and resilience for coping. They may begin to adjust their service goals to make them more realistic and achievable, given the short duration of many community learning periods. And even with their adjusted goals, they begin to find pride and satisfaction in their efforts and achievements. They begin to realize that if they have touched one life, even for a moment, they have accomplished a great task. And to the amazement of many workers, they begin to see how those within the community have touched them, taught them, and made lasting impressions on their curricula, their personal memories, their motivations, and their future goals.

As they bring their work to an end for the semester, workers feel mixed emotions that include both relief and sadness, but the lasting impressions, as well as the lessons learned, make it all worthwhile. Most of them, if they had it to do all over again, would not hesitate.

Appendix A

Sample Journal Reflection Questions

LABEL EACH JOURNAL ENTRY

Each entry in the file should be labeled with the date of visit. Some students have titled their entries or added other personal touches.

PROCESSING OR TAKING NOTES

It is probably *not* a good idea to take notes for your journal while you are engaged at your service-learning site. The best time to process is right after your service-learning for that day, and then perhaps at any time you think about your observations and experiences. Entries should be double-spaced, and each entry should be dated. It is imperative that service-learners refer to children, teachers, or others by initials only and not by name to maintain their confidentiality.

LENGTH OF ENTRIES

There is no set or required length for each entry. The length should be determined by your observation and your processing of it. As you become more at ease with writing in your journal, length will become less important. You should have at least one entry for each day that you observe. You may want to add more entries between visits as you process course materials, service-learning, and so on.

FIRST JOURNAL ASSIGNMENT: INSTRUCTIONS
REGARDING THE FIRST FEW ENTRIES

The following questions are to be addressed in the first few entries of your journal and can be addressed even before your placement actually begins. Please do not fear answering honestly. There are no right or wrong responses in your journals. Thus prior to and/or over the course of your first few service-learning sessions, respond to the following questions in your journals:

1. Where is your service-learning site? How will you be getting to your service-learning site? Describe the surroundings of your site.
2. How did you come to select your particular observation site? In other words, what attracted you to this one over the others available?
3. What do you hope to learn or possibly discover about the children, adults, families, or observation site? What do you hope to observe, learn, or discover about child and adult development by participating at your observation center?
4. What are your specific duties or tasks? Are you a tutor or a peer model, or do you serve in some other capacity? What specifically will be your tasks and roles?
5. Describe the children, adults, or families (not necessarily each one, but collectively) with whom you are working in your service-learning. With how many children, adults, or families do you come into contact? What are their age ranges and school grade levels? What do you happen to know about their lives and backgrounds (their microsystems, mesosystems, exosystems, and macrosystems, i.e., immediate and larger surrounding contexts)? How might the participants be similar to one another? How might they be different from one another? Are there any that you might define as underserved or "at risk" for some reason? Why so? Why not?
6. Do you see any similarities between yourself as a child or adult and the children, adults, or families in general or individually? What are the similarities? What are the differences?
7. What developmental deficits (physical, cognitive, psychosocial, emotional, spiritual, etc.), if any, do you think the participants have? What strengths and competencies do you think they have? What have you observed in their behavior that might illustrate these deficits, strengths, and competencies? You may include a discussion of deficits and strengths in their microsystem(s), mesosystem(s), exosystem(s), and/or macrosystem(s).
8. What questions stand out in your mind most about the participants? If you had a crystal ball and could investigate any aspect of their devel-

opment, what would you want to focus on? Why? What would you want most to avoid focusing on? Why?

8. Again, please do not fear answering honestly. There are no wrong or right responses in your journal. Remember that the purpose of your journal is to help you record, discuss, and reflect upon your observation experiences without fear of being graded on content. How do you feel at this point about this service-learning experience? How do you view yourself in relation to the participants at this point? In other words, do you feel any attachment or connection (can you relate to the participants in any way)? In what areas do you relate? In what areas do you not? Why? Why not?

9. Where do you want to go from here with respect to your observations? Have any areas emerged yet that you think you might like to focus on in particular when you observe the participants? Are there any individual participants that you feel are particularly interesting? Jot down any ideas for future directions.

BASIC INSTRUCTIONS FOR FUTURE ENTRIES

In general, your journal entry should have two parts: (1) a record of what you have observed or experienced at the time and (2) your response or reaction to it. Your reaction should focus on relating what you saw to information from the course. Personal reactions in the journal are encouraged, but the central thrust of the response should be the relationship between what you saw and the human development course content as much as possible.

Note: By Michelle R. Dunlap, from her course HMD 111B Introduction to Human Development: Social World of Children and Families.

Appendix B

Methods

When I started teaching at Connecticut College, my colleagues informed me that journal logs for critical reflection were a very important part of the learning process for students who are engaged in community learning. I understood that journals would be one of several vehicles of communication between students and me regarding their experiences and learning in relation to the course. Although I was very familiar with community learning from the years I spent engaging in it as a volunteer, service-learning as a concept was fairly new to me. I began to explore and read service-learning research materials shared with me by colleagues and available through the college's consortium of libraries. I also began to understand further how critical reflection can assist students as they deal with a variety of feelings that can arise, such as boredom, disillusionment, and frustration in the course of community service (Cooper 1998; Eyler et al. 1996; Goldsmith 1993; Norrell, Kuennen, and Koeni 1997).

After students in my courses arranged their service-learning placements, I provided support for their personal reflection in two major ways. First, I required students to each keep a journal concerning their own service-learning experiences, thoughts, feelings, concerns, expectations, and connections to course curricula (see appendix A). Their journals were turned in periodically for my responses, comments, and suggestions. Second, I scheduled at least four in-class group discussion sessions during each semester. I scheduled these sessions evenly over the course of the semester so that they occurred at least once a month. For these sessions, I placed students into groups of four to six for unstructured or semistructured discussion regarding their experiences (Dunlap 1998d).

By the end of that third semester, I submitted a proposal to the Human Subjects Institutional Review Board and the Psychology Department Ethics Committee of Connecticut College for permission to collect and analyze the journals for research purposes.

At the end of selected semesters, students were invited to submit their journals to me for a study of student adjustment in service-learning settings. No mention of the study was made to them until the last day of class after journals had been submitted and returned. Confidentiality and future anonymity were guaranteed. I assured them verbally and in writing through informed consent that there would be no penalty for withholding their journals if they chose not to participate, nor would there be benefits or rewards for submitting their journals. They were assured that their participation or refusal would in no way influence their course grades in accordance with the guidelines and approval of the Human Subjects Institutional Review Board and the Psychology Department Ethics Committee of Connecticut College. Across solicited courses, 87–98 percent of students gave written permission and submitted their journals.

From the submitted journals, anonymous transcripts were created for objective data coding purposes, and the 215 journals were systematically analyzed using the "topical codes 2" method of content analysis outlined in Bernard (1994, 197; see also Manning and Cullum-Swan 1994; Shumer 1997). This method requires that each paragraph of a journal be coded for the themes that are contained in it (Bernard 1994; Dunlap 1998b). Earlier sets of journals were coded for several research studies that analyzed basic adjustment issues (Dunlap 1998a), hero desires (Dunlap 1997), multicultural issues (Dunlap 1998b and c), and affection issues (Dunlap and Coughlin 1999).

Appendix C

Guidelines Regarding Privacy
and Confidentiality

It is important that you honor the privacy and confidence of the child and family clients with whom you work. Expectations regarding privacy and confidentiality vary from site to site, and each person engaged in community learning should seek a clear understanding regarding this issue. The guidelines that are currently issued with respect to service-learning at the Connecticut College Children's Program, a model program for young children with a diverse range of backgrounds and abilities, are provided below.

1. Do not talk about clients or their families once you leave the building.
2. Refrain from commenting about or asking questions about a client during a service-learning visit.
3. If you are in another setting and are asked about a client or family, refrain from offering any information. You may want to say, "I'm learning a great deal in my service-learning work, but I can't talk about individual clients. You could speak with one of the supervisory staff members."
4. Do not give clients or their families telephone numbers or addresses belonging to you or staff members.
5. If a client or relative asks you personal questions or asks you to help them out in some way, you should consider suggesting they see an administrator so that your role as a community worker is not confused with the roles of the staff members who are responsible for the happenings of the clients or site on a day-to-day basis.
6. When you are at your service-learning site, respect the rights of privacy of clients and their families. Don't talk about the client's or the family's

"situation(s)," especially if you do not work with them yourself.

7. When consulting with other service-learners or staff, remember to talk in a private place, closing the door if necessary. Also, do not share privileged information with clients or relatives during the service-learning visit. It is the supervisory staff's responsibility to do so.

8. Generally, it is not advisable to provide client care outside of the service-learning setting while the client is enrolled in the group in which the service-learner has a placement. Service-learners never make home visits to a family's home unless under the direct supervision of or with the permission of an agency staff member. Again, your role as a service-learner is not to be confused with that of the staff members who are responsible for the clients or the site on a day-to-day basis.

Note: Adapted and printed with permission from the *Connecticut College Children's Program Student Handbook, 1999–2000.*

Appendix D

Sample Introductory Letter to Agency

Dear School or Agency Supervisor,

    The student _____ is enrolled in a human development course that I teach. I believe that service-learning experiences help enhance academic learning and vice versa—that academic learning can enhance service-learning. Therefore, I require that all of my students engage in service-learning involving children and/or families, coordinated through either the Connecticut College Children's Program or the Connecticut College Office of Volunteers for Community Services (OVCS).

    The above student is enrolled in my HMD _____ course. All students of my courses are expected to behave in accordance with the Human Development Children's Program or OVCS guidelines for behavior and performance of duties. Students of my HMD 111B Introduction to Human Development course are also asked by me to make as many connections as they can between basic course concepts and real-life human behavior and vice versa—real-life behavior and concepts taught in the course. Students in my HMD 302 Social and Personality Development course are expected to focus on social developmental issues and social cognition issues as they perform their regular service-learning duties. Students in my HMD 321 Children and Families in a Multicultural Society course are encouraged to focus their attention on multicultural concepts, issues, challenges, and resolutions. HMD 402 Social and Personality Development Research students are expected to think in terms of the implications of particular areas of research that they are pursuing for the service-learning environments and/or children and families of service-learning environments in which they are engaged.

Attached to this letter you will find an evaluation form [see appendix G] that I would appreciate your completing at the end of the student's service-learning period. Please mail it directly to me. Your evaluation will not only provide valuable information for measuring the progress of my students but it will also help me improve the design of courses in the future.

In the meantime, please feel free to contact me if I can provide you with more information regarding the service-learning objectives that I have for my students, or if you have any other questions or concerns. I thank you again for helping provide service-learning opportunities for my students.

Sincerely,
Michelle R. Dunlap, Ph.D.

Note: By Michelle R. Dunlap

Appendix E

General Guidelines for Working with Children and Families

In your work with children and families, it is important to set limits and redirect behavior as appropriately as possible. Expectations governing redirecting and disciplining clients vary from site to site, and each person engaged in community learning should seek a clear understanding of them. Listed below are general and specific guidelines for interacting with children and families that are currently issued with respect to service-learning at the Connecticut College Children's Program, a model program for young children with a diverse range of backgrounds and abilities.

1. Observe how supervisors and staff handle situations.
2. Anticipate problems.
3. Be aware of voices, manner, tone, volume.
4. Be brave; handle a situation. Supervisors and other staff will help if necessary. Generally, the correct action is taken. Instinct is often a good guide.
5. Questions and discussion are usually deferred until after the session. However, if a crisis develops, ask immediately.
6. Clean up as you go (if possible). It is a big help in maintaining order.
7. Try to keep in mind each client's special needs while working with him or her.
8. Consistency and follow-through are essential in dealing with each client.
9. Let supervisory staff know if you have any special talents or ideas that you would like to share with the clients (e.g., cooking, storytelling, arts and crafts).

10. Be friendly in your initial contacts but move toward clients slowly and quietly. Some clients need time to accept strangers and may need to take the initiative.

11. Concentrate on learning the clients' names as quickly as possible. Calling clients by their names is a good way to gain their friendship and makes you seem like less of an "outsider." In the case of older adults, observe cultural standards for addressing them (Do they prefer to be called by their first names or by a courtesy title such as Mr., Mrs., Ms., Dr., etc. ?). Whenever you can, make your name known to the clients in a natural, casual manner.

12. Meet the client at her or his level. When making suggestions, giving directions, or simply making friendly contacts with the client, preface remarks with the client's name.

13. When talking to children, bend, stoop, or sit down to permit eye contact and to counteract the "giant" impression. However, be sure to observe cultural standards regarding eye contact. In some cultures, looking at others directly in the eyes is considered disrespectful, intimidating, or confrontational.

14. In group situations, stand or sit in a position that permits you to keep the total group in view even when speaking to one client. Doing so allows you to anticipate events and is crucial to safety.

15. With children, speak in a low and pleasant but firm voice. Voice tone and level may well say more to the client about your feelings and expectations than the actual words. There may be instances when you may need to speak more loudly and firmly, but always be professional.

16. Give positive suggestions when possible. For example, "here is paper to draw on" rather than "don't write on the wall." The second statement puts the client in the wrong and merely limits behavior without giving the child clues that will encourage further learning. (In emergency situations, "Jo, stop!" may need to precede the suggestions.)

17. Avoid telling a child or other client that she is "cute," "good," "bad," or "naughty." Show approval or disapproval of a specific action (e.g., I noticed how you were able to share some of your play dough with Jo").

18. Avoid embarrassing clients with comparisons or competitive situations unless specifically directed to do so. Generally, clients should not feel that their chances for approval depend on being "first" or "best." Clients, especially children, may need reassurance of their worth. Taking cues from clients and finding their interests helps give clients successful experiences.

19. When giving reasons to child clients, you should be sure that they are logical and related to the situation. For example, "Throwing the ball indoors may hurt someone. Let's roll it at the ten pins."

20. Offer choices when possible. Saying "Joe has just started swinging. Would you like to use the slide or the jungle gym until he's finished?" gives the client positive alternative actions. You may need to support him in starting a new activity.

21. When addressing children, try to avoid offering choices unless you are ready to accept them. For example, avoid saying "you don't want to walk in the puddle, do you?" when you want the child to stay out of the puddle. In routine situations, "time to wash" or "time to go to your room now," conveys your real expectation far better than "will you go to your room now?"

22. Social behavior is learned, and adults can often help child clients with verbal cues: "Tell Gary you want to play with him." When two children are playing and a third approaches, offer a suggestion, for example, "Here comes Beth. She could help you build a larger garage; here are more blocks," which helps them accept the new child.

23. Adults are responsible for providing child clients with an environment of personal safety and psychological comfort. Limits have positive value in that they give people, especially children, a feeling of confidence and security. Limits should be made clear to children (and adults when necessary) and maintained consistently. Limits must also be appropriate to the individual needs of the client and the specific situation. We should not feel threatened when children test these limits; exploring and testing resistance is healthy.

24. Give the client only as much help as she needs. Unless otherwise instructed to do so, do not do things for the client that she can reasonably be expected to do for herself. Do not intervene when a client is struggling happily just because you could do something more easily. You may suggest ways of working and then let the client do it. However, be ready to give help before a client is overly discouraged or when, by her words or actions, she indicates she is ready to move on to more mature functioning.

25. When working with children, remember that children learn to share and take turns slowly. Knowing what it means to possess something precedes sharing it. Thus a toddler needs to learn the concept of owning an item ("mine, mine, mine") before he can share it ("ours"). When children are ready, adults can furnish verbal help. For example, "Joe has the doll buggy now; your turn is next." (Avoid, "Joe had it first.") Be sure to follow up with, "Joe, you have had your turn. Alice and Rob are waiting. You may have your turn with the ironing board."

26. Generally speaking, allow children to attempt to settle their own disputes unless a child becomes frightened or there is a danger of physical injury.

27. Be shockproof. Clients, and particularly child clients, often show feelings, use language, or express ideas and behavior that may seem

startling to others. Overreaction on your part may intensify the behavior or make it unduly important. When you are uncertain about
how you should interpret such behavior, consult supervisory staff.

28. Avoid perfumes and aftershave lotions. Some clients could be allergic
to such products.

Remember that

a. clients learn from your behavior as well as your words;
b. young children play alone and some adult clients tend to work
alone;
c. the tired or ill client may become overactive, quiet, or withdrawn;
d. keeping your "cool" may help the client recover his or hers;
e. changes in activity often prevent the need for limits; a walk, a new
game, or a new story can change a hectic atmosphere into a happier situation;
f. when involved in one activity, clients may need time to change to
another activity or routine and advance warning of upcoming
changes;
g. following a highly active period, such as free play or movement, a
quiet resting time is needed before the next activity;
h. it is your responsibility to prepare clients for the termination of
your service-learning or an extended vacation; begin talking with
them about your departure one or two sessions before your final
session;
i. discussing your ideas, observations, concerns, and questions with
the supervising staff is always appropriate.

Note that many holidays are not celebrated by the entire community.
Some service-learning sites adopt the policy that no holidays will be
celebrated within the site, whereas others try to celebrate all holidays or seasonal themes. Be aware of the celebration policies of
your service-learning environment. Some clients become overex-
cited and anxious during times of celebration and may need limits
and support during such times.

Note: Adapted and printed with permission from the *Connecticut College
Children's Program Student Handbook, 1999–2000.*

Appendix F

Collectivistic Practices and Approaches

1. A "We Are Family" model or approach may help engage clients.
2. Including "inspiration" in the environment and routines may help the clients feel more at home.
3. Providing interpersonal "safety" and connections before task completion demands and judgments are important for clients who may take a while to warm up to others outside of their referent group.
4. Respecting and making a space for a variety of communication styles while modeling additional styles will help engage those who connect with others and express themselves in different ways.
5. Inclusion of culturally relevant stories, materials, images, and role models will help the clients feel included and validated.
6. Providing detailed, vivid stories that children can connect to their own lives will also help them feel included and validated.
7. Inclusion of stories, feelings, and struggles in the children's (and their heroes') own words will help you engage clients and keep them connected to the learning process.
8. To some degree, allow for individual flair in a child's work and regularly give each child a chance to shine. This will also help the clients feel included and will validate their work.
9. Be firm yet supportive, which is an important balance to strike with all child clients.
10. Be aware of complex parenting issues. What seems authoritarian to you may be "protective" to the parents, and what seems overly permissive to you may be "child inclusive" to the parents.

11. If possible, keep parent-related activities such as parent–teacher or-ganization meetings child inclusive or child accommodative.
12. Do not assume a "deficit model." Have high expectations and do not negatively stereotype.

Note: By Michelle R. Dunlap, compiled from the following resources: Collins and Tamarkin 1990; Greenfield and Cocking 1994; Hale-Benson 1986; Hopson and Hopson 1993; Lynch and Hanson 1998; Rose 1989; Shade 1989; Shujaa 1994.

Appendix G

Sample Placement Supervisor Evaluation of Worker

College Name
Course/Department
Instructor's Name
Service-Learning Placement Evaluation

Dear Supervisor or Teacher: I would appreciate your assessment of the following student service-learner from my course. Please complete this evaluation for the student to return to me at the end of the semester. Your feedback will not only provide valuable information for measuring the progress of students but will also help me improve the design of future courses. The supervisor or teacher should mail this form by _____ directly to _____ [professor's name and mailing address].

Student name _____

Center/school/agency _____

Supervisor/teacher _____

Using the number scale, please check the number best assessing the service-learner's performance:

1. Excellent   2. Good   3. Fair   4. Poor   5. Cannot Comment

1   2   3   4   5
a. Reliability ( )( )( )( )( )
b. Motivation ( )( )( )( )( )
c. Involvement ( )( )( )( )( )
d. Commitment ( )( )( )( )( )

e. Productivity ( )( )( )( )( )
f. Cooperativeness ( )( )( )( )( )

Do you feel that this service-learner was adequately prepared to accept the responsibilities that were given? In what way(s) could this service-learner have been better prepared?

Did you feel that this experience was worthwhile for you and your classroom or agency? How did having a service-learner in your classroom or agency benefit you?

In your opinion, what can I, as an instructor, do to enhance a service-learner exchange such as this one and make it a more beneficial experience for you, your students or clients, and my students?

Do you feel that you had a good rapport with this service-learner? Why or why not?

Would you want to have a service-learner from my courses again in the future? Why or why not?

I would greatly appreciate any additional feedback. Please use the back of this sheet for that purpose. This will help me to better prepare my students for the service-learning experience. Thank you for your participation and valuable input.

Note: Adapted with permission from Tracee Reiser, director of the Connecticut College Office of Volunteers for Community Service (OVCS).

Appendix H

Sample of Site Policy on Child Neglect and Abuse Reports

POLICY ON PROTECTIVE SERVICE REFERRALS

The Connecticut State Public Act No. 205 mandates that ". . . any person paid for caring for children in a day care center . . ." report child abuse. The State also provides immunity from liability, civil or criminal. The purpose of reporting child abuse or neglect is to:

1. Protect the child.
2. Initiate prompt investigation.
3. Provide rehabilitative services.
4. Keep the family intact.

Clarification of physical abuse, sexual abuse, neglect or maltreatment:
1. **Physical Abuse** refers to the act or failure to act, by a parent or caretaker, that causes some physical injury or some impairment of future growth and development of the child.

2. **Sexual Abuse** is exposure of a child to sexual stimulation that is inappropriate for his/her level of psycho sexual development and role in the family.

3. **Emotional Abuse**, a form of maltreatment, includes "the parents' lack of love and proper direction, inability to accept a child with his potentialities, as well as his limitations . . . and failure to encourage the child's normal development by assurance of love and acceptance."

4. **Physical Neglect** refers to the failure to provide adequate food, clothing, medical attention, shelter, care and supervision, and protection.

5. **Emotional Neglect** refers to extreme lack of attention, affection and emotional support; or permitting serious misconduct; or refusal of recommended treatment of services (recommended by school officials, medical personnel, etc.).

REFERRAL SYSTEM TO DCF

1. All college students should refer concerns and issues about potential child abuse/neglect situations to the classroom teacher.

2. All injuries, child's verbal statements of injury, abuse or neglect, or unusual behavior must be reported by the Program Director, Laboratory Coordinator or classroom teacher (after consultation with the administrator) to DCF, as soon as the observation is made.

3. Typically the classroom teacher (the most familiar adult) will talk to the child in a non-threatening manner, in order to get the child's version of the incident.

4. The Program Director, Laboratory Coordinator, or the classroom teacher (after consultation with the administrator) will contact the child's parent or guardian, in order to inform them that a report of suspected abuse is being made. If parent or guardian cannot be reached, the report must be made ASAP.

5. Contact DCF at 1-800-842-2288 (Hot Line). Fax: 860-344-3048.

6. Within 72 hours, the Program Director, Laboratory Coordinator, or classroom teacher (in consultation with the administrator) will make a written report for DCF of suspected child abuse or neglect. A copy of the report will be retained for the file if this is advised by the CSF case worker after the call to the DCF Hotline. In all cases a written report will be kept in the school file (forms are in drawer behind front desk).

If DCF is currently working with the family, follow steps for referral to DCF system.

Note: Printed with permission from the *Connecticut College Children's Program Student Handbook, 1999–2000.*

Notes

1. Pseudonyms are used to provide anonymity.

2. Although definitions of service-learning tend to vary somewhat (Stanton 1987), there are several features that distinguish service-learning from volunteer efforts. Service-learning not only provides meaningful ("as defined by [the] community") service or work but also flows "from and into course objectives," is integrated into the course through critical reflection assignments, and is assessed and evaluated according to these goals (Weigert 1998, 5).

3. The term "client" is used in this book, and always with some caution. It is meant to represent the community partners with whom the community learner is actively engaged during their learning work; that is, it is used to describe those community partners whom the community learner is assigned to serve (Dunlap 1998c). The term is used to distinguish such community partners from others with whom the worker may come into contact, e.g., personnel, supervisors, or administrators. For example, as defined here, a community learning "client" might be a child whom a worker tutors but not the community partners or staff who regularly teach the child and monitor the worker while she or he is engaged with the child. A client and community learner, by their very presence with each other, are in some degree of community *partnership* and as such are engaged in tasks that are assumed to be beneficial to both of them (Dunlap 1998a).

INTRODUCTION

1. Although definitions of service-learning tend to vary somewhat (Stanton 1987), there are several features that distinguish service-learning from volunteer efforts. Ser-

vice-learning not only provides meaningful ("as defined by [the] community") service or work but also flows "from and into course objectives," is integrated into the course through critical reflection assignments, and is assessed and evaluated according to these goals (Weigert 1998, 5).

2. Pseudonyms are used to provide anonymity.

3. The term "client" is used in this book, and always with some caution. It is meant to represent the community partners with whom the community learner is actively engaged during their learning work; that is, it is used to describe those community partners whom the community learner is assigned to serve (Dunlap 1998c). The term is used to distinguish such community partners from others with whom the worker may come into contact, e.g., personnel, supervisors, or administrators. For example, as defined here, a community learning "client" might be a child whom a worker tutors but not the community partners or staff who regularly teach the child and monitor the worker while she or he is engaged with the child. A client and community learner, by their very presence with each other, are in some degree of community *partnership* and as such are engaged in tasks that are assumed to be beneficial to both of them (Dunlap 1998a).

4. Portions of Eyler, Giles, and Schmiede (1996); Goldsmith (1993); and Hatcher and Bringle (1997) provide such a focus.

5. Specific frequencies of journaled emotions and events are available in Dunlap (1997; 1998a,b; Dunlap and Coughlin 1999).

6. Wade (1997, 217–300) provides "voices from the field," a collection of essays written by a classroom teacher, a high school student, an administrator, a school program coordinator, a staff developer, a community agency member, a parent, and a statewide community learning coordinator.

7. For example, age data was available for only 58 percent of the participants. A summary of the demographic information that was available on the participants is provided in the introduction under the subheading "Setting the Context for the Work Presented Here."

CHAPTER 2

1. Although definitions of service-learning tend to vary somewhat (Stanton 1987), there are several features that distinguish service-learning from volunteer efforts. Service-learning not only provides meaningful ("as defined by [the] community") service or work but also flows "from and into course objectives," is integrated into the course through critical reflection assignments, and is assessed and evaluated according to these goals (Weigert 1998, 5).

2. Volunteerism, for example, which usually provides meaningful service, need not require mutual learning, critical reflection, or connection to course curricula. Although by definition volunteerism, service-learning, and other curriculum-based community service are not exactly the same, they may, however, share similar adjustment processes. They all frequently involve entering new situations and environments that are unfamiliar. They all require time and experience in order for adjustment to occur.

CHAPTER 3

1. I provide an evaluation/feedback form to the supervising agency personnel with whom each of my students is placed. These staff are asked to complete the evaluation/feedback forms at the end of the semester. A sample of the evaluation is provided in appendix G.

CHAPTER 5

1. See note 1, chapter 3.

References

Aboud, F. 1988. *Children and prejudice.* New York: Basil Blackwell.

ACTION/NCSL 1989. *Service-learning: A guide for college students.* Washington, D.C.: ACTION/NCSL.

Allen, B., and L. Butler. 1996. The effects of music and movement opportunity on the analogical reasoning performance of African American and white school children: A preliminary study. *Journal of black psychology* 22, no. 3: 316–328.

Anderson, C., and J. Witmer. 1997. Administrator voices from the field. In R. Wade, ed., *Community service-learning: A guide to including service in the public school curriculum,* pp. 238–249. Albany: State University of New York Press.

Barber, B. R. 1992. *An aristocracy of everyone: The politics of education and the future of America.* New York: Ballantine.

Barnes, E. 1992. High rates of hospitalization for blacks seeking psychiatric help point to cultural biases in mental health care profession, experts say. *Black issues in higher education.*

Batshaw, M. 1997. *Children with disabilities.* Baltimore: Brookes.

Belle, D. 1982. *Lives in stress: Women and depression.* Beverly Hills, Calif.: Sage.

Berger, K., and R. Thompson. 1998. *The developing person through the life span.* 4th ed. New York: Worth.

Bernard, H. R. 1994. Field notes: How to take, code, and manage them. In *Research methods in anthropology: Qualitative and quantitative approaches,* pp. 180–207. Thousand Oaks, Calif.: Sage.

Berne, P., and L. Savary. 1993. *Building self-esteem in children.* New York: Continuum.

Berson, J. S. 1997. A study of the effects of a service-learning experience on student success at an urban community college. Ph.D. diss., Florida International University, Miami.

Blake, J. H. 1997. Lilacs. In B. Blauner, ed., *Our mothers' spirits: On the death of mothers and the grief of men.* New York: HarperCollins.

221

Boss, J. 1994. The effect of community service-work on the moral development of college ethics students. *Journal of moral education* 23: 183–197.

Boykin, W., and F. Toms. 1985. Black child socialization: A conceptual framework. In H. P. McAdoo and J. L. McAdoo, eds., *Black children: Social, educational, and parental environments.* Beverly Hills, Calif.: Sage.

Boynton, D. 1997. Classroom teacher voices from the field. In R. Wade, ed., *Community service-learning: A guide to including service in the public school curriculum,* pp. 217–224. Albany: State University of New York Press.

Brehm, S., and S. Kassin. 1996. *Social Psychology.* 3d ed. Boston: Houghton Mifflin.

Bridges, W. 1991. *Managing transitions: Making the most of change.* Reading, Mass.: Addison-Wesley.

Briere, J., and D. Elliott. 1994. Immediate and long-term impacts of child sexual abuse. In C. Larson and D. Terman, eds., *The future of children: Sexual abuse of children.* Los Altos, Calif.: David and Lucile Packard Foundation.

Bringle, R., and D. Duffy, eds. 1998. *With service in mind: Concepts and models for service-learning in psychology.* Washington, D.C.: American Association for Higher Education.

Bringle, R., and J. Hatcher. 1996. Implementing service-learning in higher education. *Journal of higher education* 672: 221–239.

Brooks-Gunn, J., and G. Duncan. 1997. The effects of poverty on children. *The future of children.* Summer-Fall.

Bullock, H. 1995. Class acts: Middle class responses to the poor. In B. Lott and D. Maluso, eds., *The social psychology of interpersonal discrimination.* New York: Guilford.

Campus Compact. 1993. Rethinking tradition: Integrating service with academic study on college campuses. *Campus Compact 1993.* Denver: Educational Commission of the States.

Canino, A. I., and J. Spurlock. 1994. *Culturally diverse children and adolescents: Assessment, diagnosis, and treatment.* New York: Guilford.

Carnes, J. 1995. *Us and them: A history of intolerance in America.* Montgomery, Ala.: Teaching Tolerance, A Project of the Southern Poverty Law Center.

Caron, Barbara, ed. (1999). *Service Matters: The Engaged Campus.* Campus Compact: Providence.

Channing L. Bete Company. 1992. *About grief.* South Deerfield, Mass.: Channing L. Bete.

———. 1993. *What you should know about stress and your child.* South Deerfield, Mass.: Channing L. Bete.

———. 1999. *About emotional abuse and neglect of children.* South Deerfield, Mass.: Channing L. Bete.

Chao, R. 1994. Beyond parental control and authoritarian parenting style: Understanding Chinese parenting through the cultural notion of training. *Child development* 65: 1111–1119.

Charness, N. 1989. Age and expertise: Responding to Talland's challenge. In L. Poon, D. Rubin, and B. Wilson, eds., *Everyday cognition in adulthood and later life.* Cambridge, U.K.: Cambridge University Press.

Chasnoff, D., and H. Cohen. 1996. *It's elementary: Talking about gay issues in school.* Hohokus, N.J.: New Day Films.

Chickering, A., and N. Schlossberg. 1995. Maximizing learning beyond courses and classes. In *Getting the most out of college*. Boston, Mass.: Allyn & Bacon.

Chideya, F. 1995. *Don't believe the hype: Fighting cultural misinformation about African Americans*. New York: Plume/Penguin.

Children's Defense Fund. 1995. *The state of America's children yearbook*. Washington, D.C.: Children's Defense Fund.

Clark, K. 1988. *Prejudice and your child*. Middletown, Conn.: Wesleyan University Press.

Clary, E., M. Snyder, and A. Stukas. 1996. Volunteers' motivations: Findings from a national survey. *Nonprofit and voluntary sector quarterly* 25, no. 4: 485–505.

Clary, E., M. Snyder, and A. Stukas. 1998. Service-learning and psychology: Lessons from the psychology of volunteers' motivations. In R. Bringle and D. Duffy, eds., *With service in mind: Concepts and models for service-learning in psychology*. Washington, D.C.: American Association for Higher Education.

Coles, R. 1993. *The call of service: A witness to idealism*. Boston: Houghton Mifflin.

Coll, C. G., J. Surrey, and K. Weingarten, eds. 1998. *Mothering against the odds: Diverse voices of contemporary mothers*. New York: Guilford.

Collins, J., E. Sorel, J. Brent, and C. Mathura. 1990. Ethnic and cultural factors in psychiatric diagnosis and treatment. In D. Ruiz, ed., *Handbook of mental disorders among Black Americans*. Westport, Conn.: Greenwood.

Collins, M., and C. Tamarkin. 1990. *Marva Collins' way: Returning to excellence in education*. New York: Putnam.

Connecticut Advisory Council for Teacher Professional Standards. 1995. *A proposal to increase the number of minority educators in Connecticut*. Presented to the Governor, State Board of Education, Education Committee of the Connecticut General Assembly, September. Contact person: Cynthia L. Jorgensen, Education Consultant, Connecticut State Department of Education, Box 2219, Hartford, CT 06145.

Connecticut College Children's Program. 1999. *Connecticut College Children's Program, student handbook 1999–2000*. New London, Conn.: Connecticut College Children's Program, Box 5215, New London, CT 06320.

Conrad, D., and D. Hedin, eds. 1982. *Youth participation and experiential education*. New York: Haworth.

Coontz, S. 1992. *The way we never were: American families and the nostalgia trap*. New York: Basic.

———. 1997. *The way we really are: Coming to terms with America's changing families*. New York: Basic.

Cooper, D. 1998. Reading, writing, and reflection. In R. Rhoads and J. Howard, eds., *Academic service learning: A pedagogy of action and reflection*. San Francisco: Jossey-Bass.

Cooper, J. California 1991. How, why to get rich. In *The matter is life*. New York: Anchor/Doubleday.

Cooper, P. 1996. Thoughts on communicating in another culture. In K. Galvin and P. Cooper, eds., *Making connections: Readings in relational communication*, pp. 49–53. Los Angeles: Roxbury.

Cushner, K., A. McClelland, and P. Safford. 1996. *Human diversity in education: An integrative approach*. 2d ed. New York: McGraw-Hill.

Damon-Moore, H. 1997. Linking multiculturalism and service learning: One college's success. *Access: Improving diversity in student recruiting and retention* 5, no. 5: 1–5.

Daniel, J. H. 1994. Exclusion and emphasis reframed as a matter of ethics. *Ethics and behavior* 4, no. 3: 229–235.

Deater-Deckard, K., et al. 1996. Physical discipline among African American and European American mothers: Links to children's externalizing behaviors. *Developmental psychology* 32, no. 6: 1065–1072.

DeGenova, M. 1997. *Families in cultural context: Strengths and challenges in diversity.* Mountain View, Calif.: Mayfield.

Delpit, L. 1995. *Other people's children: Cultural conflict in the classroom.* New York: New Press.

Delve, C., S. Mintz, and G. Stewart, eds. 1990. *Community service as values education.* San Francisco: Jossey-Bass.

Derman-Sparks, L., and the A.B.C. Task Force. 1989. *Anti-bias curriculum: Tools for empowering young children.* Washington, D.C.: National Association for the Education of Young Children.

Dovidio, J. F., and S. L. Gaertner. 1986. Prejudice, discrimination, and racism: Historical trends and contemporary approaches. In J. F. Dovidio and S. L. Gaertner, eds., *Prejudice, Discrimination, and Racism,* pp. 1–34. Orlando: Academic.

Draimin, B. 1994. *Working together against AIDS.* Rosen, New York: Rosen Publication Group.

Driscoll, A., et al. 1997. *Assessing the impact of service-learning: A workbook of strategies and methods.* Portland, Ore.: Portland State University Press.

Dunlap, M. 1997. The role of the personal fable in adolescent service learning and critical reflection. *Michigan journal of community service learning* 4: 56–63.

———. 1998a. Adjustment and developmental outcomes of students engaged in service learning. *The journal of experiential education* 21, no. 3: 147–153.

———. 1998b. Voices of students in multicultural service-learning settings. *Michigan journal of community service learning* 5: 58–67.

———. 1998c. Multicultural service learning: Challenges, research, and solutions for assisting students. *Removing the vestiges: Research-based strategies to promote inclusion* 1, no. 1: 27–34. Washington, D.C.: American Association of Community Colleges.

———. 1998d. Methods of supporting students' critical reflection in courses incorporating service learning. *Teaching of psychology* 25, no. 3: 208–210.

———. 1999a. My study of prejudice: A lifelong journey. In P. Batur-Vanderlippe and J. Feagin, eds., *The global color line: Racial and ethnic inequality and struggle from a global perspective.* Stamford, Conn.: Jai.

———. 1999b. Tolerance and intolerance for African American children and families: Lessons from the movie *Crooklyn.* In J. Robertson, *Teaching for a tolerant world.* Urbana, Ill.: National Council of Teachers of English.

Dunlap, M., and B. Coughlin. 1999. College student affection issues in child- and family-focused community service-learning settings. *Academic Exchange Quarterly* 3, no. 4: 28-34.

Dwivedi, K., and V. Varma. 1996. *Meeting the needs of ethnic minority children: A handbook for professionals.* Bristol, Pa.: Jessica Kingsley.

Edelman, M. 1992. *The measure of our success: A letter to my children and yours.* New York: HarperPerennial.

Edwards, A., and C. Polite. 1992. *Children of the dream: The psychology of black success.* New York: Doubleday.

Elia, W. 1995. *Jonathan discovers universal precautions*. New London, Conn.: Lawrence & Memorial Hospital.

Elkind, D. 1967. Egocentrism in adolescence. *Child development, 56,* 361–375.

———. 1984. *All grown up and no place to go*. Reading, Mass.: Addison-Wesley.

Erickson, J., and J. Anderson, eds. 1997. *Learning with the community: Concepts and models for service-learning in teacher education*. Washington, D.C.: American Association for Higher Education.

Erikson, K. 1976. *Everything in its path: Destruction of community in the Buffalo Creek flood*. New York: Simon & Schuster.

———. 1994. *A new species of trouble: Explorations in disaster, trauma, and community*. New York: Norton.

Ewell, Peter T. (1997). "Organizing for Learning: A New Imperative." *AAHE Bulletin* (December): 3–6.

Eyler, J., and D. Giles. 1999. *Where's the learning in service-learning?* San Francisco: Jossey-Bass.

Eyler, J., D. Giles, and J. Braxton. 1997. The impact of service-learning on college students. *Michigan journal of community service learning* 4: 5–15.

Eyler, J., D. Giles, and A. Schmiede. 1996. *A practitioner's guide to reflection in service-learning: Student voices and reflections*. Nashville, Tenn.: Vanderbilt University Press.

Feagin, J. 1998. The continuing significance of race: Antiblack discrimination in public places. In J. Feagin, ed., *The new urban paradigm: Critical perspectives on the city*. Lanham, Md.: Rowman & Littlefield.

Feagin, J., and M. Sikes. 1994. *Living with racism: The black middle class experience*. Boston: Beacon.

Feagin, J., and H. Vera. 1995. *White racism*. New York: Routledge.

Federal Interagency Forum on Child and Family Statistics. 1997. *America's children: Key indicators of well-being*. Washington, D.C.: Federal Interagency Forum on Child and Family Statistics.

Fiedler, F., T. Mitchell, and H. Triandis. 1971. The culture assimilator: An approach to cross-cultural training. *Journal of applied psychology* 55, no. 2: 95–102.

Fine, M., et al. 1997. *Off white: Readings on race, power, and society*. New York: Routledge.

Finkelhor, D. 1994. Current information on the scope and nature of child sexual abuse. In C. Larson and D. Terman, eds., *The future of children: Sexual abuse of children*. Los Altos, Calif.: David and Lucile Packard Foundation.

Fiske, S. 1993. Controlling other people: The impact of power on stereotyping. *American psychologist* 48: 621–628.

Florida Co-op Extension Service, IFAS, University of Florida. n.d. *Winning ways to talk with young children*.

Foos, C. 1998. The "different voice" of service. *Michigan journal of community service learning* 5: 14–21.

Foster, H. 1986. *Ribbin', jivin', and playing the dozens: The persistent dilemma in our schools*. New York: Ballinger.

Foster, M. 1994. Educating for competence in community and culture: Exploring the views of exemplary teachers. In M. Shujaa, ed., *Too much schooling too little education*. Trenton N.J.: Africa World Press.

Furman, R. 1995. Helping children cope with stress and deal with feelings. *Young children* 50, no. 2: 33–41.

Galvin, K., and P. Cooper, eds. 1996. *Making connections: Readings in relational communication.* Los Angeles: Roxbury.

Gelmon, S., et al. 1998. Community-university partnerships for mutual learning. *Michigan journal of community service learning* 5: 97–107.

Gibbs, J., et al. 1998. *Children of color: Psychological interventions with culturally diverse youth.* San Francisco: Jossey-Bass.

Giles, D., and J. Eyler. 1998. A service learning research agenda for the next five years. In R. Rhoads and J. Howard, eds., *Academic service learning: A pedagogy of action and reflection.* San Francisco: Jossey-Bass.

Giles, D., E. Honnet, and S. Migliore. 1991. *Research agenda for combining service-and learning in the 1990s.* Raleigh, N.C.: National Society for Internships and Experiential Education.

Gilligan, C. 1982. *In a different voice: Psychological theory and women's development.* Cambridge, Mass.: Harvard University.

Gilligan, C., J. Murphy, and M. Tappan. 1990. Moral development beyond adolescence. In C. Alexander and E. Langer, eds., *Higher stages of human development.* New York: Oxford University Press.

Gillis, J. R. 1998. Cultural heterosexism and the family. In C. Patterson and R. D. D'Augelli, eds., *Lesbian, gay, and bisexual identities in families.* New York: Oxford University Press.

Goldsmith, S. 1993. *Journal reflection: A resource guide for community service-leaders and educators engaged in service-learning.* Washington, D.C.: American Alliance for Rights and Responsibilities.

Good, L. 1996. When a child has been sexually abused: Several resources for parents and early childhood professionals. *Young Children* 51, no. 5: 84–85.

Goodwin, B. 1996. The impact of popular culture on images of African American women. In J. Chrisler, C. Golden, and P. Rozee, eds., *Lectures on the psychology of women.* New York: McGraw-Hill.

Gray, E., and J. Cosgrove. 1985. Ethnocentric perception of childrearing practices in protective services. *Child abuse and neglect* 9: 389–396.

Greene, B. 1986. When the therapist is white and the patient is black: Considerations for psychotherapy in the feminist, heterosexual, and lesbian communities. In D. Howard, ed., *The dynamics of feminist therapy.* New York: Haworth.

Greenfield, P., and R. Cocking, eds. 1994. *Cross-cultural roots of minority child development.* Hillsdale, N.J.: Erlbaum.

Guggenheim, C. 1995. Video. *The shadow of hate: A history of intolerance.* Montgomery, Ala.: Teaching Tolerance, A Project of the Southern Poverty Law Center.

Hale-Benson, J. 1986. *Black children: Their roots, culture, and learning styles.* Baltimore: Johns Hopkins University Press.

Hallahan, D., J. Kauffman, and J. Lloyd. 1995. *Introduction to learning disabilities.* Needham Heights, Mass.: Allyn & Bacon.

Hanna, S. and S. Wilford. 1990, Video. *Floor time: Tuning in to each child.* New York: Scholastic.

Hansen, Edmund J. (1998). "Essential Demographics of Today's College Students." *AAHE Bulletin* (November): 3–5.

Hanson, M. 1998. Families with Anglo-European roots. In E. Lynch and M. Hanson, eds., *Developing cross-cultural competence: A guide for working with children and their families.* 2d ed. Baltimore: Brookes.

Hardgrove, C., and L. Warrick. 1974. How shall we tell the children? *American journal of nursing.* March.

Hardman, M., C. Drew, and M. Egan. 1998. *Human exceptionality: Society, school, and family.* Needham Heights, Mass.: Allyn & Bacon.

Harkavy, I., and L. Benson. 1998. De-platonizing and democratizing education as the bases of service learning. In R. Rhoads and J. Howard, eds., *Academic service learning: A pedagogy of action and reflection.* San Francisco: Jossey-Bass.

Harris, C. 1993. Whiteness as property. *Harvard law review* 106, no. 8: 1707–1792.

Hatcher, J., ed. 1998. *Service-learning tip sheets: A faculty resource guide.* Indianapolis: Indiana Campus Compact. 850 W. Michigan, Suite 200, Indianapolis, IN 46202.

Hatcher, J., and R. Bringle. 1997. Reflection: Bridging the gap between service and learning. *College teaching* 454: 153–158.

Hecht, M., M. Collier, and S. Ribeau. 1993. *African American communication: Ethnic identity and cultural interpretation.* Newbury Park, Calif.: Sage.

Helms, J. E., ed. 1990. *Black and white racial identity: Theory, research, and practice.* Westport, Conn.: Greenwood.

Hewitt, D. 1995. *So this is normal too?: Teachers and parents working out developmental issues in young children.* St. Paul, Minn.: Redleaf.

Hopson, D., and D. Hopson. 1993. *Raising the rainbow generation: Teaching children to be successful in a multi-cultural society.* New York: Fireside.

Howard, J. 1993. *Praxis I: A faculty casebook on service-learning.* Ann Arbor, Mich.: OCSL.

Hrabowski, F., K. Maton, and G. Greif. 1998. *Beating the odds: Raising academically successful African American males.* New York: Oxford University Press.

Hurd, T., R. Lerner, and C. Barton. 1999. Integrated services: Expanding partnerships to meet the needs of today's children and families. *Young children.* March.

Hybrid Productions 1997. Video. *Camp Lavender Hill: A Short Documentary about the First Summer Camp for Children of Gay, Lesbian, and Bisexual Parents.* San Francisco: Hybrid Productions.

Ingoldsby, B., and S. Smith. 1995. *Families in multicultural perspective.* New York: Guilford.

Jacoby, B. ed. 1996. *Service-learning in higher education: Concepts and practices.* San Francisco: Jossey-Bass.

Jenny, C., et al. 1999. Analysis of missed cases of abusive head trauma. *Journal of the American Medical Association* 281, no. 7: 621–626.

Jensen, R. 1998. Patriarchal sex. In S. Schacht and D. Ewing, eds., *Feminism and men: Reconstructing gender relations.* New York: New York University.

Jones, E. 1974. Social class and psychotherapy: A critical review of research. *Psychiatry* 31: 307–320.

Kahne, J., and J. Westheimer. 1996. In the service-of what? The politics of service-learning. *Phi Delta Kappan,* May, pp. 593–599.

Kanter, R., and B. Stein. 1980. *A tale of O: On being different.* New York: Harper & Row.

———. 1993. Video. *A tale of O: On being different.* Cambridge, Mass.: Goodmeasure.

Keith, N. Z. 1997. Doing service projects in urban settings. In A. Waterman, ed., *Service-learning: Applications from the research*, pp. 127–149. Mahwah, N.J.: Lawrence Erlbaum Associates.

Kendall, J. C., et al. 1990. *Combining service and learning: A resource book for community and public service.* Raleigh, N.C.: National Society for Internships and Experiential Education.

Kilbourne, J. 1987. Video. *Still killing us softly: Advertising's image of women.* Cambridge, Mass.: Cambridge Documentary Films.

Kubler-Ross, E. 1974. *Questions and answers on death and dying.* New York: Macmillan.

———. 1981. *Living with death and dying.* New York: Macmillan.

Kunjufu, J. 1984. *Developing positive self-images and discipline in black children.* Chicago: African-American Images.

Ladson-Billings, G. 1994. *The dreamkeepers: Successful teachers of African-American children.* San Francisco: Jossey-Bass.

Lamb, M., S. Suomi, and G. Stephenson. 1979. *Social interaction analysis: Methodological issues.* Madison, Wisc.: University of Wisconsin Press.

Levine, A., and J. Cureton. 1998. Personal life: Retreat from intimacy. In *When hope and fear collide: A portrait of today's college student.* San Francisco: Jossey-Bass.

Lynch, E. 1998. Conceptual framework: From culture shock to cultural learning. In E. Lynch and M. Hanson, eds., *Developing cross-cultural competence: A guide for working with children and their families.* 2d ed. Baltimore: Brookes.

Lynch, E., and M. Hanson. 1998, *Developing cross-cultural competence: A guide for working with children and their families.* 2d ed. Baltimore: Brookes.

Mabry, J. B. 1998. Pedagogical variations in service-learning and student outcomes: How time, contact, and reflection matter. *Michigan journal of community service learning* 5: 32–47.

MacLeod, J. 1995. *Ain't no making it: Aspirations and attainment in a low-income neighborhood.* Boulder: Westview.

Manning, P. K., and B. Cullum-Swan. 1994. Narrative, content, and semiotic analysis. In N. K. Denzin and Y. S. Lincoln, eds., *Handbook of qualitative research*, pp. 463–477. Thousand Oaks, Calif.: Sage.

Markus, H., and S. Kitayama. 1991. Culture and the self: Implications for cognition, emotion and motivation. *Psychological review* 98, no. 2: 224–253.

Marschark, M. 1997. *Raising and educating a deaf child: A comprehensive guide to the choices, controversies, and decisions faced by parents and educators.* New York: Oxford University Press.

McCarthy, M. 1996. One-time, short-term service-learning experiences. In B. Jacoby, ed., *Service-learning in higher education: Concepts and practices.* San Francisco: Jossey-Bass.

McIntosh, P. 1990. White privilege: Unpacking the invisible knapsack. *Independent school* 492: 31–39.

McMillen, L. 1995. Lifting the veil from whiteness: Growing body of scholarship challenges a racial "norm." *Chronicle for Higher Education,* September 8.

Meier, S., and S. Davis. 1993. *The elements of counseling.* 2d ed. Pacific Grove, Calif.: Brooks/Cole.

Mennonite Central Committee. 1995. *Free indeed: A videodrama about racism.* Akron, Penn.: Mennonite Central Committee and MCC U.S.

Mercugliano, M., T. Power, and N. Blum. 1999. *A clinician's practical guide to attention-deficit/hyperactivity disorder.* Baltimore: Brookes.

Miller, J. 1997. The impact of service-learning experiences on students' sense of power. *Michigan journal of community service learning* 5: 16–21.

Mosby, L., et al. 1999. Troubles in interracial talk about discipline: An examination of African American child rearing narratives. *Journal of comparative family studies* 30, no. 3: 489–521.

Muuss, R. 1988. *Theories of adolescence.* New York: McGraw-Hill.

National Association for the Education of Young Children. 1986. *Helping children to learn self-control: A guide to discipline.* Washington, D.C.: National Association for the Education of Young Children.

The New London Day (Newspaper). 1999. Racial and Ethnic Composition of the Region's Public Schools, 1989–98. Oct 10, 1999, p. H3.

New London School District. 1999. *New London school district: Strategic school profile, 1998–1999.* New London, Conn.: Board of Education.

Norrell, J., L. Kuennen, and J. Koeni. 1997. A college teaching practicum: An example of intentional reflexivity and mentoring. *Family science review* 10, no. 4: 290–302.

Nunnally, E., and C. Moy. 1989. *Communication basics for human service professionals.* Newbury Park, Calif.: Sage.

Nyden, P., et al. 1997. *Building community: Social science in action.* Thousand Oaks, Calif.: Pine Forge.

Office of Youth Affairs/Citizen's Forum for Achieving Results C-Far 1999. *The guide: A list of New London Resources.* New London, Conn.: Office of Youth Affairs/Citizen's Forum for Achieving Results C-Far.

Okun, B. 1996. *Understanding diverse families: What practitioners need to know.* New York: Guilford.

Orr, C. 1999. The energizing tension between scholars and activists: Negotiating class interests and academy-community divides. *Feminist Collections: A quarterly of women's studies resources special issue on academy/community connections* 20, no. 3: 2–4.

Pasztor, E., and M. Leighton. 1993. *Helping children and youth manage separation and loss.* Washington, D.C.: Child Welfare League of America.

Patterson, C. 1994. Children of the lesbian baby boom: Behavioral adjustment, self-concepts, and sex role identity. In B. Greene and G. Hered, eds., *Lesbian and gay psychology.* Thousand Oaks, Calif.: Sage.

Peters, W. 1985. *A class divided—Jane Elliott's Blue Eyes and Brown Eyes.* New Haven, Conn.: Yale University Films.

Phillips, E. 1995. Multicultural education beyond the classroom. In C. Sleeter and P. McLaren, eds., *Multicultural education, critical pedagogy, and the politics of difference.* New York: State University of New York Press.

Ploch, D. 1996. *What do you mean, my child's not perfect?: A reference manual and guide for parents and families of children with disabilities or special needs.* Uncasville, Conn.: Easter Seal Rehabilitation Center of Southeastern Connecticut.

Porter, T. 1999. Infants and toddlers in kith and kin care: Findings from the Informal Care project. *Zero to Three,* June-July.

Primavera, J. 1999. The unintended consequences of volunteerism: Positive outcomes for those who serve. In J. Ferrari and J. Chapman, eds., *Educating students to make a difference: Community-based service learning.* New York: Haworth Press.

Racial and ethnic composition of the region's public schools, 1989–98. 1999. *New London Day,* October 10, H3.

Ramsey, P. 1987. *Teaching and learning in a diverse world: Multicultural education for young children.* New York: Teacher's College.

Report of the AAHE, ACPA, and NASPA Joint Task Force on Student Learning. (1998).

Rhoads, R. 1997. *Community service and higher learning: Explorations of the caring self.* Albany: State University of New York Press.

Rhoads, R., and J. Howard, eds. 1998. *Academic service learning: A pedagogy of action and reflection.* San Francisco: Jossey-Bass.

Riggs, M., V. Kleinman, and Signifying Works. 1991. *Color Adjustment.* San Francisco: California Newsreel.

Rimmerman, Craig A. (1997). *The New Citizenship: Unconventional Politics, Activism, and Service.* Westview Press: Boulder, Colo.

Robinson, G., and L. Barnett. 1998. Best practices in service learning. *Project brief 98/3.* Washington, D.C.: American Association of Community Colleges. One Dupont Circle, NW, Suite 410, Washington, D.C. 20036–1176.

Rose, M. 1989. *Lives on the boundary: The struggles and achievements of America's underprepared.* New York: Free Press.

Rothman, M., E. Anderson, and J. Schaffer. 1998. *Service matters: Engaging higher education in the renewal of America's communities and American democracy Campus Compact lessons from the field.* Providence, R.I.: Campus Compact Brown University.

Ruiz, D. 1990. *Handbook of mental health and mental disorder among black Americans.* Westport, Conn.: Greenwood.

Russell, K. 1993. *The color complex: The politics of skin color among African Americans.* New York: Doubleday.

Ryan, M. 1999. Together, we transform the world. *Parade,* September 5, 4–7.

Saifer, S. 1990. *Practical solutions to practically every problem: The early childhood teacher's manual.* St. Paul, Minn.: Redleaf.

Schlenker, R. B. 1985. *The self and social life.* New York: McGraw-Hill.

Schofield, J. W. 1986. Causes and consequences of the colorblind perspective. In J. Dovidio and S. Gaertner, eds., *Prejudice, discrimination, and racism.* Orlando: Academic.

Schon, Donald A. (1995). "The New Scholarship Requires a New Epistemology: Knowing-in-Action." *Change* (November/December): 27–34.

Schroeder, Charles C. (1993). "New Students—New Learning Styles." *Change* (September/October): 21–26.

Scott, K. 1991. *The habit of surviving: Five extraordinary women share the conflicts and struggles that define their lives as black women in America.* New York: Ballantine.

Serow, R. 1991. Students and voluntarism: Looking into the motives of community service participants. *American educational research journal* 28, no. 3: 543–556.

Shade, B. 1989. *Culture, style, and the educative process.* Springfield, Ill.: Charles C. Thomas.

Shelley, Percy Bysshe. (1975 [1821]). "A Defence of Poetry."

Sheridan, P., G. Foley, and S. Radlinski. 1995. *Using the supportive play model: Individualized intervention in early childhood practice.* New York: Teachers College.

Shujaa, M. 1994. Education and schooling: You can have one without the other. In *Too much schooling, too little education.* Trenton, N.J.: Africa World.

Shumer, R. 1997. Learning from qualitative research. In A. Waterman, ed., *Service-learning: Applications from the research.* Mahwah, N.J.: Lawrence Erlbaum.

Sigmon, R. 1994. *Linking service-learning with learning in liberal arts education.* Washington, D.C.: Council of Independent Colleges.

Sleek, S. 1998. Experts scrambling on school shootings. *APA monitor*, August.

Stanton, T. 1987. Service-Learning: Groping toward a Definition. *National society for internships and experiential education* 121: 2–4.

Stanton, T., D. Giles, and N. Cruz. 1999. *Service-learning: A movement's pioneers reflect on its origins, practice, and future.* San Francisco: Jossey-Bass.

Stephan, W., and J. Brigham. 1985. Intergroup contact: An introduction. *Journal of social issues* 41, no. 3: 1–8.

Stewart, E., and R. Weinstein. 1997. Volunteer participation in context: Motivations and political efficacy within three AIDS organizations. *American journal of community psychology* 25, no. 6: 837.

Stewart, L., et al. 1996. Communication in cross-gender friendships. In K. Galvin and P. Cooper, eds., *Making connections: Readings in relational communication.* Los Angeles: Roxbury.

Stukas, A., E. Clary, M. Snyder. 1999a. Service-learning: Who benefits and why? *Social Policy Report* 13: 1–19.

Stukas, A., M. Snyder, and E. Clary. 1999b. The effects of "mandatory volunteerism" on intentions to volunteer. *Psychological science* 10, no. 1: 59–64.

Swann, J. 1992. *Girls, boys, and language: Language in education.* Cambridge, Mass.: Blackwell.

Tasker, F., and S. Golombok. 1995. Adults raised as children in lesbian families. *American journal of orthopsychiatry* 65, no. 2: 203–215.

Tatum, B. 1992. Talking about race: The application of racial identity development theory in the classroom. *Harvard educational review* 62, no. 1: 1–24.

——. 1997. *"Why are all the black kids sitting together in the cafeteria?" And other conversations about race.* New York: Basic.

Teaching Tolerance Project 1997. *Starting small: Teaching tolerance in preschool and the early grades.* Montgomery, Ala.: Southern Poverty Law Center.

Thomas, T. 1997. Student voices from the field. In R. Wade, ed., *Community service-learning: A guide to including service in the public school curriculum,* pp. 225–237. Albany: State University of New York Press.

Thompson, B. W., and S. Tyagi. 1993. *Beyond a dream deferred: Multicultural education and the politics of excellence.* Minneapolis: University of Minnesota Press.

Triandis, H., and L. Triandis. 1960. Race, social class, religion, and nationality as determinants of social distance. *Journal of abnormal and social psychology* 61, no. 1: 110–118.

Turner, P. 1994. *Ceramic uncles and celluloid mammies: Black images and their influence on culture.* New York: Anchor.

Turner, R. 1991. Affirming consciousness: The Africentric perspective. In J. Everett, ed., *Child welfare: An Africentric perspective.* New Brunswick, N.J.: Rutgers University.

U.S. Department of Commerce, Bureau of the Census 1992. *1990 census of population and housing summary, tape file 3A CD90–3A–10.* Washington, D.C.: U.S. Dept. of Commerce, Bureau of Census, Data User Services Division.

University of Colorado-Boulder 1995. *Service-learning handbook.* Boulder: University of Colorado-Boulder, Student Employment and Service Learning Center. Http://csf.colorado.edu/ sl/cu/handbk95.html.

Wade, R. 1997. *Community service-learning: A guide to including service in the public school curriculum.* Albany: State University of New York Press.

Wah, L. M. 1994. Video. *The color of fear.* Oakland, Calif.: Stir Fry Productions.

Ward, J. 1997. Encouraging cultural competence in service learning practice. *Service learning: Ninety-sixth yearbook of the National Society for the Study of Education.* Chicago: University of Chicago Press.

Wardle, F. 2000. Children of mixed race: No longer invisible. *Educational leadership,* December-January.

Waterman, F. 1996. Great good-byes. In K. Galvin and P. Cooper, eds., *Making connections: Readings in relational communication.* Los Angeles, Calif.: Roxbury.

Way, N. 1998. *Everyday courage: The lives and stories of urban teenagers.* New York: New York University Press.

Weigert, K. 1998. Academic service learning: Its meaning and relevance. In R. Rhoads and J. Howard, eds., *Academic service learning: A pedagogy of action and reflection.* San Francisco: Jossey-Bass.

Weinman, J. 1990. Health psychology: Progress, perspectives, and prospects. In P. Bennett, J. Weinman, and P. Spurgeon, eds., *Current developments in health psychology,* pp. 9–33. Chur, Switzerland: Harwood Academic.

Weisbard, P. 1999. *Feminist collections: A quarterly of Women's Studies resources special issue on academy/community connections* 20, no. 3. Madison: University of Wisconsin System.

West, C. 1995. Mammy, Sapphire, and Jezebel: Historical images of black women and their implications for psychotherapy. *Psychotherapy* 32, no. 3: 458–466.

White, J. D. 1976. *Talking with a child: What to say.* New York: Macmillan.

Wiley, R. 1991. *Why black people tend to shout: Cold facts and wry views from a black man's world.* New York: Carol.

Williams, M., M. Dunlap, and T. McCandies. 1999. Keepin' it real: Three black women educators discuss how we deal with student resistance to multicultural inclusion in the curriculum. *Transformations* 10, no. 2: 11–22.

Williams, M., T. McCandies, and M. Dunlap. In press. Women of color and feminist psychology: Moving from criticism and critique to integration and application. In L. Collins, M. Dunlap, and J. Chrisler, eds., *Charting a new course for feminist psychology.* Westport, Conn.: Greenwood/Praeger.

Willis, W. 1998. Families with African American roots. In E. Lynch and M. Hanson, eds., *Developing cross-cultural competency: A guide for working with young children and their families.* Baltimore: Brookes.

Wilson, C., and F. Gutierrez. 1995. *Race, multiculturalism, and the media: From mass to class communication.* Thousand Oaks, Calif.: Sage.

Wong, H. K., and R. T. Wong. 1998. *The first days of school.* Mountain View, Calif.: Harry K. Wong Publications.

York, S. 1991. *Roots and wings: Affirming culture in early childhood programs.* St. Paul, Minn.: Redleaf.

Zinn, H. 1980. *A people's history of the United States.* New York: Harper & Row.

Zlotkowski, E. 1998. *Successful service-learning programs: New models of excellence in higher education.* Bolton, Mass.: Anker.

Index

abuse. *See* child abuse/neglect; sexual abuse
adolescents. *See* high school; middle school
advice. *See* consultation/advice
affection, 101–11; developmental theories, 108–9; Erikson's theory, 109; flirtations, of adolescents toward students, 104–5; Freudian theory, 108; Piagetian theory, 108–9; toward students as hero/heroine, 103
African American female student: adolescents testing, 82; and affection of children, 107; and awareness of social status/privilege, xi–xiii; change brought about by, 52; and closure, xxii–xxiii; composure maintained by, 95; first impressions of, 26; group discussion by, 9; inspiration of children by, 92; and multicultural issues, 120, 124, 139; rapport built by, 63, 67–68; roles of, 85; and setting limits, 93–94; transportation as problem for, 7
African American male student: and affection of client, xxiii–xxiv; and child abuse, 168; and closure, 183,

188; and multicultural issues, 127; mutual learning by, 56–57; patience of, 76; professionalism maintained by, 70; reactions of, to changing clientele, 30; self-disclosure by, 75; and setting limits, xxiii–xxiv; and shocking moments, 171; and special needs individuals, 154
age, xxxii, 217n6; of clients, 162; interpersonal relationships and, xii
AIDS. *See* HIV/AIDS
Asian American female student: and guards in women's prison, xxiv–xxv; value of community service to, 7
Asian American male student, 49–50
at-risk girls, middle school role-modeling program for, 92
attachment, client's need for, 65, 77. *See also* rapport building
attention deficit disorder (ADD), 140
attention deficit hyperactivity disorder (ADHD), 48, 150, 153, 161; misdiagnosis of high-energy children, 139–41
attention of clients, 89
autism, 149–50
autonomy, 85–86

About the Author

Michelle Robin Dunlap, Ph.D., is a social psychologist who specializes in social and personality development as an associate professor in the human development department at Connecticut College. She has also served in various professional capacities with the American Association for Higher Education (AAHE), the Association for Women in Psychology (AWP), Campus Compact, the New England Psychological Association (NEPA), and the Society for the Psychological Study of Social Issues (SPSSI). She has written journal articles, book chapters, and essays about her three lines of study: college students working in urban community settings, intergroup relations, and multicultural child rearing. Her work has taken her throughout the United States, as well as to Finland and Russia. She is also coeditor of a forthcoming book with colleagues Lynn H. Collins and Joan C. Chrisler, *Charting a New Course for Feminist Psychology*, and a special issue of the *Journal of Social Issues* with Art Stukas.